Zen Women:
Beyond Tea Ladies, Iron Maidens,
and Macho Masters

To Susan)
Thanking you for
all of our
work helping
women

Grace

Zen Women:

Beyond Tea Ladies, Iron Maidens, and Macho Masters

Grace Jill Schireson

Foreword by Miriam Levering

WISDOM PUBLICATIONS • BOSTON

Susan Rautine
March 27 2010

Wisdom Publications
199 Elm Street
Somerville MA 02144 USA
www.wisdompubs.org

Library of Congress Cataloging-in-Publication Data

Schireson, Grace Jill.
 Zen women : beyond tea ladies, iron maidens, and macho masters / Grace Jill Schireson ; foreword by Miriam Levering.
   p. cm.
 Includes bibliographical references and index.
 ISBN 0-86171-475-X (pbk. : alk. paper)
 1. Buddhist women. 2. Zen Buddhists. 3. Women in Buddhism. I. Title.
 BQ5450.S35 2009
 294.3'927082--dc22
                          2009027242

13 12 11 10 09
5 4 3 2 1

Cover art is an adaptation of a rendering by Michael Hofmann of the Six Oxherding Pic-
tures described in *Wastepaper Record* by Tachibana no Someko. Cover design by Phil Pas-
cuzzo. Interior design by Gopa&Ted2, Inc. Set in Dante MT 11/14.5.

Wisdom Publications' books are printed on acid-free paper and meet the guidelines for permanence and durability of the Production Guidelines for Book
Longevity of the Council on Library Resources.

Printed in the United States of America.

This book was produced with environmental mindfulness. We have elected to print
this title on 30% PCW recycled paper. As a result, we have saved the following resources:
22 trees, 7 million BTUs of energy, 2,095 lbs. of greenhouse gases, 10,090 gallons of water,
and 613 lbs. of solid waste. For more information, please visit our website, www.wis-
dompubs.org. This paper is also FSC certified. For more information, please visit
www.fscus.org.

This book is dedicated to the memory of my mother,
Jean Rubin Rosenberg Bernstein,
who gave me her strength,
and to my grandchildren,
Jacob, Isabel, and Olivia Schireson,
who will carry it forward.

Contents

Foreword

By Miriam Levering

Years ago, after a decade of scholarly work collecting and translating the histories and recorded words of Chinese women Zen masters from China's Five Dynasties and Song Dynasty, the golden age of Zen in China, I gave a workshop on the subject at the San Francisco Zen Center. There I met Grace Myoan Schireson, a Ph.D. psychologist with many years of therapeutic experience in Berkeley, California. She was devoting her life to two great endeavors: Zen Buddhist practice and awakening, to which she was and is deeply committed; and finding out everything she could, on her own and from scholars of Buddhist women's history, about Zen's women ancestors. Over the course of our long friendship Grace has never wavered from these two commitments, bringing her remarkable energy, focus, and insight to both tasks.

Shortly after the workshop at the San Francisco Zen Center, Grace visited me to learn more about what my work had uncovered. On more than one subsequent visit she brought her inspiring interpretations of this material to my students at the University of Tennessee. Although for years I had studied Zen history as a scholar, conversations with Grace for the first time gave me glimpses of its challenges and depths. In due time my friend Grace received Dharma transmission and took up her true work as a Zen teacher in central California. Her second true work, her energetic commitment to Buddhism's and Zen's women ancestors, has also borne fruit in a series of women's Zen retreats, as well as in the extraordinary book you hold in your hands.

You could not find a more useful or more inspiring book on this subject. I look forward to offering this book to my friends and university students. What is exceptionally rich about this book is the way in which Grace brings together her psychological insights into women's motivations and circumstances, most especially the obstacles women face and the ones they create, on the one hand; and on the other hand her own insights from her experience as Zen student and teacher. Both of Grace's careers give rise to powerful, moving questions—and answers—as she engages here with women ancestors who have found ways to carry out deeply engaged and authentic practice in married life, motherhood, convent life, and as students of male masters. Grace's readings of the stories and teachings of women ancestors are of far more than mere historical interest; I believe they are of great value to women practicing Buddhism and other spiritual paths today. All along Grace has held that today's women Zen students and students of Buddhism need as women to connect with and learn from women in their living tradition past and present. In this book Grace Schireson brings women ancestors and their teachings to life, and makes the connection between them and us easy to understand. She enables them to be our teachers right away. In this book you will meet women teachers from many centuries and regions of Asia who will speak to you. Just as valuable, you will meet this book's author, herself an extraordinary teacher.

MIRIAM LEVERING *is a professor of Religious Studies and Asian Studies at the University of Tennessee, and her current work is a study and translation of the letters of Dahui Zonggao, an important figure in the development and practice of the Zen koan curriculum. She has published numerous articles on early Rinzai Zen in China and women in Chinese Buddhism including the book* Zen Inspirations: Essential Meditations and Texts; *she is also the author of* Rethinking Scripture: Essays from a Comparative Perspective.

Preface

WHEN A MALE TEACHER returned from an early North American conference of Zen teachers, one of his female students asked him, "How many women teachers were included in this conference?" The male teacher answered, "We were all women." A long, confused silence followed.

This interaction brought up the tension between female students questioning the Zen establishment about women's representation, and it also pitted the student's insight against the teacher's wisdom and authority. Women exchanged glances and silently wondered whether we as women will be empowered to participate fully in Zen or not, and more immediately, whether we can even ask this question and continue to be accepted in a Zen community in which a male teacher can say that "we are all women." Do we as women not get it, or does this male teacher not get it? Fifteen years ago the women present looked uncomfortably at one another, perplexed at our bind, but didn't challenge his answer. Today I would cut through that confusion by asking him politely, "How many of you women teachers used the ladies' room at this Zen conference?"

It took twenty of my more than forty years of Zen practice to go beyond being intimidated by that "Oneness" thing ("We are all women"), a response that Zen teachers use to wiggle out of the possibility that within Zen there is gender discrimination. Doubtless there is the One. It shows itself as rocks, mountains, and rivers—and as men and women. Or, as stated in the Zen literature, "To understand that all is one is not enough."[1] The One reveals itself through myriad unique formations—even men and women. Why was it so difficult to talk about women and their place in Zen?

My own questioning arose as a request for more information, not a complaint about unfairness. But no matter how carefully I posed the question about women and Zen's history, my questions still somehow challenged my teachers' personal authority and the teachings of Buddhism. If there were mistakes such as gender discrimination in the formation of the Buddhist institution, or if there were flaws in the Buddhism our teachers had received from their teachers, what then was the basis of their teaching authority? Understanding how volatile the questioning was becoming, I felt I had to change the course of the inquiry if I wanted to stay in the Zen community. I also felt that in order to pursue this topic I needed to make sure that I was not caught by my own self-clinging as a female Zen person. It was essential that I move beyond my personal wound, my sorrow and anger about a long history of neglect and, even worse, a purposeful elimination of women from Zen's history.

My purpose shifted. I stopped questioning what had gone wrong with Buddhism and why women Zen teachers had been excluded from the historical record; instead I began to see my function, in this current generation of Zen teachers, to be creating a conduit for these women's past practices to honor them and bring them forward. I wanted to collect the teachings from our Zen grandmothers and carry them to our Zen granddaughters—the women who were still on their way to entering Zen practice. I wanted to find my own practice as a twentieth-century Western woman. And I wanted to help contemporary Zen practice find its way to a more balanced perspective.

By moving beyond an idealization of Zen I have developed a more mature love of, and responsibility for, Zen practice. I have moved beyond the question of why and how female Zen ancestors had been erased from Zen's history. I have sought to identify these erased women and put them back in the Zen practice I loved. I believed that their story, once told, would validate their life work and at the same time correct the mistaken tendencies that had silenced their voice. And I believed that they could help me find my own voice. I was not surprised to learn that other women also longed to hear about these female Zen ancestors.

My mission became finding the traces and scraps of these individual

Zen women's stories and piecing them together. How had these women expressed Zen, and what could they teach us? By learning about their complex and contextualized lives, might my own practice take deeper root in this female body? The search became stronger for me after my priest ordination in 1998, and even more urgent as I took the teaching seat that year. What was I supposed to do? Who could I turn to as a role model? The more deeply I entered practice, the more I wished to express my own Zen practice on the most personal level. I did not want to imitate the male masters. What did I do as a female Zen priest with a husband, children, and now grandchildren? These questions led me to this current study of my own—our own—female Zen ancestors.

For about fifty years, give or take, we in the West have been trying earnestly and patiently to follow the directions of our Japanese, Korean, Vietnamese, and Chinese teachers. We have been trying to build an American Zen practice that will guide us to the depth of their understanding. We have followed their instructions for meditation, kept their daily monastic schedule, worn their traditional monastic clothing, answered obediently when called by our new Dharma names in Asian tongues, and heartily chanted their untranslated sutras. We have asked one another what these various teachers taught, we have studied their books, and we have transcribed their spoken words. Some of us have even crossed oceans to return to our teachers' home temples in Asia in order to bring the Dharma to life here at home. In some cases, we have transferred our hopes and obedience to their designated successors, and some of us have even become these successors.

The Buddha's teaching has moved across cultures, but it takes time for it to sink roots in new soil. Five hundred years was how long it took for Buddhist practice to be transplanted from India to China, and it took another five hundred years for Buddhism to take root in China. In Japan, it again took about five hundred years for Buddhism to be expressed in its own Japanese way. We are still within the first hundred years of Buddhism's Western inception, and we are watching Buddhism adapt even as we are adapting it. Clearly one of the biggest changes in Western Buddhism is the equality of women teachers. Yet all of the West's founding Asian teachers have been male. Exploring and learning about the female side of the practice widens our view of the evolution of practice.

Now that so many men and indeed so many women are teaching Zen in America, some of us are beginning to see that the Zen we are trying to follow does not quite fit who we are. Zen needs to grow if it is to serve its Western practitioners. If, when raising this concern, we fear being disloyal to our Zen ancestors, we must remember what our teachers have told us: As much as we love and live the practice, there is always more to uncover, and we need to make this Asian practice our own. Being intimate with the whole of our lived reality is actually what our teachers asked of us.

One reason the Zen literature we have studied doesn't quite fit is that it is *based entirely on the tradition of male monastic training*. From the perspective of our Asian teachers, a Zen teacher was necessarily male; all teachers that have been most esteemed through liturgy and literature were male monastics. The classic Zen literature contains almost exclusively male masters. One of my Japanese friends reported that she had asked about female Zen teachers when she was in high school in Japan and was told, simply, that there were none. Given that women comprise half of American Zen practitioners and that few of us are monastics, we must consider whether such a tradition can lead us to an authentic American Zen practice, no matter how long or how closely we follow it.

Most Zen teachers in America understand that we need to find a balance between following traditions and changing them, but some are concerned that something important will be lost in the mix. "Let's not throw out the baby with the bathwater!" is often heard regarding our need to adapt Zen practice for modern Westerners. How about if we throw out neither? At the risk of stretching the metaphor, let me suggest that we use a bigger bathtub, fill it with more bathwater, and put male and female babies in it.

For the past ten years I have been deepening my relationship with our female Zen ancestors. I wanted to know who they were, what challenges they faced, and how they were taught. When I began to teach, I wanted to know how they taught Zen as they lived it to their students. I wanted to know how I could relate to them and their practice across the divide of time and place. I wanted to put myself in their place when they faced decisions about taking care of their families, husbands and lovers, and students.

And I had many specific questions that related to my own practice: How did it affect them to be taught by men? What did they feel as they tried to fit into this male practice environment, and how did their Zen training help them with their feelings? Did their practice lives and relationships differ from that of their male teachers? Did they express the Dharma in their own way for other female students? Was their teaching consistently different from that of male ancestors?

Because I wanted to know so much about these women and their experiences both personally and in their sociocultural context, this book has many voices. I describe the women in terms of their specific tradition, their historical culture, their spiritual transformations through Buddhist practices, and their personal histories. To interpret their experiences I draw upon my perspective as an ordained Zen priest and Dharma teacher, my training as a clinical and organizational psychologist, my understanding of women's issues as a feminist, and my personal experiences as daughter, sister, wife, mother, and grandmother.

What I learned about their lives has deepened my practice and my intimacy with my roots. These women adapted their Zen practice to their lives, and their lives to their practice. They formed institutions to meet their needs and bring their practice to their communities. They found ways to support themselves and their institutions financially. In short, they faced many of the issues Westerners now face in establishing Zen Buddhism in our environment.

Part I of this book describes female practitioners as they are portrayed in the classic literature of "Patriarchs' Zen."[2] This portrait is hardly a complete representation of how women practiced Zen. We see the landscape of monastic practice, wandering monks, and the women they encounter all through the patriarchs' eyes. As the patriarchal perspective portrays them, women practice essentially to benefit and enlighten monks. The women bring forth Zen teaching for the principal purpose of training more monks.

Part II of this book presents a different view—a view of how women Zen masters entered Zen practice and how they embodied and taught Zen uniquely as women. The chapters depart from the usual presentations of male masters in terms of their lineages; the women are organized by their functioning roles (founders, working nuns, Dharma heirs of famous male masters, and so on), initially with examples of each role ordered by geographical location—India, China, Korea, and Japan. The chapter on Zen Dharma heirs has examples only from China, Korea, and Japan. In the chapter on female founders, which discusses women who founded temples in different locations, we see how women's practice developed similarly across Asia.

Part III explores how women's practice provides flexible and pragmatic solutions to issues arising in contemporary Western Zen centers. Our sincere efforts to bring Buddhism to the West have resulted in our building residential centers for Zen monastic training. These training centers provide a precious opportunity for Westerners to come to Buddhist practice, but the centers have also had difficulty offering trainings that could most broadly benefit Buddhists living with family and working in the world. Since women historically have more often practiced within a family context and also needed to earn money while practicing, their more flexible approaches may help us more effectively integrate Buddhist practice into Western lay life.

My aspiration for this project is to provide a voice for our female ancestors' broad and flexible teachings, which have been long scattered and forgotten. I hope that this collection of teachings will inspire women to express their lives more fully, inspire Buddhist practitioners to engage in their practice more authentically, and provide Western Dharma teachers with women's teaching stories and examples of adaptations and variety in Zen practice. I believe strongly, as the Buddha did, that the four orders of Buddhism—ordained monks, ordained nuns, laymen, and laywomen—best express the range of practice opportunities for Westerners. Currently, despite the heroic efforts of female practitioners, formal recognition of the *bhikshuni* order has disappeared in Tibet and Southeast Asia, and there is much discussion from scholars and practitioners regarding the pros and cons of its reinstatement. I cannot think of a more powerful argument for the reinstatement of the nuns' order than the actuality of their previous contributions—their life stories, their devotion to sustaining the order, and their living teachings today. The value of the nuns' order becomes evident as we come to know of their past accomplishments.

We have all heard Zen's male voice. Now let us hear Zen's female voice. Our forgotten female ancestors offered their lives for our practice. May we use them well.

Acknowledgments

Aᴮᴼⱽᴱ ᴬᴸᴸ, I want to express gratitude to my husband Kuzan Peter Schireson for his all-encompassing support and devotion. He often remarked that he was sharing his home with me and one hundred other Zen female ancestors. He was not only helpful as an editor, but he was unstintingly gracious as a host to all of us. I want to thank my teachers by name: Shogaku Shunryu Suzuki Roshi, Sojun Mel Weitsman Roshi, and Fukushima Keido Roshi, who revealed the Dharma before my eyes and also taught me how to settle down. There are countless other teachers, a list I will begin but will inevitably fall short of completing: Zenkei Blanche Hartman Roshi, Seisho Maylie Scott Daiosho, Zoketsu Norman Fischer Roshi, Hoitsu Suzuki Roshi, Dupont Roshi, and Dzogchen Ponlop Rinpoche. Their wisdom and patience has been essential for helping find my way and my voice. Professors Suan Miriam Levering, Patricia Fister, and Barbara Ruch not only provided translations but, through their own pioneering spirit, inspired me to persist in this research. Professor Polly Young-Eisendrath, herself an awesome force of nature, inspired me with her friendship and creative productivity.

My Wisdom editor, Josh Bartok, was superb in every way and Myogo Mary-Allen Macneil bravely assisted with the task of early edits. John LeRoy provided outstanding copyediting. Chikudo Lewis Richmond provided interesting insight into Suzuki Roshi. Surei Darlene Cohen Sensei and Enji Angie Boissevain Sensei helped reveal women's practice in our jointly taught annual women's Zen retreats, which were organized successively by Baika Andrea Pratt, Hoka Elizabeth Flora, Shoan Piper Murakami, and all the men and women practicing at Empty Nest Zendo. I would also like to thank the women and their sanghas who received, questioned, and cheered on these teachings through my presentations at their Zen centers: Wendy Egyoku Nakao Roshi of ZCLA; Myotai Bonnie Treace Roshi; Myokaku Jane Schneider Sensei of Beginners' Mind in Northridge, California; and the women of Nalandabodhi in Seattle, of Russian River Zendo in Guerneville, of San Francisco Zen Center, of Berkeley Zen Center, and of Clouds and Water Zen Center in St. Paul. I want to express my gratitude to the additional Sangha Sisters for our inspiring practice period in Japan and our loving and supportive network that was born there: Myoko Sara Hunsaker, Myozen Martie Jensen, Zenki Mary Mocine, Myoko Iva Slone, Myogen Kathryn Stark, and Zenshin Cathleen Williams. Jean Selkirk and Yuko Okumura Sensei provided insight and translation for Joshin-san, our common lineage treasure. Laurie and Alan Senauke also helped me when the chips were down. Thank you all for your encouragement.

Finally, I acknowledge the gift and the responsibility passed to us by the countless female ancestors who gave their lives to the Dharma so that their teachings could continue to flow to us today. We can barely make out their names and faces, but we can still follow the broad path that they cleared for us.

Part I

ZEN'S WOMEN:

Women
Transformed
by Zen

Women in Classical Zen Literature   1

What Is the Difference
between Men and Women in Zen?

To mention women in Zen is to jump right into the middle of a controversy about whether gender matters at all. Zen Buddhists and
their Buddhist forebears have made the revolutionary declaration that
there is no essential difference in the spiritual experience available to all
human beings, regardless of class, race, or gender. The Zen tradition was
established on core teachings that view all phenomenal appearance as
empty of fixed substance. In this context, how could gender be the basis
for any essential differentiation? Yet, Zen is historically an all-male tradition. How does the espoused theory match up with historical reality? The
troublesome question of Zen and gender comes to life in an examination
of the place of women in Zen's history.

Questions about Zen and gender can be provocative: "Feminist propa-
ganda! How could gender, an outward appearance, have anything to do
with expressions of our essential nature?" Who can find a speck of difference between the buddha-nature of a mountain, a person, or an ocean,
let alone an essential difference between the way men and women
express their true nature in Zen practice? And yet the history of Zen practice is nearly void of even a trace of female ancestors. Were there none?
If women practiced and taught, where are their records?

The obvious incongruity between this espoused ideal of a gender-free practice and the lack of information about Zen women should provoke us to look more deeply. But we are reluctant to talk about the disparity, because our lineages teach that there is no such thing as inequality in Zen. If we are respectful Zen Buddhists with deep understanding, we believe that the teaching requires us to see through all appearances of inequality as delusions.

In fact, one of the four documented disciples of Bodhidharma (the founder of Zen in China) was a woman: Zongchi, who is described by Japan's founding Soto patriarch, Eihei Dogen. Women were practicing Zen from the beginning. Most cultures have placed a variety of restrictions on women engaging in activities outside the family, such as strictures about appearing in public, limited educational opportunities, obstacles to financial autonomy, and limited agency as decision makers (requiring women to yield to fathers, husbands, or sons). And so we find fewer women than men entering Zen practice. Given this, we would expect to find a small percentage of Zen lineage ancestors to have been female. Yet their numbers are still fewer.

Miriam Levering cites a Chinese census from the year 1021 that reported 61,240 nuns.[3] Women represented approximately 13 percent of the ordained Buddhist population in thirteenth-century China, but women Zen masters comprised only 1 percent of the total number of the officially recorded monks in the transmission records. Study of later transmission records reveal that even this initially recorded 1 percent was further reduced, effectively erasing the record of the sixteen female Dharma heirs that had constituted that 1 percent. As a result, remaining records leave us with the distinct impression that Zen practice has always been an entirely male profession.

How did it happen that women participated alongside men historically but did not become an enduring part of the Zen record? How did a practice promising equality and liberation become a "Patriarchs' Zen"? Discrepancies in the historical record and the resulting incomplete and inaccurate picture of an all-male Zen history raise many questions. What were the forces that engendered such reluctance to acknowledge women's practice and erased female Zen masters from the historical record? Is that cultural and gender bias still embedded in our tradition, shaping our practice today?

Women and Early Buddhist Practice

During the Buddha's lifetime, Mahapajapati,[4] the Buddha's aunt and later his stepmother, expressed her wish to join the Buddha's order along with her numerous followers. When the Buddha refused her plea, she repeated her aspiration to Ananda, the Buddha's cousin and close disciple. Ananda tried three times to gain the Buddha's permission and was admonished by the Buddha's third refusal: "Enough!" Ananda had struck out—the rule was that any seeker could make only three identical requests—but he did not give up. Instead, he asked the Buddha if in fact women could attain enlightenment.

We are told that the Buddha eventually declared that women were capable of the same awakening as men. He agreed to allow women to enter his order, but only under a set of conditions and restrictions known as the Eight Special Rules. By including women in a subordinate position defined by these Eight Special Rules, the Buddha set two important traditions in motion: Women could leave home and could practice only with other women, and women could not establish equal or independent practice places. These rules have guided (and perhaps misguided) Buddhism from its inception and have affected the evolution of practice for women and men for over twenty-five hundred years.

The study of gender segregation and the development of two separate orders are relevant topics for all who have inherited Buddhist practice from Asian ancestors, and especially for those Western Buddhist founders who have been schooled by Asian teachers trained in the traditional Buddhist view of the nuns' status as subordinate to the monks.

The Eight Special Rules:

1. A nun even of a hundred years' standing shall respectfully greet, rise up in the presence of, bow down before, and perform all proper duties toward a monk ordained even a day.
2. A nun is not to spend the rainy season in a district where there is no monk.
3. Every half-moon, a nun is to await two things from the order of monks—the date of the Uposatha ceremony (communal confession of faults or violations of the monastic code) and the time monks will come to give teaching.

4. After the rains retreat, the nuns are to hold Pavarana (an inquiry into whether any faults have been committed) before both sanghas—that of the monks and that of the nuns—in respect to what has been seen, what has been heard, and what has been suspected.

5. A nun who has been guilty of a serious offense must undergo discipline before both sanghas, that of the monks and that of the nuns.

6. When a novice has trained for two years in the six precepts (the first five precepts plus the precept of taking one meal a day before noon), she should seek ordination from both sanghas.

7. A nun is not to revile or abuse a monk under any circumstance.

8. Admonition of monks by nuns is forbidden; admonition of nuns by monks is not forbidden.[5]

These Eight Special Rules established the women's order as secondary and subordinate to the monks' order. Rules 2 and 5 established the nuns' dependence on the monks' guidance and the nuns' vulnerability to the monks' sanctions. Rules 7 and 8 specify that a nun is never to correct a monk. It is said that the one rule Mahapajapati protested was rule 1, that even the most senior nun was junior to the most junior monk. During the Buddha's lifetime it appears that nuns lived with these rules and were acknowledged for their accomplishments even though their practice was dependent on the monks. As we shall see, over time the nuns' institutionalized dependency confined them in a secondary position, impeded their ability to support themselves, and made it difficult for their order to continue.

Discussion of women in early Buddhism mirrored old cultural stereotypes that collided with Buddhist egalitarian principles of liberation for all beings. Alan Sponberg has suggested that Buddhism moved from a psychologically astute observation of sexual cravings and attraction (for example, describing how cravings for sex could be observed and not acted upon) to outright psychopathological misogyny.[6] Ascetic misogyny in early Buddhism described a woman's unremitting intention as "to ensnare a man," and this diverted attention away from the inevitability of desire and one's own responsibility for that desire to the object of the desire: women.

Westerners need to decide how to work with difficult passages in the Buddhist canon. There are four ways to consider the meaning of the apparently misogynistic remarks by the Buddha in the scriptures.

1. The Buddha, a perfectly realized being, made these remarks in a teaching context that we cannot reproduce or precisely imagine, since we weren't there. We may read his seemingly misogynistic remarks without being troubled by them.

2. Later Buddhists inserted these words into the Buddhist canon. The Buddha, a perfectly realized being, would never have made such remarks. Nevertheless, the teachings should not be questioned.

3. Later Buddhists inserted these words into the Buddhist canon. We may address the negativity of these remarks provided that we clearly state that these and other misogynistic remarks do not come from the Buddha, a perfectly realized being, but come from other, less realized Buddhists at a later time.

4. The Buddha was a spiritual genius manifesting the most complete awakening that may unfold for a human being. He was, however, a human being and was therefore still living with his own karmic consequences and psychological reactivity, as evidenced by these remarks. He was therefore susceptible to a perception or belief that women's sexual power could lead his monks astray to the detriment of his newly formed order. The Buddha's tendency to objectify women and sexuality as a negative force needs to be considered as we transplant Buddhism to the West.

Westerners may choose not to examine the relevance of the early Buddhist attitude and customs toward women, but not without consequence for the transplanting of Buddhism to the West. In this work, my approach tends to take the fourth view, keeping in mind that one cannot be certain that twenty-five-hundred-year-old quotes are accurately attributed. We would do well to examine these misogynistic passages according to the Buddha's own standards and advice to the Kalamas, villagers who asked him how to assess a spiritual teacher:

> Rely not on the teacher but on the teaching. Rely not on the words of the teaching, but on the spirit of the words. Rely not on theory, but on experience. Do not believe in anything simply because you have heard it. Do not believe in traditions because they have been handed down for many generations. Do not believe anything because it is spoken and rumored by

many. Do not believe in anything because it is written in your religious books. Do not believe in anything merely on the authority of your teachers and elders. But after observation and analysis, when you find that anything agrees with reason and is conducive to the good and the benefit of one and all, then accept it and live up to it.[7]

Sponberg proposes that early Buddhists found the denigration of women familiar and natural because it conformed to an earlier Hindu view: if a person is born a female this is because of karmic forces leading to a lower rebirth. This view is encountered even today. At a contemporary Western Tibetan practice place I was once asked why we should be interested in studying the teachings of female ancestors since it is understood that being born a woman is considered within Buddhism to be an inferior birth. As women, how should we respond to this? Do we justify this Buddhist belief and consider how amazing it is that, despite our inferior female birth, we can teach the Dharma? Or do we consider that discrimination and prejudice were smuggled into our enlightened teachings and practice?

This view, along with the need to protect monks from women's ensnaring ways, seems to have been incorporated into early Buddhist thinking and formed part of the basis for the Eight Special Rules. Early Buddhists believed ordaining women would create major obstacles for the acceptance, credibility, and continuation of their new order within the Hindu tradition. Allowing women equal entry would disturb the prevailing culture and threaten power relations in the future. To resolve the contradiction—that Buddhist women have equal capacity to awaken but are unequal participants—women were granted limited entry to ordination with a second-class status.

The Eight Special Rules significantly limited the development of women's practice over the longer term. For one thing, they limited opportunities for the development of female teachers. Under these rules nuns were not only junior to monks without exception but also depended on monks for training and so could not become fully independent Dharma teachers. Furthermore, the rules had significant and lasting implications for the status of nuns. Nuns' practice was not considered first-rate, and certainly not equivalent to monks' practice. This made it difficult for nuns to attract followers and receive the donations necessary to support their practice. Throughout history, nuns' convents were impoverished whereas monks' monasteries, with their first-class status and well-recognized teachers, received greater donations and attracted more powerful supporters.

To this day the implicit judgment that nuns are second-tier practitioners may account for some of the relative lack of interest Westerners have displayed in studying early women Zen masters and their convents, practices, and leaders.

But if women were forbidden to practice with men, how did some women manage to become practice leaders and masters, as reported in the classic Zen literature? Clearly, at least some of the Eight Special Rules must have been bent or broken. If so, this may be related to the fact that early on Zen based its teaching on innate wisdom uncovered through meditation and declared itself not dependent on sutras or written word. Like all other Buddhist schools, however, the earliest Zen communities took direction from Buddhist scriptures mandating separate orders for men's and women's practice. On the other hand, exceptional male masters manifested Zen's intention to be free from doctrine and taught women alongside monks. We find that some of these exceptional teachers had female disciples and even female Dharma heirs.

Still, most Zen teachers respected the division of male and female orders practicing in separate temples. The Confucian tradition of male ancestor worship in China further reinforced the androcentrism and male-female inequality derived from the Hindu tradition. Confucian values also engendered additional practices of honoring male Zen masters as if they were familial ancestors. Even today, gender-differentiated and segregated practices continue to be pervasive in most Asian Zen temples.

The Zen Master as a Manly Man

What we learn from classical Zen literature most emphatically is that all Zen masters are heroic. Levering has noted this use of male-gendered language to describe a Zen master's essence. On the one hand, all beings, without exception, are capable of enlightenment. On the other hand, any being who attains the Way is *chang-fu*, or a "manly man."[8] The heroism of Zen masters is both the source of their determination to practice and the fruit of their spiritual accomplishment. Zen masters predominantly come in one flavor—the heroic manly men. What does this say about the female Zen master?

The women depicted in classic Zen literature appear, just like the men, in the one-dimensional role of male hero. However, they lack almost all of the human, personal characteristics that help us connect and identify with their male Zen master counterparts. Happy as we are to know that Zen women existed, we find virtually no details through which to form a personal connection with them. They appear as manly embodiments of Zen transformation, but we don't know how they were transformed or who they were before they came to practice. We learn nothing about how they found their way in such difficult times. We are left to wonder what they were really like and whether they can serve as useful role models for female practitioners today. In short, we have no substantial information on just how these women practiced *as women.*

Contemporary women reading about these women in the classical Zen literature may find the macho portraits less than inviting. How many contemporary women really wish to become transformed into female clones of male Zen masters? If women do wish to become *chang-fu,* is this a healthy aspiration or further evidence of internalized self-deprecation? For many women, the image of the heroic manly woman may in fact be unrealistic, unattainable, or even undesirable.

Perhaps early female Zen masters were anomalies. Could a women, raised as a woman, become a tough-as-nails female version of a male Zen master? Perhaps the early Zen women were exceptionally heroic before they ever entered practice.

As Levering has explained, we always hear about women's Zen contributions in (male) conquest language. All distinguishing female characteristics seem to disappear in the light of Zen. We are without any image or archetype of a female or a feminine Zen master. As Levering notes, while classic portrayals show that Zen included women, Patriarchs' Zen never became androgynous, incorporating the varied experience of both men and women as a way of enriching the tradition.

The next chapter presents women from the perspective of classic Zen literature. We learn nothing about how they live as women, but we learn how they are transformed by Zen, how they serve to transform Zen monks, and how they serve to highlight great Zen masters.

Women Meeting Monks

2

Nuns Who Could Be Men

Two women, Moshan Liaoran (ca. 860) of Ruizhou and Liu Tiemo (ca. 870), exemplify the role of women identical to male Zen masters. Both have been completely transformed into male Zen heroes; both are *chang-fu*. Like the macho stereotype of a thoroughly masculine, overly muscled "he-man," we could dub the image of this tough-as-nails female type a "she-man." We are told that they are women, but we hear not even a hint of female identity, behavior, or life experience. Their personalities match those of the strongest male masters.

Moshan Liaoran:
First Full-Fledged Female Zen Master

Zen Master Moshan Liaoran was among the first women to be included in the American Zen curriculum. She is one of the few female Dharma heirs in the records of the male lineage.[9] Although we know nothing of Moshan's early life, her life as a woman, or how she came to practice Zen, her status as a teacher is unquestionable. Moshan's awakening to her buddha-nature transcended her gender and her circumstances, and this is made manifest by her teaching words, teaching style, and position as a teacher in Sung dynasty China. We first meet Moshan in an exchange with Guanxi Zhixian.

Zen Master Moshan Liaoran of Ruizhou [who was abbess of her own temple] was a Dharma heir of Gao'an Dayu (ca. 800). One day the monk Guanxi Xian arrived at Mt. Mo, where Moshan taught, and said, "If there's someone here who's worthy, I'll stay here. If not, I'll overturn the meditation platform!" He then entered the hall.

Moshan sent her attendant to query the visitor, saying, "Your Reverence, are you here sightseeing, or have you come seeking the Buddhadharma?"

"I seek the Dharma."

So Moshan sat upon the Dharma seat [in the audience room] and Xian entered for an interview.

Moshan said, "Your Reverence, where have you come from today?"

Guanxi said, "From the road's mouth [an undefiled place]."

Moshan said, "Why don't you cover it [that mouth]?"

Guanxi didn't answer for some time. Finally he asked, "What about Mt. Mo [Moshan]?"

Moshan said, "The peak isn't revealed."

Guanxi asked, "Who is the master of Mt. Mo?"

Moshan said, "Without the form of man or woman."

Guanxi shouted, then said, "Why can't it transform itself [become a man]?"

Moshan said, "It's not a god or demon [wild fox spirit]. So how could it become something else?"

Guanxi then submitted to become Moshan's student. He worked as head gardener for three years.[10]

For the first time in the history of Zen we encounter a full-fledged female teacher, teaching a man at her own temple. There is little to explain how this happened; we do understand, through Guanxi's challenge to her authority, that her status was unusual. Moshan, head of a temple, surrounded by her students and monastic formalities such as ascending the platform in the Dharma hall to meet Guanxi, was apparently able to teach both male and female practitioners in her temple. This is a flagrant infraction of the Eight Special Rules. Through her skillful Zen words she asserted her authority and simultaneously revealed

Guanxi's arrogance. Cleverly connecting the road to the person before her, she pointed out his (big) mouth: "Why don't you cover it?" Or, why are you so crude? By criticizing, and indeed teaching, a male monk, she was also in violation of the Eight Special Rules. After all, if she couldn't correct male students, how could she point out their mistaken views?

In response to Moshan's verbal slap, Guanxi paused and redirected his questioning to Moshan in her role as Mt. Mo—as the abbess and therefore the personification of the mountain and peak of the temple. "If I am crude by opening my mouth," he asked, "how do you express yourself?" She answered: "The peak is not revealed." Or, "I am not pointing to myself, my position, or my ability. To understand the peak, the essence of my teaching, you need to penetrate your own confusion, and whatever has covered this peak from your view. I have no need to show off to you, to point to this, the peak, but you may uncover my teaching by seeing through your own delusions."

This must not have been the first time Moshan had been challenged because of her gender; she skillfully uncovered Guanxi's sexist attitude, and his sticking to his view that he would be the judge of her skill. There was something arrogant in his approach and it was Moshan's job to help him see through it. Suspecting a lurking sexist attitude, she had put forth a preemptive strike and stated that what she was teaching was "without the form of man or woman." She confronted Guanxi's challenge to her teaching based on her suspicion that he would question her authority because she was a woman, and she positioned herself to address his concern. Guanxi asked her, in effect, "What are you, a woman, doing in this position? What does a woman teacher have to offer?" She responded on the level of absolute reality. Gender is not what teaches the Dharma; what there is that teaches, what there is to teach, goes beyond gender. And yet gender exists—why would you need to change that? Wisdom pours forth from everything so why not just accept each voice? What needs transformation when neither man nor woman is what specifically teaches the Dharma? Existence itself teaches the Dharma.

Buddhist scriptures, following earlier Hindu beliefs, assert that a female form must transform to a male form to achieve buddhahood, but here Moshan refutes it.[11] On the level of the absolute, there are no genders; on the level of relative reality, there are just many different forms. Why then would these forms need to transform? This exchange about the essential, formless, genderless quality of *it* established Moshan as a Zen master, and it simultaneously validated women's ability to teach Dharma in the face of Buddhist superstition.

Moshan has been an ongoing inspiration to women practicing Zen in China, Korea, and Japan. Her quick wit and penetrating teaching liken her to a male Zen master. Today we are taught in Zen lectures that women can equal men in Zen. In Moshan we meet the first one who clearly *was* equal.

Iron Grinder Liu:
Her Active Edge Was Sharp and Dangerous

Iron Grinder Liu (Liu Tiemo, ca. 870) was a student of Guishan (d. 853). It is not a coincidence that *iron* appears in her name. She embodies the stereotype of a hardhearted iron woman. Her name is variously translated as Iron Grinder, Iron-Grinder, and Iron Grindstone—the translations all allude to her ability to reduce the strongest matter to dust.

Rosabeth Moss Kanter in her study of how women are perceived in corporate America found that women entering male-dominated organizations survived via their relationships to men in stereotypical roles as mother, pet, or seductress.[12] If a woman did not enter the familiar and familial role of wife, mother, or sister, she was seen as a kind of monster. Kanter uses the term "iron maiden," the name of a medieval torture device, to describe a woman focused on organizational results who didn't offer enough relationship to suit the male power structure—a woman perceived as too authoritative, emotionally disconnected from the familial role, and unyielding. Such a woman, according to Kanter, was viewed as made of iron, not flesh and blood.

Classic Zen literature emphasized Liu's toughness—her well-trained, honed Zen mind. She was described as performing like a grinding wheel. When a Zen monk met her, sparks would surely fly.

> The leader of a congregation, named Iron-Grinder Liu, came to visit Zen Master Zihu.
> Zihu said, "I've heard of Iron-Grinder Liu. They say you're hard to contend with. Is that so?"
> Iron-Grinder Liu said, "I daren't presume so."
> Zihu asked, "Do you turn left or right?"

Liu said, "Don't tip over, Master."
Zihu immediately hit her.[13]

Iron Grinder taught at her own temple and was known for her ferocious Dharma. In this exchange with Zihu, she demonstrated that she could not be caught with words of praise or disparagement. She reminded Zihu that his wondering about "left or right" would throw him off balance, pull him into the world of dualistic thinking and comparison. Was she difficult or easy to deal with? Zihu asked her. When she corrected him he resorted to his own trademark: a beating with the stick. As a ferocious woman Zen master, she did not exempt herself from physical beatings. These did not diminish her strength or her ability to stand without tipping. Master Fojian commented in the *Book of Serenity*, "She let Zihu wield the stick, but though she appeared soft, she had steel-like strength."[14]

Iron Grinder lived in a hermitage just a few miles from her teacher and frequent sparring partner, Guishan. She is remembered for her enigmatic exchange with Guishan, a conversation that did not rely solely on words; we sense their deep connection—his laying down and her leaving—as their meaning. Their verbal exchange does not say what they meant, nor mean what it says. It represents two Zen adepts communicating through terse verbal and nonverbal exchange. Nothing was wasted; they understood each other thoroughly, and they responded completely.

> Iron Grindstone Liu went to Guishan.
> Guishan said: "Old cow, so you've come!"
> She said, "Tomorrow there is a communal feast on Mt. Tai; are you going?"
> Guishan lay down.
> Liu immediately left.[15]

Liu and Guishan embody the unspoken intimacy of the Zen teacher-student relationship: she an "old cow," he the old water buffalo—as he refers to himself elsewhere. They enact the relationship usually ascribed to male student and teacher. We witness an interaction that could have taken place between two men—except, of course, that he calls her "cow."

Both teachers stay close to their hermitage, close to their practice, close to their easeful samadhi. They have little need to participate in community gatherings. Liu clearly knows that neither of them will be attending the "big event" on Mt. Tai, since it is six hundred miles away with only one day left to travel there. She asked him whether he was going only so that the two of them, teacher and student, could mutually express their peace and contentment in the Dharma. They needed neither the ceremonial nor the conventional accolades of the Zen community. Just let go.

Guishan had found a way to teach and empower this talented woman just as he taught men. We know that their relationship continued, that they most likely lived in close proximity, but that she probably had her own practice place. Reputed to be "dangerous," she completely inhabited the stereotypical role of the heroic, powerful male Zen master. From her familiarity and acceptance of the use of the stick, we see that she had been treated like a man.

Did Iron Grinder's embodiment of *chang-fu* represent the only type of woman that could ascend to the position of Zen master, or did her personality include qualities outside this stereotype? Was she an Iron Grinder before she came to Zen, or was her toughness the result of Zen training? Did Zen create Iron Grinders, or did Iron Grinders gravitate to Zen practice? We might even wonder whether this stereotype of the single-minded, strong "she-man" ever existed as described.

Token Nuns: Establishing Zen as a Truly Liberated Spiritual Institution

When the Buddhist female order took root in China through the leadership of the first Chinese monks, it had to contend with Confucian ideals about human relations, including the submission and seclusion of women. Later this submission of Buddhist women was transferred to Japan. Occasionally Zen teachers have cited women who had been allowed to participate in male monasteries as examples of enlightened practice. These few women are referred to, in contemporary language, as tokens—the symbolic but not genuine inclusion of a minority representative.

Eihei Dogen, the thirteenth-century Japanese Soto Zen founder, insisted in his essay "Raihaitokuzui" (Attaining the Marrow) that Zen needs to be freed from gender stereotypes if it is to truly offer complete awakening.[16] He preached that if monks experienced enlightenment on the meditation cushion without examining their own sexist views, they limited and hindered their boundless realization with self-serving, ignorant prejudice and superstition. Dogen insisted that monks who attempted to integrate their experience of enlightenment, while at the same time maintaining conventional and small-minded attitudes—for instance, the banning of women from the holiest temple sites[17]—were just "stupid people who insulted the Dharma."

To prove that these negative and limiting stereotypes of women did not reflect reality but instead represented provincial cultural stereotypes, Dogen cited powerful Zen women who were accepted by the Chinese Zen establishment and he contrasted these women's participation in Chinese Zen to the superstitious and ignorant Buddhist practices he experienced in Japan as he established his first temple. We see these Sung dynasty Chinese women through an outstanding teacher's vision of gender-free Zen. Once again, unfortunately, we learn nothing about the women's identities as women or how they entered or achieved recognition in an all-male system. We are grateful to Dogen for his understanding of the problem of Zen women's inequality and his wish to remedy it.

In this essay Dogen mentions two other Chinese women: Zongchi and Miaoxin.

Zongchi:
First in the Zen Tradition

The Chinese nun Zongchi (ca. 550) demonstrated Zen's ability to train women alongside men from its earliest inception. Born in the early to mid-sixth century, Zongchi was the sister of an important Chinese king,[18] and has occasionally been described as the daughter of Emperor Wu of the Liang dynasty of sixth-century China.[19] We know of her, through Dogen, as one of Bodhidharma's disciples. Bodhidharma, of course, is the Indian monk who brought Zen practice from India to China and is often referred to as the first Chinese patriarch. Bodhidharma's encounter with Emperor Wu and his subsequent founding of Shaolin temple are widely accepted as the founding of Zen in China.

Bodhidharma was surely familiar with the Buddha's admonitions regarding separate practice for women. It is not known how Zongchi became his disciple, but it appears that he taught her alongside his male disciples at Shaolin temple.[20] In the *Shobogenzo* chapter called "Katto" (Twining Vines),[21] Dogen names her as one of Bodhidharma's four equal Dharma heirs. We can only assume that Bodhidharma's confidence in the depth of his own awakening allowed him to seemingly dismiss the traditionally observed Buddha's Eight Special Rules.

Zongchi is an example of an early female pioneer who had the opportunity, probably through her aristocratic family, to study with a great master and practice alongside his male disciples as one of them. Miriam Levering, in her essay on Dogen's "Raihaitokuzui,"[22] contends that Chinese accounts of Bodhidharma had originally described Zongchi as a full Dharma heir, but that history tended to downgrade her equality, placing her in the third or fourth position among Bodhidharma's four students. This view tends to depict her as a kind of placeholder, a female token illustrating the potential for Zen's undiscriminating wisdom in action.

Zen lineage records, the official story of the patriarch's mind-to-mind transmission, continued through another of the four disciples, but Dogen emphasized that the teaching of each of Bodhidharma's four disciples was complete. Even though we remember and recognize only one of Bodhidharma's successors, Huike, as a lineage holder, Dogen considered Zongchi equally endowed with understanding.[23] Interestingly, according to the records, she was also able to recite the whole of the Lotus Sutra from memory.

Zongchi's only recorded teaching is a single discussion with Bodhidharma. The discussion occurred after Bodhidharma's nine years in China when he gathered his disciples and asked each one to express his or her practice realization. The nun Zongchi said: "My understanding now is that it is like the joy of seeing the buddha land of Aksobhya: it is felt at the first glance, but not the second glance."[24] Bodhidharma's teaching emphasized a direct experience of one's own nature. He acknowledged her remark and said to her, "You have my flesh." Zongchi's teaching articulated direct experience that cannot be duplicated by description or review or conveyed through explanation or instruction.

Although Dogen referred to her as an example of an early lineage holder, we learn nothing more of her life or her teachings after the discussion at Shaolin temple.

Miaoxin:
Enlightened Seventeen Monks

In "Raihaitokuzui" Dogen extolled another nun, Miaoxin (ca. 880), as a powerful example of a woman who enlightened men. She studied with Guishan's Dharma heir, Yangshan (d. 883). This is a tantalizing detail: Guishan's teaching relationship with Liu Tiemo (Iron Grinder Liu) may have helped Yangshan teach and recognize Miaoxin's ability, perhaps "like father, like son." We can guess that since both Liu Tiemo and Yangshan studied with the same teacher, either Yangshan knew Liu Tiemo personally, or he knew his teacher's respect for her.

Although Dogen could not have personally witnessed Miaoxin's admittance to Yangshan's temple, since her assignment there occurred several hundred years prior to his birth, he declared with certainty that none of the monks present disputed her selection. Dogen also recounted the teaching she later offered to seventeen monks who had come to call on her teacher, Yangshan:

Once she [Miaoxin] was working in the administrative quarters and seventeen monks [on pilgrimage] from the Shoku district came to see her master [Yangshan]. They wanted to climb the mountain right away, but it was too late and they had to spend the night at the administrative quarters. At night they began to discuss the famous story of the Sixth Patriarch and the wind and the flag. [One monk says the flag is moving, one monk says the wind is moving, the Sixth Patriarch says, "The flag is not moving, the wind is not moving, you are moving your mind!"] All of the seventeen monks gave their respective opinions, but all were off the mark. Miaoxin, on the other side of the wall, overheard their discussion and said, "It's a pity that the seventeen blind donkeys have worn out so many pairs of straw sandals on pilgrimages and still cannot even dream about the Buddhadharma." A little later Miaoxin's male attendant told them her response to their discussion, but none of them were dissatisfied or resentful about it. On the contrary, they were ashamed at their lack of attainment of the Way. They straightened up their robes, offered incense, made prostrations, and sought her instruction. She said, "Please come closer." But before they could come closer, she shouted, "The wind is not moving, the flag is not moving, the mind is not moving!" When they heard that, all of them reflected on their own hearts, then bowed to her in gratitude and became her disciples. Soon after that they returned to Seishu without even visiting Yangshan. Truly, Miaoxin's level is not surpassed by the three sages and ten saints, and her actions are those of one who transmits the right stream of the buddhas and patriarchs.[25]

Miaoxin embodied the confidence and penetrating wisdom of a traditional Zen master. Seeing that the monks were wallowing in dualistic analysis, she set them up to directly experience *"what moves?"* by asking them to physically move forward to experience that which actually moves. Before they could respond to her instructions she caught them by surprise: Wind doesn't move, flag doesn't move, mind doesn't move—what moves? The nondualistic experience of "what moves?" caught the monks in mid-movement, opened them to a direct experience of life's continuous and all-pervading movement.

Dogen portrayed a woman embodying the Zen master's role who gained recognition by teaching in a way that enlightened monks. Not only was the teacher Miaoxin masterful, but the inquiring monks were not caught by dualistic judgments about whether to invite a woman to teach them. Dogen encouraged his own monks to change their provincial thinking, to be open-minded to the teachings of women. He ends his essay with these admonishments to his audience regarding a mythical female Buddhist teacher, a woman who transforms herself into a male Buddha: "She should be venerated, honored, and respected like all the Buddhas and *tathagathas*. This is the ancient practice of the Buddhist Way. Those who do not know this are to be greatly pitied."[26]

Dogen's attempts to overcome discrimination against women among his followers show that some Zen teachers have historically strived to venerate male and female enlightened beings equally. Without Dogen's efforts to teach his monks to see beyond their prejudices, we might have lost the story of Miaoxin and her inspirational teaching, which remains influential to this day. Japanese Soto nuns used Dogen's seminal teaching and "Raihaitokuzui" to encourage twentieth-century

Soto bureaucracy to recognize them as equal participants in the Soto Zen institution.

Women Who Humiliated Monks

Sometimes women's Zen teachings catalyzed monks to deeper investigation of the Dharma, as we have seen in the stories of Moshan and Miaoxin. Another class of Zen stories involve women who manifest their ability by showing monks their own foolishness—holding a mirror to the monks' inability to be present in the moment of everyday activity. In these stories Zen monks learn to survive the worst embarrassment of all—defeat at the hands of an unknown and often untrained woman's Dharma words. Even the names of these women—except for one nun named Shiji—have been lost. Some of these women teachers, who often lacked even basic ordination, fit the mother stereotype and are known to Zen students as "tea ladies." Others fit the "iron maiden" stereotype of a mean old lady. Both types act as anonymous agents of change that push a monk in the right direction—toward greater perseverance and humility—with a little slap.

Shiji:
A Brief Visitor Who Unsettled Juzhi

Recounted in the teaching record of the monk Jinhua Juzhi (Japanese: "One Finger Gutei"), we find the story of the mysterious nun Shiji (ca. 900). Shiji, whose name means "reality," played a pivotal role in Juzhi's training through her brief visit to his hermitage. Strong, silent, and thoroughly penetrating, she is a classic iron maiden: invulnerable, without need of relationship, and completely self-confident.

> When Juzhi [was living in a hermitage] in eastern China a nun named Shiji came to his hut. When she got there, she went straight in; without taking off her hat, she walked around his meditation seat thrice, holding her staff. "If you can speak," she said, "I'll take off my hat." She questioned him three times, but Juzhi had no reply. Then as she was leaving, Juzhi said, "It's late—would you stay the night?" The nun said, "If you can

speak, I'll stay." Again Juzhi had no reply. The nun then walked out. Juzhi said sorrowfully, "Though I'm in the body of a man, I lack the spirit of a man." After this he determined to clarify this matter.[27]

This nun tested her understanding by challenging Zen monks (and perhaps nuns) she encountered in remote hermitages. Juzhi, tongue-tied, could not bring forth a word of Zen. He was a man and his challenger was a woman, but he could not show the true Zen he-man spirit, which *she* could. Trounced by a woman—how disturbing! But Juzhi was honest with himself about his deficiencies, and he was fair-minded. He was willing to learn from this visiting nun whom he saw as his Dharma senior.

At nightfall Shiji left the hermitage and traveled on, we know not where. She was unconcerned for her safety in this remote location, although it seems that Juzhi was. Her pursuit of Zen proceeded without hesitation. Her mission was to live and travel solely to expose the Dharma. But whereas we can follow Juzhi's development as Zen master, Shiji's training and teaching career were lost.

The Tea Lady: Deshan Refreshed

Deshan's tea-cake lady (ca. 850) is one witty example of a scholarly monk's comeuppance through the barbed insight of an unnamed old woman, a mother type. The tea lady, who sells pastries, softens up Deshan's arrogant defenses and sends him off to Zen Master Longtan for a more complete ego annihilation. It should be noted that the Chinese word for the pastry she served also means to "refresh" or "lighten" as well as "point to the mind." Perhaps this tea lady had practiced with the great Longtan and been refreshed by his awakened mind. We learn nothing of her training through this story or any other.

Deshan (819–914), a scholar-monk who lectured on the Diamond Sutra in China, became a famous Zen teacher. The Diamond Sutra teaches that the realization of buddhahood occurs through concentrated study of the conduct and practices of the buddhas over countless eons, and that right conduct must come forth from unselfishness and helping others. When Deshan heard that the Zen masters of southern China were teaching that the mind itself was Buddha, he resolved to travel to "destroy this crew of Chan [Zen] devils." Deshan felt study was being overlooked by these devils, whose only concern seemed to be teaching how the mind appears in this very moment as Buddha. Full of himself, and carrying a big load of scholars' commentaries, Deshan stopped on the road for a snack of tea cakes an old woman was selling.

He put down his commentaries to buy some refreshment to lighten his mind. The woman said, "What is that you're carrying?" Deshan said, "Commentaries on the Diamond Sutra." The woman said, "I have a question for you. If you can answer it, I'll give you some pastry; if not, you'll have to buy it somewhere else." Deshan agreed. The woman said, "The Diamond Sutra says, 'Past mind can't be grasped, present mind can't be grasped, future mind can't be grasped.' Which mind does the learned monk wish to lighten [refresh]?" Deshan was speechless. The woman directed him to call on Longtan.[28]

This tea lady understood that Deshan was loaded up with scholarly writings and self-importance. She taught Deshan that Zen was not to be found in his academic studies, but right here in this very moment of interaction. She helped break down the heavy barrier of righteousness he wanted to inflict on the southern Zen school. This old lady dealt in tea cakes—or mind pointers—daily, so perhaps Deshan was not the only smarty-pants to fall prey to the old granny's Zen barb.

Sen-jo and Her Soul Are Separated

Sen-jo, also known as Seijo, the subject of Case 35 in the *Mumonkan*, seems to illustrate both the mother and the tea lady roles.[29] Sen-jo is not a Zen practitioner—or indeed even a real person. In fact, she is a character from a kind of Chinese ghost story. But her story, used in the context of a Zen koan, illustrates the extreme pressure that women experienced when they had to choose between their obligation to family members and their aspiration to self-realization through practice outside the home. This is a theme for many of the female practitioners who appear in the next section on women's Zen. While Sen-jo struggled between her father's choice of her husband and her own heart's desire, many female practitioners struggled between their desire to enter a Zen temple and their parents' demand that they enter married life. Sen-jo could either follow her heart and disappoint her family or obey her family and betray her heart. Either way, the suffering would be overwhelming.

Sen-jo, the daughter of Chokan, was raised expecting that one day she would marry her cousin Oochu, with whom she had played since early childhood. So when Sen-jo's father, Chokan, announced that Sen-jo was to marry another, both were heartbroken. Oochu, unable to bear watching Sen-jo marry another, got a boat to leave the village. As he was departing, he saw a shadowy figure running alongside the shore. He was delighted to see that it was Sen-jo, who joined him in the boat. The two journeyed far away, where they were wed and had two children.

As time passed Sen-jo longed to see her homeland and be forgiven by her parents. Oochu took her back to their native village, and he left her in the boat while he met with her father to apologize for their disobedience.

Chokan, astonished, asked Oochu, "Which girl are you talking about?"

"Your daughter Sen-jo, Father," replied Oochu.

Chokan said, "My daughter Sen? Since the time you left [our village] she has been sick in bed and has been unable to speak."[30]

The story is resolved when Sen-jo leaves the boat and meets the Sen-jo who had been sick in bed. The two parts of the self meet, merge, and become one person again. The teachings on this story illustrate how women represent the strongest side of emotions, devotion and obligation. When a woman can face her own path directly she can become unified with her true purpose. Zen commentaries on this case suggest that we are fooled by separating ourselves into parts or separating our lives into parts. They use this women's story, rather than that of a man, since women are more powerful symbols of emotion and obligation to others. Oochu seems to have walked away from the uncomfortable family machinations without difficulty, but leaving home was torment for Sen-jo, who felt the separation keenly. Only through the deepest practice, the story tells us, can we perceive our unified and true self in the midst of our own longings and relationships.

The Old Lady Who Burned Down the Hut

In this story of unknown origin an old woman enlists a seductress to check out an old monk. Often retold by Zen teachers, it illustrates how true compassion is superior to mere renunciation of desire.

> There was an old woman in China who had supported a monk for over twenty years. She had built a little hut for him and fed him while he was meditating. Finally she wondered just what progress he had made in all this time. To find out, she obtained the help of a girl rich in desire.
>
> "Go and embrace him," she told her, "and then ask him suddenly: 'What now?'"
>
> The girl called upon the monk and without much ado caressed him and asked him what he was going to do about it.
>
> "An old tree grows on a cold rock in winter," replied the monk somewhat poetically. "Nowhere is there any warmth."
>
> The girl returned and related what he had said.
>
> "To think I fed that fellow for twenty years!" exclaimed the old woman in anger. "He showed no consideration for your need, no disposition to explain your condition. He need not have responded to passion, but at least he could have evidenced some compassion."
>
> She at once went to the hut of the monk and burned it down.[31]

Zen masters like to ask their students, "Why did the old lady burn down the hut?" A nameless old woman, a mother figure who has been providing nourishment and support to a monk, tests an experienced but unsuspecting monk. She finds his practice barren. She was a strict teacher in disguise. She would have burned down the hut and beaten the old monk if the girl had seduced him. But the callous way he rejected the young woman indicated only coldheartedness. If this monk's practice had helped him to transcend his desire, he would have had the resources and empathy to question the young woman's inappropriate and out of context desire. Why was she so attracted to a solitary old monk? Didn't he know he was not exactly a sex symbol at his age, in his circumstances?

This story helps us see women in the role of practice checkpoints. Has a monk snuffed out his humanity by practicing austerities? Like the nun Shiji who tested Juzhi, this old woman tests the monk's lifetime wisdom. Neither Shiji nor this old lady believed that a monk's hut-dwelling lifestyle is proof of enlightenment. They want to know how a monk responds to the unpredictable. What does a monk do when a person becomes confused and needy? How does he balance his feelings of passion and his role as a vessel of compassion in the service of all beings? This old lady knows there is a difference between repressing feelings and letting go of them. She knows that there is a difference between austerity and genuine nonattachment. And she shows that providing a hut for a monk can be giving him a place to hide, not a place to practice.

On one level, we can see this old lady as a manifestation of the Great Mother; she provides for our needs, and when the time is right, she takes everything away. There is also something in her that this book will address later: the difference between male and female spirituality. A theme in female spirituality is the actual embodiment, not just the conceptualization, of wisdom and compassion. The old woman questions how the monk embodies wisdom, cares for other human beings, and shows he is fully human. The Great Mother, or the embodiment of female spirituality, highlights issues of interdependence, relationships, and sexuality. While the Buddha and his followers emphasized the cooling of passion, the life of nonattachment free of desire, women more often concern themselves with the hands-on engagement with life's messiness.

Yuzen's Shakedown

Stories illustrating the power of nuns and laywomen to humiliate did not end in the Chinese classical period of Zen. When he was young, the Obaku Zen monk Yuzen Gentatsu (1842–1918), who later became the abbot of Myoshinji temple in Kyoto, had an unfortunate run-in with a nun he was traveling with. Yuzen recounted his experience:

> I was young then, speaking nonsense and boasting greatly. To my surprise, the nun showed the knowledge and experience of an equivalent amount of training. Her calm opposition quickly

silenced me. I couldn't say anything in reply to show any Zen understanding. The nun harshly demonstrated my ignorance. At her sarcastic words all I could do was make the sound, *Guu*—. The chagrin at the time was severe, if there had been a hole, I would have crawled into it. It lasted a long time and inspired me to work harder.[32]

"*Guu*"? This sounds like baby talk. Yuzen, stupefied by the nun's "calm opposition," found himself face-to-face with an awakened and confident nun who he seemed to experience as an iron maiden. No place for Yuzen's charm or boasting here! Yuzen was inspired to return to his basic practice with more determination, but there were other consequences to this encounter. Sadly, Yuzen developed a lifelong dislike of nuns, and we may surmise that what happened to Yuzen happened to others. The Eight Special Rules forbid nuns to correct monks. Corrections from women are therefore particularly difficult when monks are taught to see women as inherently incompetent.

Nuns and Laywomen Questioning Great Zen Masters

Some women's encounters with well-known Zen monks highlight these masters' teachings. Found in the Zen masters' records, these women are anonymous. In these stories the woman has found a way to work with a great master, but she serves only as a foil to demonstrate his flexible mind, teaching ability, or his humanness. These discourses show that the great male teachers are equally skillful whether they are teaching monks, nuns, or laywomen, regardless of the question asked.

Zhaozhou's Nuns and Laywomen

Zhaozhou Congshen (878–987, Japanese: Joshu), one of the greatest Zen masters of all time, was so deft with words that his followers said "he emitted sparks from his lips and had a boneless tongue."[33] He could not be trapped in verbal discourse; he always spoke clear truth regarding practice instructions. Whether women raised questions about Zen or questions specific to gender issues, his answers hit the mark and he pointed the way. He answered all questions with nothing extra. Through these encounters with female students, we get a view of Zhaozhou's warmth and playfulness.

The first encounter presents an anonymous nun pursuing Zhaozhou with all her might. When she tries to corner him, he just laughs good-naturedly.

> A nun asked, "Setting aside the explanations given until now, please instruct me."
> The master shouted, "Burn an iron bottle to ashes!"
> The nun then went and poured the water out of an iron bottle and brought it to the master saying, "Please answer."
> The master laughed at this.[34]

With this elegant gesture, we may hear this anonymous woman saying, "Okay teacher, if burning the iron bottle explains things, let's see how you do it! Practice what you preach!" We may infer from this story the nun's familiarity and freedom within Zhaozhou's monastic setting. She knows where to find the iron bottle, feels free to dump the water out, and comes back to confront the teacher. She felt right at home at Zhaozhou's temple; we can almost see the nuns practicing right there with Zhaozhou and his monks.

On another occasion, Zhaozhou faced the taboo issue of sexuality with one of his nuns.

> A nun asked, "What is the deeply secret mind?"
> The master squeezed her hand.
> The nun said, "Do you still have that in you?"
> The master said, "It is you who have it."[35]

When she asked him to reveal the deeply secret mind, the true self, he is thoroughly unafraid of intimacy (even with a nun) and reaches out to touch her with his hand. The gentle side of Zhaozhou is exposed in this first move; he offers a touching teaching, not a put-down. One life touches another; the intimate flow of interconnection is right here and now. This is our true, unbounded Buddha nature, intimate and secret beyond words. Since a monk touching a nun or woman is forbidden by Buddhist monastic rules, Zhaozhou's gesture indicates a deeper connection, deeper truth. Perhaps prompted by Zhaozhou's intimacy, the nun's question "Do you still have that in you?" can be heard to bring up sexuality or at the very least a need for human contact. He and she are not only Buddha and Buddhi,[36] but man and woman as well. Whether she is questioning his motivation or inquiring about his sexuality's whereabouts, the nun wants to know: "Do you still have it? Zhaozhou, does sexuality, or even the need for human affection still arise in you after all this practice?" This is a question for all of us: What becomes of sexuality, our human tenderness and longing, after many years of practice? Do we still have it? Is that okay? How is it expressed in an enlightened Zen master?

The nun also challenged the master personally: "Hey Zhaozhou, are you some kind of old lecher with your nuns, after all this enlightened practice?" Zhaozhou rang clear as a bell when he questioned her "secret mind." "You have got it yourself, nun!" He still does not put her down. He points her back to her own experience of "it." Without rancor he suggests that she examine her projection. He returns the idea of desire to her side of the encounter, and at the same time he takes her deeper, making it clear that she must investigate her own secret mind.

The occasion of one of Zhaozhou's harshest remarks to a woman was in response to a Zen granny who brings up the Buddhist superstition about women's bodies and the five hindrances.[37]

> An old woman asked, "I have a body with the five hindrances. How can I escape them?"
> The master said, "Pray that all people are born in Heaven and pray that you yourself drown in a sea of hardship."[38]

Ouch! A tough pill to swallow for women of Zhaozhou's era, after thirteen hundred years of Buddhist discrimination. The medicine is strong: Forget yourself; pray for others. No matter how tough your situation, it won't do any good to feel sorry for yourself. Why keep claiming your position as victim? There is no escape from the present condition, as long as we cling to our ideas of self and seek an escape from suffering. Instead of dwelling on why you can't get ahead, pray to stay behind. Break your habitual pattern of *wanting* to get ahead, a pattern that just results in more clinging to your own suffering. Stop looking to fix your situation, and find your freedom right here in this overflowing sea of hardship. Stop fighting difficulty and sink into acceptance. Zhaozhou's diagnosis is harsh: "Old lady, as long as you believe this nonsense, you're sunk!"

Zhaozhou's answer addressed the potential whininess of this old woman. In the presence of one of the greatest Zen masters of all time, is this all she can ask? Is her pattern to bitch about how hard her life has been made by the Buddhist doctrine of five hindrances? Zhaozhou is teaching women; he's not promoting superstitions about women. Why does she bring up this complaint when he has stretched the Eight Special Rules to allow her and other women to practice with him? If she is trying to push Zhaozhou's nose in the unfairness that women encountered in Buddhist practice, he's clearly not having any of it.

Which is perhaps, a problem: while Zhaozhou's attempts to enlighten this woman can be appreciated, something is missing from his answer to her question. He did not question the role of these superstitions within Buddhism. In my opinion, teachers need to acknowledge problems within their traditions and try to bring about change. In this exchange Zhaozhou neither addresses these harmful superstitions nor vows to change them. Today, more than a thousand years distant from his teaching, we can only wonder about what other ways he might have found to address these superstitions. She asked this question because she had an opportunity to seek greater clarity from Zhaozhou on Buddhism and the culture in which she lived. Had he encouraged this kind of question from his sangha? We are left wondering what else might he have said about this matter?

From a contemporary perspective, we may imagine that Zhaozhou was beyond the usual superstition and ignorance about women, but we can only wonder what else he might have done to change or inform the Zen tradition as a whole about these inequities. An important element of Buddhist practice is how practitioners, especially masters, honestly address institutional blind spots.

Perhaps the women in the preceding story and in this next one are identical. He got her; now she gets him.

> The master went out [for a walk] and ran into a woman who was carrying a basket.

The master asked, "Where are you going?"

The old woman said, "I'm taking bamboo shoots to Zhaozhou."

The master said, "When you see Zhaozhou, what will you do?"

The old woman walked up and slapped the master.[39]

Zhaozhou directly meets each person whether he is in the temple or out for a walk. His teaching style has permeated many of the people surrounding the temple. Outside the temple, and unafraid of this old lady, he is undefended, and he lets her slap him. They must have known each other well. Her slap, like a mother to an impudent young son, seems to say, "Don't be so full of yourself, Zhaozhou. I too know how to approach and deliver a Zen greeting!"

Hakuin Accepts It All

Hakuin Ekaku (1686–1768), with his intense, lively, and inclusive style, revived Zen in Japan at a time when it had become moribund. He lived in a plain temple in a small village where he interacted freely with monks, nuns, laymen, and laywomen.

Early in his career as a celibate monk, Hakuin became a target for the accusations of a pregnant and unmarried young woman. Priests during Hakuin's lifetime were known for their corrupt behavior, including having sexual relationships during a time when such relations were expressly forbidden for monks and nuns. Accused and disgraced before his congregation, Hakuin, in all of his encounters with the family, just asked "Is that so?"

Hakuin was falsely accused by a local girl of being the father of her illegitimate child. Hakuin said nothing in his defense just "Is that so?" When the irate girl's father demanded that Hakuin raise the child, he readily accepted, saying "Is that so?" Hakuin gently cared for the infant without complaint, taking it along on begging trips with him, and silently endured the scorn heaped on him by villagers. Eventually the girl was stricken with remorse and confessed the truth—a young neighbor was the father, not Hakuin. When the girl's mortified father begged forgiveness for the false accusation, Hakuin replied calmly "Is that so?" and handed the baby back.[40]

Hakuin embodied Zhaozhou's advice to accept the rough seas of hardship while protecting and caring for his tormentors. Hakuin had no need to protect his virtue or his practice from character slurs. He demonstrated courage, compassion, and lack of attachment to other people's opinions. Unconcerned about Buddhist rules against family life, he took on the baby's care just like any devoted mother. Hakuin exemplified flexibility and selflessness as he continued his Zen practice with the baby, despite the false claims of the young woman, the family's distortion, the real father's evasion, and the villagers' harsh judgments.

An egalitarian teacher, Hakuin was celebrated for offering instruction to the local people in his village of Hara. He believed that Zen practice could extend to everyone. He tried to counter people's "magical" belief in a Pure Land[41] after death by anchoring Pure Land concepts to practice in this moment. This next story tells of his encounter with a mother type:

> One morning an old lady experienced *kensho* [Zen awakening] while cleaning up after breakfast. She rushed over and announced to Hakuin, "Amida has engulfed my body! The universe radiates! How truly marvelous!"
>
> "Nonsense!" Hakuin retorted. "Does it shine up your asshole?"
>
> The tiny old lady gave Hakuin a shove and shouted, "What do you know about enlightenment?"
>
> They both roared with laughter.[42]

Crude language and a shove capture the intimacy of the village Zen master with his congregation. Testing the old lady's awakening, Hakuin uses unconventional colloquial language to see if she is in some fantasy world. She feels genuinely at ease and responds with a shove and a rebuke, and they both celebrate with laughter. Their naturalness and intimacy should be an inspiration for contemporary practitioners.

Even though official Buddhist rules for nuns did not allow them to practice in monasteries under male teachers, the records of these two outstanding male Zen masters, Zhaozhou and Hakuin, show us the lively practice possibilities they afforded to women through inclusive and broadminded teaching.

In this chapter we have extracted a few women's experiences from the documents of Patriarchs' Zen, the accepted basis of Zen Buddhist practice. In the patriarchs' world there are no female Zen masters—only the occasional appearance of an exceptional woman. In this all-male world of practice, a small number of women highlight the ability of male teachers, surprise or embarrass monks into acknowledging their lack of understanding, and find their way into positions within the Zen institutions.

Women's potential for spiritual leadership in their own right is the subject of the next section of this book. The focus shifts from how Zen shaped women to how women shaped Zen.

Part II

WOMEN'S ZEN

Introduction to Women's Zen   3

THERE IS SOMETHING heretical in categorizing Zen by gender. After all, the word *Zen* just means "meditation." Yet we talk about Japanese Zen, Western Zen, Rinzai Zen, Soto Zen, Obaku Zen, and so on, each of which emphasizes different aspects of practice. When we lump all these categories of Zen together, they comprise Patriarchs' Zen. Is there an equivalent "Matriarchs' Zen"? What does the sum of these two streams offer to contemporary Western Zen practitioners?

To explore this, I suggest we look beyond classic Zen literature to answer three key questions:

1. Were there separate institutions for women's Zen practice?
2. Did female Zen teachers leave teaching words beyond the literature of "Patriarchs' Zen"?
3. Were there authenticated Zen Buddhist female teachers whose lives and teachings were left out of the story of "Patriarchs' Zen"?

We can answer all three questions in the affirmative. Women's Zen assumes no categorical differences between male and female attributes. The existence or nonexistence of elusive traits that characterize men and women has long been argued. It is not the aim of women's Zen, or of this book, to prove that the feminine is in any way superior to the masculine. The intent of this chapter is to present a body of female Zen masters' work in the form of writings, artistic contributions, Zen institutions, and additional Zen practices.

Part I of this book, "Zen's Women," portrayed women as supporting
players in the story of Patriarchs' Zen. This section, "Women's Zen," creates and expands Zen practice in its own first-person female voice.
Women go beyond the limited familial and supportive roles that constel-
lated around Patriarchs' Zen to offer a unique embodiment of Zen at the
same time that they embody their female identity. Because women's Zen
developed in the same cultural milieu as Patriarchs' Zen, we can see how
women's Zen was innovative or unique. Women's Zen incorporated
women's abilities and issues into Zen practice, finding ways to express
and practice Zen as women rather than as token participants in an all-
male Zen institution. Women found ways to include family training and
their own style of leadership within convents, in their own homes, and in
their own small hermitages. They did not just imitate the macho Zen
heroes; they expanded the job description of the enlightened (and not
always monastic) female Zen master to include: loyalty to family, commitment to married sexual relationships, continued work in the lay community, and socially engaged Buddhist projects.

When we shift our view of women from their *relationship* roles (as
mother, sister, wife, or iron maiden without family ties) to their *functional*
roles (as founders, innovators, managers, and artists), we see that women
make unique contributions to those excluded from a monastic setting.
We see beyond a view of women as "unsafe" whenever they depart from
the roles of nurturing mother, sister, or lover.

A Women's Zen Lineage

Until recently, Western Zen women have assumed that few if any female
teachers preceded them. Part of this misunderstanding comes from the
scarcity of women in classical Zen literature. (A few such rare birds have
already been mentioned in the previous section of this book.) Another
source of this misunderstanding derives from documents of the Zen sect
which suggest that the teachings passed from male master to male disciple without listing a single woman.[43]

This male Zen order claims to trace its teachers' lineage back to the
Buddha, though most scholars dispute the veracity of a continuous lineage.[44] The female order makes no such claim to continuity. From the time
of the first nuns in India led by Mahapajapati Gotami (the Buddha's aunt

and stepmother), the women's order has struggled to survive, dwindled to virtually nothing, and at times almost vanished.[45] Like a stream gone underground, the women's order would seem to disappear, only to surface later in a different location. Looking beneath the surface, we see that women did not sustain their lineage single-handedly, rather, their Zen order was repeatedly reinvigorated by open-minded male Zen masters. The complex relationships that have connected women to a variety of teachers will be discussed and illustrated in chapter 7.

There is no formal or continuous lineage of female Zen teachers tracing back to the first Buddhist woman, Mahapajapati. We do find evidence of its persistence, but no linked relationships from teachers to disciples. The discontinuity of the women's lineage had many causes, including the hazardous nature of travel for women, the rape and capture of woman as sex slaves, the restrictions placed on women's participation outside the home by Confucian culture in China and Japan and Hindu culture in India, the lack of convents, and, of course, by the Eight Special Rules. Finally, discrimination against women and conservative views forbidding women to work outside the family system may have resulted in the erasure of women masters from Zen records during particularly misogynistic periods of history.[46]

The Origin and Transmission of the Female Zen Buddhist Order

The women's Zen order descended from the first women who practiced with the Buddha Shakyamuni. Special rules and services practiced in current female Zen orders throughout Asia can be traced to this original Buddhist women's order. Mahapajapati's reputation and influence were so strong that several hundred years after her death, in a set of poems commenting on the earliest account of her life (in poems found in the *Therigatha*), she was referred to as the Buddhi Gotami (in contrast to the male Buddha Gotama). In the *Theri Apadana*, Gotami expresses her belief in women's spiritual potential. Just as Patriarchs' Zen traces back to Shakyamuni Buddha, so Matriarchs' Zen traces back to Mahapajapati Buddhi. And just as the male Zen monastery evolved from the Buddha's order, so the Zen convent derived from the Buddhi's order. Women practitioners in China, Korea, and Japan all referred back to Mahapajapati and what she accomplished. Unfortunately, the ways in which this order might have provided for gender-differentiated practice has been lost to Western Zen practice and scholarship.

The male lineage follows the transmission of Buddhism from India to China, to Korea, and then to Japan via traveling male Zen and Buddhist masters, but the transmission for the female order differs. The nuns' order in India did not carry Buddhism to Chinese women. After monks brought Buddhism to China, Chinese women studied Buddhadharma with men and then created their own convents. Later, early Chinese nuns tried to replicate the ordination process that had been developed for Indian nuns. Similarly, Chinese nuns did not bring Buddhism to Korean women. Korean men went to China and brought Buddhism to Korea, and Korean women were ordained by the first Korean monks and later formed their own convents.

The transmission from Korea to Japan was a little different. Perhaps surprisingly, the first ordained Buddhist practitioners in Japan were not men, but women. The strength of women's spiritual influence in Japan was probably due at least in part to the ancient cult of Japan's female goddess, Amaterasu, the sun goddess in the Shinto pantheon of deities. Amaterasu was given credit for inventing the cultivation of wheat and rice, the use of silkworms and the loom, and for sending her grandson to earth to pacify the Japanese people in a time of war. The Japanese emperors are said to descend from Amaterasu. Women were the early intermediaries in this Japanese folk religion.

From this brief study of how Buddhism traveled from India to Japan and then from Japan to the West, we see that women worldwide are indebted to male teachers. Yet left out of this history of Buddhist transmission is male Zen teachers' indebtedness to the women who showed pioneering monks that women could not only practice sincerely but spread the Buddhadharma in unique ways. The Zen lineage (according to legend) began with the Indian monk Bodhidharma bringing Buddhist practice to Chinese men and—as we have seen—at least one woman. He and his successors ordained women in Tang dynasty China. Korean and Japanese monks traveled to China and brought back Zen teachings. Japanese monks brought Zen to the West and taught both men and women. Currently, there are many female Zen teachers in the West, but there is no separate established female order. Most Western Zen women do not even know that a female order existed.

Functional Roles for Women in Buddhism and Zen

Not surprisingly, women practicing Zen under similar conditions across Asian countries developed similar means of practice and inhabited a similar range of roles. Six common conditions combined to help shape the development of women's functional roles across Asia:

1. Women were excluded from male monasteries. Often there were no convents, so women developed alternative types of training and practice settings.
2. Women faced familial obligations and legal restrictions regarding their right to leave home, and thus needed to find a way to practice at home.
3. Women who did manage to leave home and form convents struggled for financial support, since convents were defined by early Buddhism as second-rate institutions;[47] as a result, they developed ways to combine means of financial support and practice.
4. Women faced unique safety issues. The threat of rape limited their mobility and participation and their consequent recognition and accreditation in the Buddhist world. By limiting women's ability to travel, the continuity of their association and lineage were also limited.
5. Women were often officially identified as having lesser abilities (both by their communities and in Buddhist scriptures), so they were discouraged from taking the tonsure, or, if tonsured, their teachings were not valued in the community.
6. Women's lack of education limited their ability to study sutras. Only educated women—which is to say women of high socioeconomic status—had access to Buddhist practice.

Consequently, women found creative ways to participate in training even when their efforts were not culturally sanctioned or deemed appropriate by family or position. They found ways to practice that did not require celibacy, home leaving, or retreat from the world. And so, within the context of these constraints, we can define six distinctive functional roles inhabited by women Zen teachers:

1. *Founders:* Women who founded and developed a system of convents or institutions where women could practice separately from men as the Buddha had originally directed.

2. *Supporters:* Women in highly placed political and economic positions who helped build, support, and influence Buddhist practice.

3. *Convent nuns:* Women who joined established convents and expanded practice techniques for the sake of women and the community in general.

4. *Nuns who practiced with men:* Women who practiced with male teachers in male monasteries, strengthening the tradition, passing on their own original teachings, and expanding our understanding of how to relate to a teacher, but leaving no female lineage.

5. *Family nuns:* Ordained women who developed practice places outside institutions, while living at home and caring for parents, children, or other family members. There were also ordained women who taught about sexuality—nuns whose teaching allowed for the integration of sexuality and practice from their own experience.

6. *Working nuns:* Women who supported themselves financially by applying their Zen training to a profession.

Across Asia we can find these functional roles filled by outstanding female Buddhist and Zen Buddhist practitioners, first in India, then in China and Korea, and finally in Japan. Most Zen lineages trace their descent through male ancestors from India, China, and then Japan, but when women are included in Zen's transmission, we see the first Buddhists in Japan received their ordination through Korea.

Historically, Buddhism traveled to Korea earlier than it did to Japan, and according to early Japanese records, in the year 584, the first ordained Buddhists in Japan were Japanese nuns who received their ordinations first from Korean missionaries, and then traveled to Korea for more formal training.[48] While Buddhism may have existed in Japan prior to the ordination of these young nuns, their formal Korean ordination and training marked the first Buddhist clergy and formal teaching by Japanese Buddhists, and it traces the transmission of Japanese Buddhism through Korea.

The fact that our first Zen Buddhist ancestors in Japan were women is little known. The Zen practice of Westerners in some respects resembles that of Zen's female ancestors. Like many of our female ancestors, most Western Zen practitioners live outside Zen monasteries and face financial and logistical obstacles. A wider historical perspective, one that encompasses those women and their accomplishments, will deepen our understanding of Zen and enhance our practice opportunities in intimate family relationships and at work. Our women forebears offer inspiration and an encouraging model of flexible participation that is highly relevant to Zen in the West.

The following chapters in this part of the book consider the six categories of women Zen practitioners listed above. Examples will be presented of each functional role, in the order of Zen's historical transmission from India to China, Korea, and then Japan.

Founders and Supporters 4

Founders Cultivating Buddhist Practice Prior to Zen

IN THIS CHAPTER I discuss how Zen women have built open and supportive practice environments. I consider the accomplishments of Zen Buddhism's early female founders in three areas: their demonstration of leadership, their expansion of Buddhist practice, and response to women practitioners' needs.

Mahapajapati: Leader of the Assembly

Women who became nuns in the earliest Buddhist order sought the spiritual liberation that Zen calls enlightenment. This pursuit was outside the usual realm of women's lives; indeed, it was an almost inconceivable quest, considering women's limited legal rights, polygamous marriage customs, and the dominant cultural view of women as objects of sensual extravagance, familial duty, or both. Early Indian Buddhist nuns describe their awakening and sense of freedom as the simultaneous realization of what they were and what they were not; they realized their true nature as enlightened beings, and they realized they were neither imprisoned underlings nor seductive objects trained to serve family and husbands.

All Zen women are able to practice due to the efforts of one woman, the Buddha's stepmother Mahapajapati Gotami. Because she sought awakening and moved beyond the restrictions defined by her family relations, Mahapajapati gained entry for women into the Buddhist order. She established an authentic Buddhist vocation for women and made ordained practice possible for women willing to follow her example.

Mahapajapati continued to inspire women as Buddhism spread to China and beyond. The first Asian founding nuns, Jingjian in China, Sassi in Korea, and Zenshin-ni in Japan, attempted to authenticate what they could learn from traveling monks in order to follow Mahapajapati. These founding nuns broke free of traditions (and sometimes family demands) to start convents and further the ordination process for women.

Mahapajapati was born of nobility into the Koliyan clan near the foothills of the Himalayas.[49] She is first in a long tradition of early Buddhist female practitioners whose privileged position gave them access to Buddhist teachings. We can guess that her birth preceded Shakyamuni Buddha's by about fifteen or twenty years. At the time of her birth, it is said to have been prophesied that she would lead a great assembly, and that she would also mother a great secular or religious leader. *Pajapati* means "leader of great assembly," and *Maha*, which also means "great," was added to her name for her role in leading the women's order. Both she and her sister, Maya, were married to the same man—the Buddha's father, Suddhodana. Mahapajapati was his second wife even while her sister was alive. When her sister died, after giving birth to the baby who became Shakyamuni Buddha, Mahapajapati became Suddhodana's queen and principal wife and, even though she was the Buddha's biological aunt, she became his stepmother.

Although Mahapajapati was married to the ruler of the Shakya clan, she was no stranger to hardship. She shared a husband with a sister who died in childbirth. This situation would strain any woman emotionally. She also had to share her home and her husband with his other wives and later with her stepson's wives (before Siddhartha left the palace to begin his spiritual search).

Siddhartha—son, husband, father, prince, and heir to clan leadership—felt it necessary to leave home to pursue spiritual liberation. As the awakened Buddha, he described family life and political responsibility as a prison from which one must be liberated. In order to liberate oneself, the Buddha taught, we must cut off our attachments to position and family responsibilities, leave home, and join his newly founded order.

The Buddha viewed this path to liberation as something exclusively for men; women were objects to be repudiated in the quest for awakening. Given his view, it is easy to imagine that his female relatives had some firsthand lessons in suffering. In today's psychological terminology, we might surmise that Buddha's wives and family members suffered significant abandonment trauma when he left home and declared that doing so was the essential step to liberation.

When the awakened Buddha returned home, he found that his stepmother, Mahapajapati, and his principal wife, Yashodhara, as well as other women from his household, wanted to follow the home-leaving path he advocated. Hadn't they learned firsthand from the Buddha the pain of attachment in the emotional realm? Hadn't they learned that happiness based on loving relationships was impermanent and ultimately unsatisfactory? Hadn't they truly understood the cost of their emotional attachment—to him—and hadn't they heard the solution directly from him?

Consider this excerpt from a prose poem written in modern times, from the imagined perspective of the Buddha's wife Yashodhara:

> Tell me one thing, Yashodhara, how did you contain the raging storm in your small hands? Just the idea of your life shakes the earth and sends the screaming waves dashing against the shore. You would have remembered while your life slipped by, the last kiss of Siddhartha's final farewell, those tender lips.[50]

These words call attention to the women's side of home leaving (abandonment). Buddha's last kiss, signaling the end of their marriage, described the other side of the Buddha's life. Yashodhara was in fact a real person, a wife in love with her husband, not just an object of desire to be transcended. This view of the Buddha's wife as a cast-off has yet to be addressed in Buddhist studies—she remains (in the scriptures) simply the one who was left. The problem highlighted here is that home leaving, regardless of one's marital status or the ages of one's children, was advocated exclusively for men as the only way to practice authentically. Home leaving not only bestowed special rights and status to men, it typified women as objects that could (or should) be left behind. This complex and shadowy relationship, which positions men as subjects and women as objects, deserves explicit investigation (see chapter 8 below).

Early Buddhists believed that ordaining women would create difficulties in the prevailing culture. Who would raise children if women also were allowed to leave home? Did women even have the right to leave a

[handwritten margin note: enraged?more responsibility!]

man? How would outraged husbands respond to a religious order that supported women as independent agents? For these early Buddhists, ordaining women as home leavers was too radical and troublesome. Initially of course, as we have seen, the Buddha would not even consider including his female relatives on his great path of liberation.[51]

While we can appreciate the gravity of these challenges, we cannot forget that, on behalf of the caste of untouchables, the Buddha tried to change the system. He fought against ancient Brahmanic limitations on behalf of male untouchables' admission to his Buddhist order. It is interesting that the Buddha was evidently more concerned about the imagined negative effect of women on his order than that of the untouchables.

Mahapajapati alone is credited with founding the Buddhist female order, and her continued pleading with Buddha is especially noteworthy considering that women of her time were trained to be socially submissive. She brought her request for the creation of a female order to the Buddha three times. When he refused for the third time she departed in tears. She had exhausted her ability to make a request—three times was the rule—but even then she did not give up. She cut off her hair, put on the same saffron robe worn by the Buddha's male followers, and led a group of female followers a hundred and fifty miles barefoot to the Buddha's training monastery in Vesali to silently demonstrate, weary and with feet bloodied by the walk, the depth of their spiritual aspiration. Was it Mahapajapati's personal strength, a vision evoked by her exposure to Buddhist practice, or the promise of liberation that empowered her and her followers to defy orders, to endure physical hardship, and to stand up for women's rights (at a time when even the term "women's rights" did not exist)? All of these conditions may have combined with her deep maternal devotion to other women's welfare, catalyzing her to take action. Mahapajapati, who could have led a life of material comfort and private spiritual inquiry, risked her family standing to challenge the Buddha for the sake of women who had fewer options than she had. This combination of empathy for women less well off, willingness to sacrifice her own entitled status, and personal strength are all characteristic traits of the early Buddhist female founders.

The Buddha had advised Mahapajapati not to set her heart on Buddhist ordination for women.[52] Indeed, her aspiration was rebuked by the greatest spiritual leader of the time, her own stepson and nephew. Risking censure and rejection, she defied conventional rules of behavior as mother and widow and embarked on her journey. This action, being willing to risk it all, is a familiar step on the path to becoming a Zen matriarch.

Traditionally, to be accepted within cultural conventions, a woman must honor conventional relationships. To serve any other purpose, even a deeper one, a woman must risk disapproval by loved ones and society. As we saw earlier in the story of Sen-jo, a woman risks being separated from her soul when she follows her own aspirations. In contrast, for men, the hero's journey is accepted as part of the male identity, allowing men more freedom to come and go from family life. Family and loved ones may mourn, but they await the male hero's return. For women who follow this path, ostracism or worse is often the fate that awaits them.

The second characteristic of the female Buddhist founders was the creation of a role for rejected women. Some of Mahapajapati's own aspiring nuns were women who had been discarded—widows and retired prostitutes, for instance. What a heart-rending sight these worn-out and determined women must have been as their march approached the Buddha's camp. And yet the Buddha, presented with enslaved women seeking liberation, continued to deny their admission to the order.

Mahapajapati inspired the confidence of her followers, but she also needed to move Ananda and the Buddha. Without Ananda's support, women may have been excluded entirely. As Paula Arai skillfully documented in *Women Living Zen*, Japanese Zen nuns, in recognition of the depth of Ananda's compassionate act, today perform a special ceremony of homage to him. There is also some evidence that Ananda experienced criticism regarding his relationship to and support for women.[53] Ananda paid a price for his intercession on Mahapajapati's behalf, and the accounts of the First Council suggest he was ahead of his time.

Gaining the support of an influential male insider is a third characteristic in the story of women's Zen. Many women determined to study Zen had to plead their case to a male insider. Even after the establishment of the convent, a woman entering the Zen Buddhist tradition often had to convince the male establishment to allow her to work with a teacher. But in the case of women who founded orders where there were none, no matter how skillful a female founder was, her words had to find sympathetic male ears. Mahapajapati's words and example are underscored in the *Theri Apadana*,[54] which was written more than one hundred years after her death and includes the Buddha's sermon praising her accomplishments. The Buddha acknowledges Mahapajapati for her deep wisdom; indeed, she was wise enough to know when to oppose the Buddha's view and when to accept his special rules. The Buddha came to understand the value of the nuns' order, praised her "as a nun of great renown."[55] In addition to saying she was "most wise, with wisdom vast and wide," the Buddha acknowledged that she had mastered "great powers." While women are often extolled for wisdom and compassion, it is rare that their "powers" are celebrated.

Mahapajapati's willingness to continue in the face of hardship—to lead her followers a hundred and fifty miles barefoot to make her request—is a noteworthy detail. Contemporary women are often taught to protect themselves, be cautious, and avoid difficult or dangerous physical situations. Through the standards described for female beauty during the Buddha's lifetime, this protective stance—preserving female delicacy and refinement—was also the case during Mahapajapati's lifetime. This conditioning can create obstacles for women attempting to participate in a man's world. Even today, women are warned not to walk alone, and never to look directly at a man, for fear of encouraging rape. Women are warned against becoming overly muscular, strong, and/or callused—because this would make a woman unattractive to men.

Another celebrated attribute of Mahapajapati is that she saw inherent value in those who had been marginalized by her culture. Women of the Buddha's day were viewed as property of men and had few if any legal rights. Mahapajapati not only stood up for women's right to join the Buddhist order, but also saw value in women who were rejected as worthless by her society—widows, the old prostitutes, and divorced or abandoned wives.

This is a useful model for contemporary women who, when entering male-dominated organizations, sometimes overzealously seek male approval while competing with or undermining other women. Women sometimes see female participation in an organization as a zero-sum game. Recognizing that status for women is hard to come by; they seek to eliminate other women vying for position. Mahapajapati provides an example for such women, who may need coaching to learn to support one another in patriarchal settings.

In a poem summarizing her years of practice, she revealed balanced respect for the Buddha and his order without forgetting how her sister, who gave birth to the Buddha, offered salvation to humanity through her own flesh and blood. Honoring her family life, she both experienced and transcended emotions simultaneously, an important teaching for all practitioners. She did not repress her feelings, and neither did she let them interfere with her intention to seek ordination and recognition for herself and other women. Through Susan Murcott's translation of the earliest nuns' poems, the *Therigatha*, we gain access to Mahapajapati's practice experience:

> Homage to you Buddha,
> best of all creatures,
> who set me and many others
> free from pain.
> ...I have been
> mother, son,
> father, brother,
> grandmother;
> knowing nothing of the truth
> I journeyed on.
> ...But I have seen the Blessed One;
> this is my last body,
> and I will not go
> from birth to birth again.
> ...Maya gave birth to Gautama
> for the sake of us all.
> She has driven back the pain
> of the sick and dying.[56]

As we can see here, Mahapajapati does not repress or abandon feeling—she inhabits her loving roles and is affected by their tenderness. She experiences the arising of emotions within an expanded view; she is not caught by her feelings as something unique to her identity but rather identifies them as her journey to awakening.

Women, who often experience themselves as having strong emotions, can learn from Mahapajapati's example that they do not need to betray or repress their feelings. Many women live without finding or following their deepest aspirations. Deeply involved in familial roles, they lose their sense of direction. Contrast this tendency with men's culturally supported ability to find their life's work even within the context of familial demands: Men often follow their aspirations without difficulty, whether they stay connected to the family, limit their participation in it, or abandon it altogether. Women, on the other hand, often must choose one or the other—aspiration or family life. Mahapajapati struggled to make sense of family responsibility—recounting many lifetimes of being caught by family roles and finally finding her deepest spiritual aspiration.

Illuminating the path of liberation, her poignant reference to her own sister's early death connects us to our human condition. Whether or not we follow the Buddhist path of liberation, we are inevitably vulnerable to the loss of loved ones. Mahapajapati reminds us that without these unsung heroes—the mothers who courageously bear children at the risk of their lives—we would have neither monks, nor nuns, nor buddhas.

The First Chinese Nuns

Jingjian: "Pure Example"

Jingjian (ca. 292–361) and other early Chinese founders of orders have been documented in Kathryn Tsai's translation of *Lives of the Nuns*.[57] Jingjian insisted on establishing the legitimacy of her ordination and set an example for other pioneer nuns who sought to establish the nuns' order in China. She carefully studied the records of the nuns that preceded her in India, to live up to their standards, and then she found her own way.

According to the *Lives of the Nuns*, Jingjian was the well-educated daughter of a government administrator in northwestern China, widowed as a young woman and left impoverished and financially responsible for her family. To earn money she taught lute and calligraphy to the children of noble families. Devoted to formal study, she left home to pursue Buddhist training.

Like other upper-class Buddhist female founders, Jingjian probably first learned about Buddhism at home. Buddhist teachings inspired her, but she couldn't find anyone nearby to study with. Later she met the monk Fashi at his monastery, received teachings on the Dharma, and experienced a great awakening.

Jingjian eventually found her way to monastic practice. By then her husband was deceased; what became of the family she supported can only be conjectured. We do know, however, that she became a model for women entering convent training and for other Chinese female aspirants.

Jingjian initially practiced with male monks until she learned that there was a different set of rules in the Buddhist scriptures between *bhikshu* and *bhikshuni*,[58] monk and nun. The requirements for nuns' ordination had not yet been established in China, but Jingjian decided to receive the tonsure anyway by taking the ten fundamental precepts that were available for monks.[59] She was then about thirty years old.

At this point Jingjian resolved to deepen her practice. She could have continued in the role of "little sister" within a male monastery, but she glimpsed the possibility of a different kind of freedom. She had learned that women had previously established independent roles as *bhikshunis*. Although she had taken ordination as a monk (since there was no other path), she attempted to authenticate the *bhikshuni* practice by examining available records and making contact with Buddhist practitioners.

In a historic move, Jingjian and twenty-four other women who had first studied along with the male monks established the independent Bamboo Grove Convent for nuns—perhaps the first Buddhist convent in China. She was not yet designated as a teacher, but she was well respected by other nuns and considered more reliable than some recognized male leaders. Women followed her even before her official teacher status was granted. She helped establish a pattern of female leadership devoted to maintaining the order for women. Jingjian and her nuns wished to create a solid vocation for women within the Buddhist tradition. Finding details about the ordination of nuns in newly translated materials, she resolved to follow this tradition. She learned that nuns took five hundred vows and had to be ordained by both monks and nuns. Since a nun's order had not yet existed in China, where would the necessary nuns come from? Some senior monks objected to Jingjian's intention to establish a formal ordination process for women, since as yet there were no nuns in China. (Interestingly, the same problem has arisen in contemporary Asian countries where the *bhikshuni* order has died out. Monks argue that without nuns to perform the full *bhikshuni* ordination, there is no way to restart the order. Even though the *bhikshuni* order has survived in China and nuns from China could come to Burma or Thailand for the ceremony, this is not yet encouraged and sometimes not allowed.)

Nonetheless, Jingjian prevailed, seeking more formal recognition for women while sidestepping the male hierarchy's objections. Like Mahapajapati, she invented a way to establish formal status, quietly rebelling against the disapproving higher-ups. And, like Mahapajapati, she gained the monks' respect and support.

Another parallel between Jingjian and Mahapajapati: just as Mahapajapati was supported by Ananda, Jingjian was supported by the foreign monk Tanmo Jieduo. He performed ordination for Jingjian and three other nuns despite recorded objections by other monks. This ordination established Jingjian and her followers as the first official female Buddhist nuns of China. Where there's a will, there's a way. It seems that this event was recognized as significant by the Chinese historians; like many spiritual stories, the first nuns' ordination in China is said to have been marked by the appearance of the supernatural. It is written that at the time of the event a "remarkable fragrance and perfume filled the air." It is also recorded that this fragrance returned to Jingjian at the time of her death. Just before she died she smelled this same perfume and saw a misty red cloud. A woman holding a five-colored flower in her hands descended from the sky. *Lives of the Nuns* offers an account of Jingjian's final moments:

> [Jingjian said to her followers:] "Manage your affairs well in the future. I am taking leave of you now." Clasping their hands she bid them farewell and then rose up into the air. The path she traveled looked like a rainbow going straight up to heaven. At that time she was seventy years old.[60]

Zhixian:
"Wise Virtue Unafraid"

Zhixian (ca. 300–370) was a practicing Buddhist nun remembered mainly for her courage in facing a hostile bureaucrat. She exemplifies female founders who endured physical hardship for the sake of practice. In her locale there was a bureaucrat who was bent on destroying Buddhism and reestablishing Taoism as the sole spiritual practice. (At this time Taoist and Buddhist followers were competing for dominance.) This administrator required all nuns to report for questioning or face defrocking. His hope was that this demand would reduce the population of practicing nuns so his Taoist practitioners could prevail.

Zhixian was the only able-bodied nun to report; all other nuns who could leave the area did so. Remarkably, the Taoist bureaucrat approved of both Zhixian's understanding of monastic regulations and her practice. Unfortunately, he also was smitten by her refined beauty and eloquent speech. He attempted to use his physical power and authority to insist that she have sex with him. Zhixian refused. The administrator stabbed her more than twenty times. She fell to the ground unconscious and was revived by others after he left.

Zhixian had the founder's spirit—she risked her own life in order to protect the nuns' right to practice. Zhixian recovered from the attack and continued her practice and eventually attracted many followers who joined her in the West Convent of Ssu Province.[61]

Huizhan:
"Deep Wisdom Establishing Blessings"

Huizhan (ca. 320), another founding nun in this early Chinese order, was traveling over a mountain pass when robbers attacked her. Apparently she had been practicing devotions to the bodhisattva of compassion, Guanyin. It is reported that after she called out to Guanyin, the attackers' hands were paralyzed. Unable to attack her, they still wanted to take her robes. Demonstrating a lack of attachment and an abundance of compassion for the robbers, she threw off her outer robe and inner skirt, which left her clothed but exposed to the weather. We are reminded of the well-known stories of a later Zen master, Ryokan, who offered his meager possessions to robbers.

Whether or not we accept the presence of the supernatural in this account, her determined founder's energy is impressive. Faced with obstacles, she continued to develop her practice. We are told that she laughed at her predicament as she completed her journey over the mountain to pursue her training. Her practice eventually became well-respected and she was invited in the year 344 by the minister of public works to found the Establishing Blessings Convent.[62]

The First Ordained Buddhist Founders
in Japan and Korea

The male Zen lineage acknowledges that it originated in India, recognizes that it was transmitted to China, and proposes that from China it traveled to Japan. Korean transmission is often left out of the Japanese account, but historical records that include women show the movement of Buddhism from China to Korea and then to Japan. Early Chinese Buddhism, prior to the first recorded Japanese ordinations, spread to Japan through diplomatic interactions with Korea sometime after the fourth century. Official records show that the Korean king Song sent Buddhist scriptures and a Buddha statue to Japan in the middle of the sixth century (ca. 570). The earliest Japanese interpretations of Buddhism blended it with their own native deities, the *kami*, and the use of Buddhist practice to ward off illness and other disasters for the protection of the elite and of the developing nation. Japanese Zen later traces its roots from China through the early twelfth- and thirteenth-century male founders Eisai, Dogen, and Enni Benen, but as we have seen, the first ordained Japanese Buddhists were actually sixth-century women who had been taught by Koreans.[63] Even though traditional and accepted accounts of the Zen lineage do not acknowledge these women as early Buddhist founders in Japan, their activities as the first ordained Buddhists in Japan prepared the ground for later developments in Japanese Buddhist practice. We'll explore their stories in more detail later in this chapter.

To understand how Buddhism came to Japan, we must look to Korea. Buddhism had reached the early Korean nations (Koguryo, Paekje, and Silla) in the third or fourth century through the monk Ado (also known as the Black Barbarian Mukho-ja).[64] Ado, born in Korea, was descended from a Chinese father. He trained in a Chinese monastery and returned to the Korean peninsula after his ordination. He brought Buddhism with him, which later moved to Japan through Koreans who trained Zenshin and her associates. Little is known about early Japanese and Chinese founding women, and even less has been recovered about their Korean counterparts. Nevertheless, a 2004 Korean conference of international scholars was held in Seoul to emphasize the importance of this task.

Sa-ssi, the First Ordained Korean Nun: "Village Wisdom"

Sa-ssi (ca. 430) was ordained by Ado, whom she met through her brother, Morye. Morye, described as a simple and compassionate villager, hid Ado from pursuing Koreans intent on exterminating the bearer of this revolutionary new religion before it spread. Sa-ssi went on to establish the order of Korean nuns and their training convents. Her story mirrors that of many early Buddhist women: she was exposed to the teaching through her family, took official ordination with a male teacher, and went on to found a convent. The separate nuns' order that she founded continues to flourish in Korea today.

Zenshin, Zenso, and Ezen, the First Japanese Buddhists

In most Asian Buddhist countries, monks established the practice of Buddhism, after which women created an order following their example. In Japan, three Japanese women took the tonsure in 584. It is exceptional that in Japan women created the first Buddhist order. Their ordination was held in Japan and attended by a Korean layman (formerly a priest) and an old Korean nun. The Soga empress Suiko offered her palace as a Buddhist temple.[65] The ordination of these three nuns and their teaching initially inspired their followers and supporters to undertake the construction of Buddhist temples.

The first ordained Buddhist in Japan, whose Dharma name was Zenshin, was a young Japanese girl, born Shima, daughter of Shiba Tatto. She was ordained at the age of eleven along with two other girls who might have been her friends or attendants.

Due to warring political clan factions and supporters of the emperor and Shintoism, within a few years the political tide turned against these first Buddhists. In 587 a powerful lord who opposed Buddhism, Mononobe no Moriya, encouraged local residents in the destruction of their Buddhist temples. He insisted that a current epidemic was caused by Buddhist practice, which betrayed the native Japanese allegiance to Shintoism. The first three nuns were publicly defrocked, stripped of their ordained status, and beaten.

When Moriya no Mononobe was later defeated by the pro-Buddhist Soga clan, the nuns' humiliation and political ostracism came to an end. The same three young nuns applied for and received permission in 587 to travel to Korea, then known as the kingdom of Paekche, to continue their Buddhist studies and receive full *bhikshuni* ordination. The formal *bhikshuni* ordination required ten fully ordained monks and ten fully ordained nuns. If indeed these young nuns received the full *bhikshuni* ordination, this means that a fully ordained nuns' practice functioned in Korea at that time. The training associated with full *bhikshuni* ordination took a minimum of two years according to early Buddhist customs for nuns.[66] After ordination the nuns returned to Japan in 590. The number of converts to Buddhism and ordained nuns increased under Zenshin's leadership.

The fact that the first Buddhists in Japan were women linked to Korean nuns has been left out of the usual story of Buddhism's transmission across Asia. The adversity these young women endured to give birth to Buddhism in Japan has also been forgotten. Like Mahapajapati before them, these women persisted in practice through hardship and humiliation. They looked after the health and welfare of others through chanting sutras. They demonstrated courage, perseverance, and a commitment to founding temples for women.

Homyo, a Korean Nun in Japan: "A Chanting Missionary"

Besides supporting Buddhism through material efforts, monks and nuns were expected to use their spiritual powers to bring about healing. Women found acceptance in this early Buddhist role owing to the well-established female shamanic folk traditions of Korea and Japan. Even after Zenshin had established a convent in Japan in 590, there is evidence Korea continued to send nuns to Japan. The Korean nun Homyo (ca. 656)[67] purportedly cured an important Fujiwara aristocrat through recitation of the Vimalakirti Sutra, a sutra that revolves around the Buddha's visit to an ailing layman. The services that early Buddhists provided for Japanese aristocrats included some education on the complete Buddhist order, including laypeople, ordained monks and nuns, and visiting Korean missionaries. As Japanese Buddhist temples assumed political and social roles of greater importance, male clerics took over temple management. Because Buddhist scriptures were written in Chinese, a language most Japanese women were not taught, the nuns began to be pushed aside by better-educated males who did read Chinese. Lack of education for women, seventh-century Confucian and early Hindu condescension, and a fundamentally negative Buddhist institutional view of women as less capable than monks combined to cause the decline of early Buddhist convents as compared to monasteries. Nonetheless, Japanese women continued to find a variety of ways to practice.

The first Buddhist women were successful in founding Buddhist temples in Japan at least partly because women at that time often acted as spiritual mediums in the Shinto tradition, conveying the wishes of the indigenous deities to the people. Women were quite powerful in the family and enjoyed authority in their marriages. Forty years after Zenshin's ordination, there were forty-six Buddhist temples in Japan with 816 monks and 569 nuns. Japanese Buddhism owes much to the dedication of these young women who continued to deepen their training and their practice despite being beaten and threatened. They created a new religious opportunity and a new sociocultural position for women in Japan: the ordained Buddhist nun. While the power of women has waxed and waned throughout Japanese history, these early female founders embodied the possibility of women becoming spiritual pioneers.

Royal Supporters for Buddhism

Starting with Queen Mahapajapati, royal and otherwise privileged women have used their power and position to assist the birth of Buddhist practice. An understanding of their contribution widens our view of what is required to spread Buddhist practice in the West. Affluent and highly placed women created practice opportunities, and some of them engaged in Buddhist practice themselves. Then, because of their highly visible positions, they helped Buddhism gain wider acceptance. Empress Wu Zetian (625–705) reigned over the flowering of Chan Buddhism in China; Queen Sondok (610–47), the first female queen to reign in Korea, sponsored the building of Buddhist monuments; and Empress Komyo (701–60) supported early Buddhism in Japan before the Zen school was established.

Empress Wu Zetian:
"Daughter of Heaven"

Empress Wu lived in the Tang dynasty (618–906), a time of relative free-dom for women in China. Her name *Wu Zetian* means "Wu Equals Heaven." At that time women were not required, for instance, to bind their feet or otherwise lead lives of submission. Her rise to the throne after the death of her husband Kao Tsung was described by her Confu-cian critics as ruthless, but her actual reign was seen as beneficial to the Chinese people. Most notably for our purposes, she established Bud-dhism as the state religion in 691 and sponsored Buddhist practice by inviting Buddhist scholars to China, building Buddhist temples, and com-missioning Buddhist cave paintings. She also developed the Chinese mer-itocracy tradition of application for government positions through taking competitive exams, and she strengthened government support for public works.

Wu is the only female monarch in China's history, and before she could officially take power as head of state she needed to create an image or a role model for a woman ruler; there had been none previously in China. She had the intelligence and political acumen to realize that she must ele-vate *all* women in order to create and inhabit her role. She sponsored scholarly biographies of famous women, elevated the status of the mother, and made use of Confucian writings celebrating a mother's com-passion to promote her own ability to relate to her subjects. She also rein-terpreted traditional Chinese symbols in a way that allowed women legal rights to power. Empress Wu, who clearly studied and practiced Bud-dhism herself, either wrote or had written on her behalf the following introduction to the translation of Buddhist doctrinal teachings:

As for one's essence, she neither arises nor ceases. As for the characteristics, she has no past or future. Correctly practicing the stations of mindfulness, the thirty-seven constituents [of enlightenment] is her practice. Sympathy, compassion, joy and equanimity—the four unlimited virtues—move her heart. The power of expedient means is inconceivable; the unifying policy has many facets. Merging with the great Emptiness is the limit. How much less can the multifaceted [government] policy be exhausted? Entering the smallest infinitesimal point has no name which can be expressed.[68]

In this piece of writing, Empress Wu integrates the needs of the kingdom with her own spiritual practice. While we don't know whether she explicitly followed these instructions in integrating Zen mind into her daily life on the throne, we do know what she accomplished as a ruler in difficult times. She negotiated peace settlements with the Turks and the Tibetans. She led China to success in conflict with Korea. By lowering the tax burden, she avoided uprisings. It is thought that she relied less on nepotism than other emperors; her advisors were well selected and appropriate to her cabinet. She was a competent ruler who used her power to lift the status of both women and Buddhism. She created a role for a female leader where there was none, and she used that role to support the development of Buddhist wisdom.

Queen Sondok:
"Princess of the Moon and Stars"

Queen Sondok is a legendary and beloved figure in the history of Korea and Korean Buddhism. The daughter of a king who had no son, she was the first Korean woman to rule as queen—and one of only three women in Korean history who did so. While a female Korean queen may have made Korea's Confucian population uncomfortable,[69] Sondok was widely revered by both the Korean shamanistic and Korean Buddhist traditions. Indeed, it may be that Korea's strong female shamanic tradition served as a foundation to empower Sondok's rule as queen.

The fourteen years of her reign, 634–47, were marked by violence and war. She strengthened ties to China, sent scholars and monks to China, and built Buddhist temples in Korea. In addition to studying Buddhism with Chinese monk missionaries, she studied astronomy and is credited with building the first observatory in Asia—hence she was called the Princess of the Moon and Stars. She also improved life for her subjects. She was known for her powers of premonition, including her correct prediction of the hour and day of her death. She passed the throne to her female cousin Chindok, who ruled from 647 to 654.

Yung-Chung Kim, a modern scholar, tells a story illustrating Queen Sondok's intuitive skills, her wisdom, and her compassion for her subjects.

Queen Sondok went up South Mountain for a picnic [on horse-back with Ch'un-ch'u]; she noticed flames and smoke rising to the sky. Upon inquiring of her attendants, she learned that Yu-sin was about to burn his sister to death because an illicit love affair had resulted in her pregnancy.

The Queen looked around and noticed that Ch'un-ch'u was as pale as death. "So it was you [who impregnated her]!" she said. "Go quickly and save the girl!" Ch'un-ch'u leaped on his horse and galloped quickly to Yu-sin's house, shouting, "Queen's order! Queen's order! Do not put her to death!" And so Mun-hui was saved.

A few days later Ch'un-ch'u and Mun-hui were formally married.[70]

Sondok lived and reigned in a time when strict Confucian morality was applied to women. Only the female participant in a premarital affair faced the death penalty. This anecdote illustrates Sondok's everyday wisdom. Not only did she embody wisdom and compassion on a large scale by supporting Buddhist temples, she did so on a personal scale, as in this example of protecting just one life.

Empress Komyo:
"Divine Light of Compassion"

Komyo was the wife of the Japanese emperor Shomu and did not herself reign on the throne. One of this couple's largest joint accomplishments was building the Great Buddha (Daibutsu) that still stands in Nara. During their reign, the government supported a system of Buddhist temples for monks and nuns, obviating the need for the renunciants to seek alms or survive by donations. Komyo initiated many projects for nuns, such as actively working for the welfare of orphans, sufferers of Hansen's disease (leprosy), those injured by war, and the economically underprivileged. Empress Komyo herself took the tonsure at the ordination platform of Todaiji in 749.[71]

We know that Komyo's mother, Tachibana no Michiyo, had also taken Buddhist vows to protect the health of the previous empress, Gensho. Tachibana renounced her wealth to become a nun after the death of her husband and the empress's illness. Tachibana lived until Komyo was

thirty-three and was said to be a strong influence on Komyo's development. Komyo watched her father develop a state-supported Buddhism.
Komyo consciously chose to model herself after Empress Wu of China.
She surpassed her role model's involvement in Buddhism by being the
first ruler to build a national network of nuns' convents.

Empress Komyo also was (and still is) revered as a hands-on embodiment of Guanyin (Japanese: Kannon), the bodhisattva of compassion.
She personally provided care to Hansen's disease patients and built hospitals that provided free medicine for the poor. Legend tells us that she
heard a voice warning her, "Empress, be not vain," and the voice commanded her to build a bathhouse for the poor and sick.[72] Apparently at
that time she took the vow "I myself will personally cleanse the bodies
of one thousand people." This kind of intimacy, while apparently perceived by some at the time as unseemly for a queen, was not so unusual
for a female Zen ancestor. For Komyo, helping another trumped holding
to propriety.

Though appearing in the section in this book on royal supporters,
Empress Komyo can also be seen as a founder. She established Hokkeji
Convent in the early eighth century by converting her father's residence
on the outskirts of Nara. Hokkeji was the flagship of the national convent
system and considered the female counterpart to Todaiji Monastery.
Housed in Hokkeji is an eleven-faced Kannon image modeled on the face
of Komyo. Hokkeji Convent continues the work of Komyo by caring for
those in need. Today the Hokkeji nuns work on Braille texts for the blind
and make protective amulets for pregnant women.

Korean Royal Wives: the *Nuns* **Hyeogyeong** and **Hyegyeong**

The nun Hyeogyeong (1440–1521) was known as Queen Song of Korea
prior to her ordination. Another nun of the same era, Hyegyeong, was a
concubine to the Queen Song's husband, King Tanjung (r. 1452–55). The
two knew each other through their relationship to the king. Tanjung was
later deposed and killed by his guardian uncle, who became King Sejo
(1417–68). Queen Song, later to become the nun Hyeogyeong, immediately fled the palace to take refuge. She went to the first nunnery established in Seoul, Ch'ongyongsa.

Hyeogyeong began working as a dyer to support the temple, but was found and approached there by the murderous uncle Sejo, who wished to make amends for his violence by offering her financial support. Repulsed by her husband's murderer and by his offer of financial support, Hyeogyeong traveled further to the small temple Mit'asa (established ca. 1047).

King Tanjung's concubine, Kweon (whose ordination name was Hyegyeong) escaped with the Queen Song to Mit'asa's neighboring nunnery Pomunsa, founded in 1115 by Korea's national teacher Tamjin expressly for nuns' training.[73]

Both these women became nuns when difficult circumstances destroyed their home life. Neither wished to have any association with their husband's assassin despite the protection he offered. Importantly, both transcended their previously competitive familial roles and joined together for mutual safety and Buddhist practice, establishing nunneries that continue in Korea to this day. Their friendship under difficult circumstances illustrates the beneficial power of women committed to principle. Korean nunneries have continued to offer protection for women, and safe haven during political upheaval.

The Buddhist "Wheel-turning monarchs" introduced in this chapter embody a distinctive role for women in general and for Buddhist women in particular. Women with extraordinary worldly power kept their attention focused on their spiritual development and on the welfare of others. They demonstrated their competence in national and international diplomacy and lived as caring human beings developing themselves through Buddhist practice. Often a woman is taught that wanting to be successful or powerful means that she is selfish or shallow and will lose touch with her identity and function. These women demonstrate the lie in this stereotype.

Through their examples, we see financially independent women who will not sell their integrity or their freedom of expression in exchange for safe haven and companionship. We meet women who do not lose their spirituality and humanity in the context of abundant finances—women who use their power to deepen their spiritual development, their compassionate relationship to their community, and their personal responsibility to others.

Early Zen Dharma Heirs   5

Establishing Women's Zen Lineage in China, Korea, and Japan

THE FIRST FEMALE Zen masters emerged in China, Korea, and Japan when Buddhism began to form different sects and schools, and in this chapter female Zen Dharma heirs from China, Korea, and Japan are presented in that geographical order. Each school of Buddhism emphasized a different aspect of practice, with the Zen school emphasizing seated meditation, or *zazen*. Other schools focused on scriptures such as the Lotus Sutra (Pure Land) or the Avatamsaka Sutra (Kegon), on walking pilgrimages (Tendai), or on esoteric Vajrayana rituals and symbols (Shingon). Because the Zen school is based on meditation practice, it is not dependent on literacy or knowledge of scriptures. Mastery of meditation does not favor males or females and is not inherently related to educational advantages, power, influence, physical strength, or wealth.

In Zen, every meditator sits down with her- or himself, using her or his own body-mind awareness, to reveal both inherent buddha-nature and the personal habits that obscure its flourishing. Men and women equally can realize this inherent awakened state through meditation. As meditative awareness stabilizes, it becomes a potent means of freeing practitioners from restrictive self-concepts. Meditation illuminates and dissolves limiting self-concepts related to familial roles, gender roles, or internalized self-images emerging from cultural stereotypes or other sources. Buddhists express it this way: All defilements are *self-liberating* in the great space of awareness. We open this space of awareness, and simultaneously see and release ourselves from self-intoxicating ideas—the very ideas and feelings that create the self-identity that limits our freedom.

The accomplishments of the first female Zen masters answer several important questions pertinent to women seeking liberation: How do women find their way in a male-dominated institution? What was it about Zen training that liberated them? What words of wisdom did they leave behind? These words should matter to contemporary women. Modern women's self-help groups and feminist therapy are concerned with, for instance, liberation from rigid familial roles, restrictive cultural stereotypes, and internalized negative images. These interpersonal, cultural, and intrapsychic traps limit women's personal/spiritual expression and affect women's ability to survive and thrive personally, professionally, and financially. Studying how Zen practice can free women from these traps and help them learn to express their freedom is instructive not only for Zen practitioners but for all women concerned with liberation.

The lives and teachings of these female Zen masters, while not articulated in classical Zen literature, are presented here thanks to more recent translations. Like early Buddhist founders, female Zen founders established temples for women and were recognized as Dharma masters by monks and nuns, laymen and laywomen. Additionally, from this lineup of early Zen teachers we receive our first female Zen teaching words, presented within the life context of an actual woman and her own life story.

Zengo, as these teaching words are called in Japanese, are the concise teaching words of a Zen master. They are the direct personal expression of the teacher's Zen mind, the mind of realization distilled from years of practice expressed concisely.

Unlike teachings explored in the previous section, "Zen's Women," in this section, "Women's Zen," women's teaching words are contextualized within the details of their early lives and training experiences, embedded in the real-life stories of actual women's efforts, suffering, and transcendence. By studying these female masters, women can relate more fully to familial tensions, difficulties with institutions, and personal sacrifices inevitably encountered by female practitioners.

Zhiyuan Xinggang:
Chinese Linji Dharma Heir

Xinggang (1597–1657), whose family name was Hu, was an only child born to a scholarly family. Although both her parents were religious, they refused their daughter's request to enter the religious life and remain unmarried. She had shown early promise as a poet, and from young girl-hood spent long hours worshipping at the family altar by reciting the name of the Buddha. At eighteen, Xinggang found herself engaged to be married, again despite her requests to enter the religious life. Her parents-in-law expected her to continue the family line through birthing children. This responsibility, not foreign to women today, was considered an essential filial duty in China.

Xinggang's intended husband died before they were married, and as seventeenth-century Chinese custom dictated, she was sent to live with his parents (her intended in-laws) to fulfill her duties as a daughter-in-law. Living with her in-laws, she could not put aside her religious desire and spent long periods on her knees before the Buddha, weeping and praying that she be allowed to find her way to Buddhist practice and enlightenment before she died.

Her religious fervor included periods of fasting and depression. This behavior frightened her parents and her in-laws, who responded by forbidding her religious fasting. Xinggang, now twenty-six, seized control of her life through a desperate measure. She gave up eating and drinking altogether. Finally, faced with her demise, her family allowed her to begin formal training at a local temple with the elderly master Tianci Cixing.

Xinggang's early life reveals tantalizing similarities to other Buddhist female ancestors, and it raises questions that apply to contemporary young women. Her biography presents a woman determined to follow a religious path. Her early ability and determination were blocked by her family. Were they trying to protect her from her own extreme behavior, or did her behavior become so extreme because she was imprisoned by filial duty? With a view four hundred years distant, it is difficult to say. The record suggests, however, that through Zen practice she eventually became functional, useful, and stable as a Zen teacher.

The Buddhist scholar Rita Gross discusses Buddhism's stance vis-à-vis marriage and procreation in her book *Soaring and Settling*. Without the support of feminist writings, and with little external assistance, Xinggang charted an alternate course: a life free of marriage and procreative responsibilities. Her highly original journey suggests she had a genuine religious calling and that only she could find her own true life—through answering that call. Did the sight of a young girl devotedly engaging in daily worship frighten her parents? They must have wished for a healthier balance or a more conventional life for their sensitive and precocious daughter. Viewing Xinggang through her family's eyes, one is sympathetic to a parent unsure of what to do with a daughter who prays and weeps daily at the Buddha's altar for long periods. Today parents might well insist on psychotherapy, in which she might be diagnosed with an eating disorder. Xinggang's parents must have wondered whether she was somehow unbalanced or perhaps even possessed by negative forces. They may have seen her as desperately needing the stabilizing effects of a structured family life. We can imagine them crossing their fingers and offering their prayers, once they relented and allowed her to participate in Buddhist training, perhaps hoping that it would be "just a phase."

Passive-aggressive forms of resistance such as withdrawing from family interactions, and self-destructive assertions of will such as refusing food, seem to be a first line of defense for women pursuing their own way despite family wishes. Gender differences related to strength, temperament, customs, laws, and safety issues limit women from prevailing by brute strength, running away, or otherwise rebelling against a system that binds them. It is, after all, hard to imagine a grown young man in similar circumstances behaving in quite the same way. A young man would simply run away from home to pursue his spiritual training (following the Buddha's example) instead of going on a hunger strike. As we study female Zen ancestors, we see again and again that women used passive-aggressive resistance and acts of self-destruction to oppose family or institutional obstacles and accomplish their spiritual objectives.

Today, thankfully, women have other options; they have the legal right to lead their own lives, including whether to marry or not, and they can for the most part travel safely pursuing their goals. Still, the choices even contemporary women face are painful if they cut across familial expectations that demand adherence to conventional roles.

It is interesting to compare Xinggang's story to how women today may struggle to follow a calling that conflicts with family wishes. Understanding the burdens that women face in unfolding an autonomous life may help us find a more flexible view in diagnosing or even labeling difficult behaviors in women's development. We also can identify more sympathetically with a family's terror and refusal to allow Zen training when we consider Xinggang's disturbed behavior (for example, her refusing to eat) through today's view of anorexia in young perfectionistic women.

Such a wider perspective can be helpful to contemporary Zen teachers who guide young women with family conflicts. Teachers need to understand that women have often been raised differently than men, and that women's adjustment to Zen may be more complicated as they relate to the sangha in ways that replicate their entangled family conflicts.

Xinggang's formal training with old Master Cixing meant living at home, taking care of her in-laws, and keeping an eye out for her own parents. After seven years with Cixing, Xinggang was ready to take her practice to the next level: formal ordination and residential practice. In 1630, when she was thirty-three, Xinggang felt confident enough to visit Cixing's teacher at Mount Jinsu Monastery, where more than three hundred monks practiced together with Master Miyun Yuanwu (1565–1641).[74] It is a rather intimidating image—a lone woman approaching a large male training institution on her own.

Xinggang had a typical initial interview with Master Miyun Yuanwu. She raised her lifelong spiritual question: "Where is the place where I can settle myself and establish my life?" This was the question that she used as a koan for meditation.[75] Master Yuanwu, in typical Zen master style, declared that he was sparing her the thirty blows that she deserved. He also brought up the case of a talented and irreverent Tang dynasty Zen teacher, Thirteenth Daughter Zheng,[76] perhaps to encourage her. Zheng has a sharp tongue, confronts her teacher repeatedly, is put in her place, and yet persists until she has a breakthrough.

Master Yuanwu's mention of Zheng suggests that he had some familiarity with women's practice—he knew about Zheng and he believed that Xinggang would benefit from knowing about this woman's practice. Perhaps he used the example of Daughter Zheng to motivate Xinggang to continue despite the obligatory rejection of the initial interview. The story of how Zheng is scolded but eventually becomes a Dharma heir helps us to understand Miyun's approach with Xinggang. Initially Xinggang's confident responses, like Zheng's, were soundly rejected in her interviews with the master. Perhaps Master Yuanwu was saying, "I am rejecting you. That's necessary, but other strong female students were also rejected and went on to prove themselves." He both corrected and encouraged her. In Master Yuanwu, Xinggang had found an able Zen master who was prepared to teach her, but through this relationship we are reminded of the extra obstacles facing a woman pursuing Zen practice.

Xinggang's mother was still alive, and since the requisite three-year mourning for her father's death was not complete, Master Yuanwu sent Xinggang home to complete her filial duties. Master Yuanwu had himself abandoned responsibility for parents, wife, and children thirty-five years earlier when he had left home to study Zen, but he imposed different standards on Xinggang. She returned home to care for her parents, and after her mother's death returned to Master Yuanwu for formal ordination.

What can we make of this example of double standards? Are there two standards regarding men and women, even in the eyes of the enlightened Zen master? Does Zen, a practice promising liberation, enact forms of bias and thereby oppression? Or was Yuanwu wise to encourage Xinggang to complete her care for her parents, conjecturing that as a woman she had different emotional needs? There are really two questions worth unpacking here: Can a teaching that promises enlightenment practice what it preaches? What does a practitioner do when the Zen institution seemingly talks the talk but doesn't walk the walk?

We must remember that all institutions are composed of human beings—people who have absorbed the habitual thought patterns of their own culture. In practicing Buddhism, it is urgent that we not confuse our love for the practice of enlightenment with the actions that occur within its institutions. Today we have rules and federal laws protecting minorities (as well as women) and grievance committees within Zen centers to help address inconsistencies and inequities, and to point out and correct gender and other forms of discrimination. Even now, we see how our culture obscures issues, how men and women in institutions cannot see, much less correct, their blind spots. Sometimes the teachers and the institution reflect an enlightened mind, and sometimes they do not. The question of how to address these blind spots as Zen develops in Western centers will be discussed later, in part III.

The question of what to do when the institution fails to turn toward its blind spots, or when the rules and committees fail us, needs to be addressed by each practitioner. For practice to deepen, we need to understand that disappointment and problems are part of our growth. The Buddha himself taught that unsatisfactoriness is a basic truth of human existence, and we must come to realize that Dharma institutions and even Zen masters are not exempt from this reality. The Buddha taught that we all suffer in ways that can't be helped but can be understood. Not every unfair situation can be identified and regulated, but we must learn through practice to work with disappointment and with our unfulfilled desire. Sooner or later we have to face difficulty as an inevitable part of every life. What resources will we call on to face our pain? Where do we go for help?

Early Zen Dharma heirs like Xinggang offered some answers to these questions. She found a way to practice with rejection, to build confidence in her path, and to pursue liberation. Living the Zen life means settling ourselves in our meditation and finding a way, even when our path is blocked. Like Xinggang, we can find resolution by returning again and again to our commitment to rely on spiritual practice itself to guide us to deeper wisdom and resolution. Xinggang continued deepening her spiritual practice and nourishing her resolve even when her Zen mentor rejected her request for admission. She did not abandon her calling; she just took a detour, practicing at home until conditions changed. When hardship itself is embedded within our practice realm, we learn to trust the practice more deeply—to recognize there is nowhere else to go. When hardship occurs in our relationships or work, we turn toward the Three Treasures—Buddha, Dharma, and Sangha. But when the disappointment occurs within the realm of the Three Treasures, we must let go of our demand that Buddhism meet our needs perfectly. We begin to truly meet our suffering and rely on awareness itself to guide us.

This was an essential skill for Zen women; they could not afford to take (perceived or actual) inequity personally. The opportunity to practice was precious, but not perfect. Xinggang teaches us that the ability to deepen commitment despite obstacles is essential for anyone determined to awaken through spiritual practice. After one has deepened and settled, clarity and courage arise. At that time, appropriate action, whether it be a protest or an alternate route, will find its expression in our life.

After taking care of her family responsibilities and returning to Yuanwu, Xinggang was ordained. For a while, she couldn't seem to find a way to work through her koan; she couldn't find an "entry way" with Yuanwu. But she followed her path right through the center of her difficulties, unimpeded by lack of rapport with the teacher. She remained committed to her intention and she moved ahead, continuing her training and finally experiencing awakening with one of Master Yuanwu's senior disciples, Master Tongshen (1593–1638). Xinggang began studying with Master Tongshen when she was thirty-six years old. After a year of practice, she had her first breakthrough with a famous Zen koan: "What was your original face before your mother and father were born?" Her breakthrough came only after surviving a week of nonstop meditation during which "she redoubled her efforts and began to spit blood and found it impossible to eat or drink."[77] (We note the reappearance of Xinggang's extreme behavior and physical/psychological symptoms, not an uncommon occurrence for Zen practitioners on the edge of a spiritual breakthrough.)

After further illumination she composed the following verse: This is Xinggang's first *zengo*, the fruit of her developing poetic ability.

Before my parents had been born
Emptiness congealed, clarity complete,
From the start there is nothing lacking:
Clouds scatter dew over the blue heavens.[78]

Here she addresses the subject matter of her koan, woven together with her experience of the unending flow of life. Awakening to life—hardships and all—is paired with the beautiful image of clouds scattering dew over the blue heavens. Obstacles and years of struggle had been thoroughly digested and transcended. Her koan, "What was my face before my parents were born?" is ironically pertinent to a woman struggling to find her independence within the web of filial duties. Parents, no parents: there is nothing missing in the web of life or in any relationship between earth and heaven.

Later, Xinggang teaches another student with the same koan that facilitated her awakening. In this poem, we hear her giving practice instruction to a student regarding this koan:

Understand the ordinary mind, and realize one [who] is naturally complete.
    Ask urgently who you were before your father and mother were born.
    When you see through the method that underlies them all,
    The mountain blossoms and flowing streams will rejoice with you.[79]

In these practice instructions Xinggang describes the process of training and the experience of awakening. First, through meditation, find the place from which to observe the mind at work. From the position of practicing beyond self and method, realize that there is nothing missing, that this awareness itself is complete and connected to all consciousness. This awareness is naturally present, underlying all experience. We don't need to "believe in it"; we can experience it through urgent and focused meditation practice. Once awareness is stabilized, with concentrated effort we can inquire, "What is it that has poured from the source through this very mind at this very moment?" The result of effortful inquiry and deeply concentrated awareness will without fail reveal the transformative energy flowing and connecting all consciousness in oneness. This realization expresses itself just as spring blossoms and streams flow. It manifests as the life force everywhere.

Xinggang's awakening was recognized and deepened by her teacher Master Tongshen. Later she was presented with the staff and robes, symbols of her authenticity as a Dharma teacher in the Linji lineage. Xinggang was forty-one years old when she received the Dharma staff, known also as the "wish-fulfiller." She composed another poem in connection with the Dharma transmission ceremony:

> Fingers fold around the "wish-fulfiller," the lineage continues;
> As both past and present disappear in a dazzling emptiness.
> When one understands the nature of the true "wish-fulfiller,"
> Then the unchanging Absolute will rest in the palm of one's
> hand.[80]

Here Xinggang uses the symbolism of the Zen master's staff to describe the freedom resulting from awakening. Understanding and abiding in unified reality, the Dharma holder knows the true meaning of happiness. She is not separate from anything; true fulfillment is not dependent on satisfying wishes. This true fulfillment comes through the transformation of disappointments encountered along the way; the true happiness bestowed by the "wish-fulfiller" is the gift of having nothing more to wish for. With realization of oneness, everything is right here in her hands. Her ease is based on perceiving, experiencing, and inhabiting the continuity of life as it arises in the present moment.

Like traditional Zen masters before her, Xinggang went into seclusion after she received Dharma transmission. It is not clear whether Xinggang received directions from her teacher to "hide her light" after her awakening had been verified, as many Zen masters did, and that this subsequently was why she decided to go into retreat for nine years, but we know that she returned to the small hermitage near her parents' graves, where she had begun her formal practice. Once more she engaged in ascetic practices in seclusion.

Ascetic practices were advocated by the eminent Linji master Gaofeng Yuanmiao (1238–95), whose words she often quoted. These practices, known as *siguan*, "enclosure as if dead," involved restricting oneself to a hermitage, usually for a period of three years of solitary meditation practice and rituals. Seclusion, recommended to Xinggang during her training, resembles the historical and contemporary long hermit retreats done in the Tibetan tradition. After her period of seclusion, Xinggang expressed her deepened sense of liberation in this way:

I lived in deep seclusion with few comforts but determined to persevere. My body [seated upright] with grave dignity, [I made no distinctions between] inner and outer. I pushed against emptiness, cutting off entanglements. Once the [distinction between] inner and outer was gone then all entanglements were dissolved. When there is neither shape nor form, one sees oneself face to face, and can gather up [a great] kalpa in a single point and spread a speck of dust over the ten directions. [Then one experiences] no restrictions, no restraints, [and is] free to go where one pleases.[81]

Through concentrated effort, she was able to release troubling thoughts and emotions. Finding her place in vast awareness, she slipped away from the distinctions of perceived and perceiver, self and other, here and there, and past, present, and future. This experience and the resulting confidence removed restrictive concerns and empowered her freedom.

Xinggang became an official Linji Dharma heir, awarded this formal status by her teacher. Her lineage authenticity is documented by her formal status, and her teaching words reflect the strict Linji style. But her softened teaching style departs from that of her male lineage predecessors.

Linji's "take no prisoners" Zen is known for its shouts and blows and its emphasis on full exertion for enlightenment. While Xinggang's perseverance and exertion in training are consistent with the Linji style, her teachings emphasize urgency without harshness. She speaks of joy in practice and of compassionate service, and her disciples express warmth and tenderness.

Xinggang taught both lay disciples and ordained students that liberation is a life-and-death struggle. She emphasized the hard work required for spiritual development through meditation and koan practice. Rather than just speaking of the hardship, however, she articulates the other side as well:

> There is no greater suffering than to be caught up in the bustle of worldly affairs, there is no greater joy than cultivating the way with one-pointed mind. The Way is no other than the greatest joy in this world. Abandoning the Way to seek out pleasure is like throwing away food and seeking hunger![82]

Xinggang taught that what we usually think of as fun and interesting—worldly seeking—is actually suffering. She believed that seeking liberation, which we associate with renunciation and hardship, is actually joyous. Xinggang offers this kind reminder for Zen trainees and other spiritual practitioners: the hardship we experience is not a result of the practice or its inevitable physical difficulties. Our suffering is caused instead by our inevitable human desires for having things our own way, and by our addictions to worldly pleasures that only result in more suffering. Xinggang reframed the difficulty of Zen training so that we can see the result of our habitual misperception. Her emphasis on joy is a welcome addition to the Linji tradition's usual focus on shouts and blows. We get the urgency and directness of Linji Zen with the warm flavor of delight.

Xinggang's disciples openly express intimate feelings toward one another and toward their teacher, a rarity in Zen literature. Emotion is particularly noticeable in the records of Xinggang and three of her seven Dharma heirs: Yigong Chaoke (1620–67), Yikui Chaochen (1625–79), and Yichuan Zhaoke (d. 1656). Yigong, Xinggang's most senior nun, wrote these verses when Xinggang died:

MOURNING THE NUN WHO WAS MY MASTER

I.

The moon sinks west as autumn comes to a close;
The fly-whisk untouched lies at the head of her seat.
Outside the window, the branches of a single tree weep;
A wind rises and rain drips mournfully in the meditation hall.

II.

For the past twenty years, she has been our teacher,
Truly unique and alone, her staff flashing up and down.
When did the smoke from her quarters dwindle away,
Leaving her children and grandchildren as they were before?[83]

The reference to children and grandchildren has a ring of intimacy and nurturing beyond the usual relationship between Zen master and disciples. We sense Xinggang's vitality as the staff flashes up and down, and the tenderness of the single tree's weeping. Xinggang's successor, Yigong, openly expresses her vulnerability, sorrow, and loss regarding her teacher's death. We also see the maternal relationship Xinggang shared through her strong teaching role with her "children and grandchildren." While this ephemeral life expressed as the dwindling of smoke is a classic Zen reference, we do not find herein the "no coming or going" that is often expressed in the traditional Zen poem without a sense of deep personal feeling. In this poem, we encounter genuine human feelings of loss.

Yigong also expressed her feelings in a poem when her Dharma sister Yichuan died only two years after their teacher's death. Here, in another example of Yigong's *zengo*, are her memorial words mourning the death of her Dharma sister, Yichuan. Yichuan had also studied with Master Xinggang.

Alas! There was no one like you my Dharma sister, the monk from Banruo. Your heart was like that of a naked child, your actions like those of the ancients...you were clever while appearing awkward, wise while appearing stupid, eloquent while appearing inarticulate, iron-strong while appearing soft. You treated others as you would treat yourself, and fully exhausted the possibilities of both man and heaven. You and I shared the same way of life, but you have abandoned me and entered the realm of the deathless.[84]

Again, this tender, detailed description communicates Yigong's painful personal loss and sense of abandonment. Interestingly, Yigong refers to her Dharma sister as a monk, emphasizing Yichuan's primary relationship to practice that transcended her gender. While Yigong acknowledged the realm of the deathless in authentic Zen style, she willingly exposed her emotional vulnerability as she endured the loss of her Dharma sister.

Giving comfort to monks in distress is not the usual role of the Zen master, but Xinggang's teaching includes a vivid example of Zen tenderness and caretaking. On a visit to Jinsu, the temple where she had trained, Xinggang found the monks there "suffering greatly from the cold."[85] Xinggang and her nuns spent the next several months at their convent sewing leggings for all the monks. In Linji-style Zen, we expect to hear about the benefits of practicing with heat, cold, and mosquitoes—among other trying circumstances. According to the traditional Zen perspective, all these obstacles drive the concentration deeper.

Even Shunryu Suzuki, the modern founder of Japanese Soto Zen in America, had "toughen-up" advice for his American students at one of the first Western monasteries (around 1970) when they complained about the winter cold: "Use zazen to make heat!" While the monks who wore Xinggang's leggings also needed to learn how to "make heat," perhaps they would avoid frostbite by making heat while wrapped in the nuns' knitted compassion. Xinggang's rigorous training style, practicality, and warmhearted compassion make a powerful teaching combination.

Zen women have had to find innovative methods to continue their practice. They have practiced all manner of resistance to convince family members to allow them to leave home to practice. They have approached and bargained with multiple male teachers until they found one who would accept them. They have found ways to circumvent rules when their ordinations were blocked. They have made the most of family connections. They have outsmarted captors when they were physically dominated by invaders. They have developed new forms of practice combining home life and brief monastic visits. Xinggang's life is a wonderful example of how a woman can continue practicing and how women's Zen can expand the expression of Zen to emphasize tenderness, vulnerability, and nurturing in addition to liberation through heroic strength.

Myori Beophui Sunim:
The One Great Korean Nun Master

Myori Beophui (1887–1975) is the only nun that the current Chogye order in Korea has accorded the status of master, equal to the great historical male Korean masters. She joined the Mitaam Convent at the age of three after her father died; she had been carried there on her grandmother's back. This gesture of extreme body-to-body intimacy with her grandmother, and the complete abandonment which immediately followed, surely left its mark on this little girl. It is hard to imagine the devastating conditions that would require leaving a child behind and the entire family's heartache that followed.

Beophui was first ordained with novice status when she was fourteen years old, and she took full *bhikshuni* vows at age twenty-one. She traveled to train with Master Man'gong when she was twenty-five and was greeted by him with "I knew a meditator like her was coming."[86] She was admitted to his practice community, and after being acknowledged for her deep awakening she was named his first female Dharma heir. She opened a path for other women to follow as the first female head master of the nuns' meditation hall. According to the same Chogye order sources, the nun Song'yong Sunim, who later trained the Western practitioner Martine Batchelor, claimed that Beophui slept no more than two hours a night and worked with a hoe by moonlight. While she left many successful nun students, she never gave a Dharma talk, choosing instead to make her life's work an expression of the Buddha's way. According to her disciple Song'yong Sunim, when Beophui was asked about the Dharma she would pretend as if she didn't know. With Beophui and other nuns that follow, we note that chronic emotional deprivation in women may be linked to their inability to take the formal teaching seat and speak.

Beophui was a great leader and inspiration for Korean nuns. Perhaps her reluctance to speak from a teaching platform about Dharma came in part from her immersion in the Joseon dynasty culture that had preceded her—a five-hundred-year policy of *namjon yeobi*, or "respect men, abase women"—as well as her early childhood abandonment and loss of family.

Her dedication to eighty-five years of monastic life inspired the practice of many Korean nuns. No doubt, Beophui Sunim knew something of the Zen women who preceded her; she had nine strong female Dharma heirs.

Mugai Nyodai:
Japanese Rinzai Founder of the Imperial Zen Convent System

The existence of Mugai Nyodai (1223–98), a Linji / Rinzai Zen master, was accidentally discovered by the Japan scholar Barbara Ruch. Surveying a book of portraits of Zen abbots, Professor Ruch was stopped in her tracks when she saw Nyodai's clearly feminine facial features. What was a woman doing among all these male Zen abbots? After seeing this portrait, Ruch focused her research on Nyodai and her heritage. She created the Institute for the Study of Medieval Japan to answer the questions that Nyodai's existence raised. Her institute is almost entirely focused on finding, translating, studying, and disseminating the work of Mugai Nyodai and the temples that were part of her lineage. We can see Barbara Ruch herself as one of our modern-day female founders.

Professor Ruch's experience mirrors the discovery process for many of us who have stumbled across our first tidbit of women's Zen. At first we are surprised to discover that Western women are not the first women to practice and teach Zen. We may feel anger at what appears to be the intentional suppression of this valuable ancestral material. As we get to know these women, perhaps sadness arises for their neglected lives and works. Just as Dr. Ruch has established her institute, we may begin to uncover the work for ourselves, to pass through our emotional cycles, and to resolve to do our part to bring this material to light.

How do we begin to understand these women's teachings, the suppression and omission of their work, and the new view of Zen that emerges when they are included? How could a purportedly awakened practice support the repression of their teachings? Perhaps we have idealized the Zen institution and its story, or perhaps we are simply new to finding out about these mistakes. Uncovering this work provides us with new inspiration for Zen practice and changes our relationship to our own Zen institutions. Finally, Zen itself is changed by the inclusion of this material and our new embodiment of the practice it inspires. How we might integrate the uncovering process into current Zen institutions is a topic covered in part III.

Returning to Mugai Nyodai, she ordained as a nun in her fifties, was well educated in Chinese and Japanese classics, and had been married to a feudal lord. Her husband was killed in battle and his clan was destroyed. We don't know for sure whether she began her Zen studies during or after her marriage. We do know that she studied Rinzai Zen with the eminent Japanese teacher Enni Benen (1200–81) of Tofukuji Monastery, also known as Shoichi Kokushi, and the Chinese teacher Wuxue Zuyuan (1226–86), also known in Japanese as Mugaku Sogen or Bukko Kokushi. She had an impeccable Japanese Rinzai Zen lineage, having been recognized by Mugaku as one of his two Dharma heirs. She was the first woman in Japanese history to be recognized as a Rinzai Zen master, and she went on to found Keiaiji temple after the death of her father and the exile of her husband. Keiaiji grew to include more than fifteen subtemples.[87]

Mugai's training with Mugaku Sogen is historically well documented. The scholar Anne Dutton, in an unpublished paper, has tried to explain why, despite Mugai's accomplishments as a Dharma heir and subtemple founder at Engakuji,[88] she seems to have been virtually erased from the lineage.[89] The answer seems to be that Muso Soseki, her Dharma nephew, was apparently responsible for eradicating all traces of Mugai Nyodai from the Engakuji history. We can conjecture that she was removed in an effort to strengthen the concept of a singular, linear Zen succession. It appears that Muso Soseki was interested in promoting, preserving, and consolidating Mugaku's lineage through only one of Wuxue's Dharma heirs, his own teacher Koho Kennichi (1241–1316). When Mugai Nyodai received transmission, she was an equal to Muso's teacher, Koho Kennichi; both were Dharma heirs of Mugaku Sogen. It appears Muso sought to eliminate the record of Abbot Nyodai's status and contribution in favor of his own teacher's record.

The representation of the Zen lineage as continuing through one main male Dharma heir has essentially made women invisible throughout Zen's long history. This unhealthy tendency may show up in today's Western Zen lineage charts. For example, Kapleau Roshi's first Dharma heir, a woman, Toni Packer, has been removed from some renditions of his lineage. This is an awkward situation; according to some, Toni's revisions to Zen practice were accepted by Kapleau but rejected by his practitioners, so she left the center. Toni Packer eventually formed her own school of meditation practice outside the Zen school. Nevertheless, the fact remains that she was the first Dharma heir in Kapleau's American school of Zen. Will her name be lost to history?

I have also seen some records of Taizan Maezumi Roshi's Dharma heirs where the name of a female lineage holder, Charlotte Joko Beck, is missing. Joko Beck was discouraged by Maezumi Roshi's inappropriate behavior during his struggle with alcoholism, for which he made a public apology to his sangha. She broke off with her teacher and founded her own Zen school, the Ordinary Mind School of Zen, outside of Maezumi Roshi's direction. However, she was Maezumi Roshi's Dharma heir and should be recognized as such in an accurate history of Western Zen lineage. Before retiring, Joko passed her Soto Zen lineage on to her Dharma heirs, which allowed them entry into the American Soto Zen Buddhist Association and community.

Repudiation of lineage and inability to remain within the traditional hierarchy may have similarly affected other historical Zen women. While there are reasons to both innovate and to move away from corrupt power structures, the presence of women in a historical lineage can support the practice of women who follow, just as their courageous innovations and departures may be more fully appreciated within their lineage context.

Mugai Nyodai's training at Tofukuji with Enni Benen also brings up a recurrent theme for early Zen women: their exclusion from the male monastery based on potential or imagined impropriety, and these women's dramatic fight for inclusion. Imperial convent records suggest that, threatened with exclusion from training at Tofukuji, because the presence of a woman might distract the monks training there, Mugai Nyodai burned her face, and only then gained entry. This particular form of self-mutilation, face burning, is a recurrent theme in the history of women's Zen, discussed in detail in chapter 7 below through the example of Ryonen Genso. Ryonen also burned her face and may have learned of this gruesome temple entry technique through studying historical records of Mugai Nyodai.

The story goes that Zen Master Enni Benen was amenable to Mugai Nyodai's training at his male monastery, but his disciples caused a ruckus. Coming from a wealthy family, she then offered to sponsor the construction of a convent within the grounds of Tofukuji as a remedy, but this did not pacify the monks who continued their harassment. Mugai then scarred her face with a hot iron. Her self-mutilation was a declaration of her sincerity and lack of interest in using feminine wiles. Ruch conjectures that one can see the burn when viewing the lifelike statue made in her image, evidenced by the droop of her right cheek.

Education and freedom to travel were often class privileges of the female Zen founders; although useful, these privileges were not always necessary for gaining access to Zen training. Women, like their male counterparts, became deeply motivated to practice Zen only through learning about it. Because women in Asian cultures were often confined to their homes, access to education and to Buddhist teachings also came through family acquaintances—connections to literati and to important Buddhist teachers. Unlike their male counterparts, women had less freedom to be out and about. They were less likely to meet a Zen student or teacher through their everyday activities. It is not surprising that Zen's female pioneers tended to come from privileged families connected to educated laypeople who had access to accomplished Buddhist teachers.

Female Zen founders used their class privilege to travel to authentic teachers. Their education was useful in reading sutras, understanding Zen lectures, and in evaluating with whom they should study. Later, as they became teachers, their education gave them the confidence and the ability to articulate their teachings. Education and Zen practice helped women move beyond the narrow-minded prejudice and social constraints of their times; it exposed them to historical examples of egalitarian women's practice and gave them the polish and credibility necessary to be respected in the Zen tradition. Exposure to training helped these founding females develop a shared purpose: to create a community of like-minded women seeking the Way.

In Zen, where Buddhist understanding could sometimes trump social position and power, a woman devoted to meditation itself, with the strong support of her teacher, could develop a deep practice and make a significant contribution. Sincerity and being a good judge of character could go far in supporting a woman's Zen practice once she found her way to a Zen teacher who granted her entry. The early founders' understanding that a woman could benefit from Zen, regardless of her educational or social background, must have encouraged them to develop convents specifically to help women practice. In other words, women of privilege witnessed and experienced the oppression of their gender and then became motivated to offer Zen practice to other women—regardless of their social class—as a remedy.

Besides her dedication to establishing convents, Mugai Nyodai is also remembered for her own powerful awakening experience, expressed in her poem to her teacher, Wuxue; Mugai Nyodai, seeing her true self, expressed it delicately as a *zengo*. In her poem, she described the difficulties faced before awakening—trying to practice without genuine understanding. Pulled by desire, the karma of previous actions, and life circumstances, she wandered as if lost from one activity to the next without finding the authentic Way. Experiencing oneness through Zen awakening, we finally realize our inherent relationship to the natural world and understand our uniquely human function in life. Our human function is to express and embody this oneness in everything we do. Our life, this human-embodied oneness, is an expression of enlightenment symbolized by the moon. It is powerfully bright and reflected everywhere, but like the floating clouds, it moves on, peacefully changing form just as we do. Here is Mugai Nyodai's *zengo*, addressed to her teacher to express her enlightenment.

> Understanding nothing,
> I lost my way.
> But now I see I, too, am one
> With the moon on the water
> And the floating clouds.[90]

Soto Zen Female Founders

We can name some of the founders of today's Japanese Soto Zen nuns' order, but sadly, we are without their teaching words. Paula Arai in her book *Women Living Zen* has helped us to trace our lineage, from women's Soto Zen practice today back to the historical female founders in Japan. As a member of the Soto Zen school, I was delighted to learn about my ancestors but disappointed not to be able to hear their voices. Once we acknowledge these early Soto Zen founders as placeholders in the women's Soto lineage, we can advocate for some translated record of their teachings.

The women's Soto Zen order was established by several women who both studied under and influenced the early Soto Zen masters Eihei Dogen and Keizan Jokin. The founder of Soto Zen, Eihei Dogen (1200–53), advocated in his essay "Raihaitokuzui" the importance of recognizing women's equal teaching ability in the Dharma.[91]

At the same time that Dogen was advocating for women, the Zen school was also excluding women from its training temples. Stranger and sadder yet, Eiheiji, the temple Dogen founded in Fukui, Japan, currently has no training facilities for women. Until recently, the Soto Zen school enforced many inequalities in nuns' status relative to monks'; despite Dogen's writings about gender equality in the thirteenth century, discrimination against women persisted in the order he founded through the twentieth century. For example, around 1900 the Soto Zen school gave monks an average stipend of 180,000 yen a year in financial support, while nuns received on average only 600 yen each year.[92]

Despite Dogen's strong support, and his willingness to train women in his order, it was not until several generations of practitioners later that Dogen's male disciple Keizan transmitted the Dharma to a female heir (ca. 1325). Dharma transmission is a spiritual and institutional acknowledgment of mastery. It was Keizan who transformed Dogen's preachings about women's equality into the reality of authentic and independent women's practice, and it was also Keizan who transformed the Soto Zen school by including women and laypeople more fully.

Keizan is said to be the mother and Dogen the father of Soto Zen. We can infer several meanings to the attribution of a motherly status to Keizan. Dogen conceived the practice and perhaps planted the seed of Soto Zen, but Keizan nurtured it by adding ceremonies to make it more inclusive of laypeople. In this sense, it was really Keizan who gave birth to the Soto Zen tradition in Japan. This characterization may also refer to the way Keizan attributed his spiritual faith to his own mother and grandmother, making no mention of his father's spiritual guidance. Keizan's image as a mother may also express something of his nurturing tenderness toward the underdogs—women and lay followers. What follows is an expanded view of Soto Zen through the women in Keizan's life.

Myochi:
Keizan Zenji's Granny

Myochi (ca. 1225) was an early supporter of Eihei Dogen. It is believed that she was a lay disciple of Dogen's own first Zen teacher, Myozen, and that she gave financial support to both Myozen and Dogen and attended their lectures.[93] Her connection with Dogen, even before Keizan's birth, helped to build the very practice path Keizan later chose to follow. Her faith in Zen influenced both Keizan and his mother, Myochi's daughter Ekan, to follow the Zen path. Keizan declared that Myochi's faith led him to become a novice monk at Eiheiji at age seven. It is not known whether Keizan ordained at that early age because of his grandmother's urging or because he wanted to honor her death.

Throughout his life, Keizan felt that it was the faith of his grandmother and his mother that karmically supported his practice. He believed in their faith as a tangible energetic force that sustained his practice and teaching. He also praised his female financial supporter, Sonin. Indeed, Keizan believed a teacher's karma depended both on his faith and on his supporters. Keizan said that a teacher with a powerful message still needed attention and financial contributions. He also believed that material supporters of Buddhism should be honored in the same way we honor the Buddha.

We learn from Myochi and Keizan that our own dedication to supporting practice, even in the midst of family responsibilities, may add depth to the unfolding path of Western Zen. We can support the transplanting of Zen to America through both financial contributions and sincere practice. Like Grandmother Myochi, we can help support teachers in whom we have confidence without becoming resident members of a Zen monastery.

We can never know just what aspect of Zen practice will be nurtured by our genuine practice effort or whether our efforts will leave no trace at all for those to come. As it turned out, Myochi's devotion not only supported Soto Zen's foundational teachers but guided her grandson, Keizan, who later became a Soto Zen founder himself.

Ekan Daishi:
Plum Blossom

Keizan's mother, Ekan (d. ca. 1314), was a fervent devotee of Kannon, the compassionate bodhisattva who vowed to save all living creatures and was thought to be capable of assuming many forms to teach and lead. Ekan's devotion to Kannon was influenced by her mother, Myochi. Ekan kept a figure of the eleven-headed Kannon by her side and prayed to it regularly. We are told she prayed fervently to Kannon for a baby. After years of failing to conceive, she finally became pregnant and attributed her pregnancy to Kannon's intercession. She found herself pregnant at age thirty-seven, after dreaming that she had swallowed the morning sun. She then prayed to Kannon that she might bear her child safely, if that were to be useful to humanity; she asked Kannon to cause the infant to wither in her womb if he had no benefit to beings. She continued daily prayers and recitations from the Kannon Sutra until, in the year 1264, she gave birth to Keizan on her way to the lying-in chamber (delivery room) at a Dharma hall dedicated to Kannon. Ekan later became abbess of a Soto convent, Jojuji, and a strong influence in the development of the Soto Zen sect through her guidance and interventions with her son. Keizan's writings mentioned both her strong faith and her stern admonitions regarding his youthful arrogance when he first rose to power. She noticed when her son was getting too full of himself, and she made the necessary verbal corrections. Praising his mother and grandmother, Keizan gave them the credit for his career as a Soto monk. He believed that their faith provided the influential power through which he was ordained, founded Yokoji temple, and helped to propagate Soto Zen across Japan. Ekan was devoted to teaching Buddhism to women and founded another temple: Hooji. Reflecting the respect for women's practice that Ekan helped Keizan to develop, the abbacy of Hooji was passed to Ekan's niece Myosho by Keizan.[94]

Ekan is an example of the flexibility of many women ancestors' path to Zen practice and the far-reaching influence of early nuns. The same potential exists today for female practitioners who may begin life tending a family, develop a sincere practice, and then follow their inner compass into monastic training later. Although Ekan had been a wife and mother, she sought ordination. She was not limited by her familial role; within that role she developed her own aspiration and became a role model for her son Keizan and for other women.

The Japanese Soto Zen nuns' order, descended from Keizan's mother, has an affinity for the plum blossom, which they use as their symbol. The plum tree is the first to bloom in early spring, and its delicate blossoms often meet with snow and cold. It is said that the plum blossom teaches us how to be gentle even in the harshest conditions. Even though women's practice and women Zen teachers historically have been disregarded, subordinated, and underfunded, women's Zen has persisted in expressing its strength through compassionate practice, as we will see in many of the examples that follow. While various male Zen sects have become warriors, attacking other temples in open sectarian hostility, female Zen practitioners have been decidedly nonsectarian. They have been faithful both to the fundamentals of Zen nonattachment and to the bodhisattva vow to revere life—to save all beings through their engaged practice with orphans, sufferers of leprosy, and abused women.

Unlike some of the limitations faced by Myochi, in today's Zen practice any Zen student can express her strong faith and develop exemplary ethical standards from her position as a wife and mother. Developing faith and daily practice within a family context can take deep root in a formal training place when the opportunity becomes available. Besides her own individual contribution, Ekan used her familial role as a positive force. Keizan, so affected by the depth of his mother's practice, was said to vow to help women's practice in the three worlds and the ten directions. While women are certainly not limited to finding meaning only through their children's accomplishments, the combination of Zen training and family training has much potential.

Ekyu Daishi:
The First Female Soto Zen Dharma Heir

Keizan praised Ekan's devotion to teaching women and honored her example by giving one of his female disciples, Kinto Ekyu (ca. 1325), the first Soto Dharma transmission to a woman.[95] In order to support Ekyu's training, Keizan translated Dogen's explanations on the Buddhist precepts from *kanji* to *hiragana*—apparently Ekyu's education, like that of many women of her time, did not include Chinese characters, the *kanji*. *Hiragana*, also known as women's script, is a phonetic syllabary, designed for use by people who were not fully educated.

From Ekyu we learn that lack of sophistication does not hinder deep practice. If a woman has not had sufficient education or lacks training, her contribution may still blossom within Zen. Ekyu found her way to a supportive teacher who made important texts available to her despite her illiteracy in Chinese characters. After developing deep roots in Soto Zen practice, Ekyu was able to lead other women and become the first female Soto Dharma heir.

These early Soto nuns helped create the possibility of Zen practice for women today. At times their personal life was secondary to their awakening and to the opportunity they were creating for other women to awaken. Female Zen practitioners today may feel encouraged and guided in practice, knowing that other women will practice more seriously because of their dedication.

Facing Aggression and Hardship

Zhixian, as we have seen, faced an administrator's investigation and endured an attempted rape and knife attack. Xinggang practiced despite frightening physical symptoms. Zenshin endured public defrocking and insisted on further training anyway. These female founders' courage in the face of life-threatening circumstances was based on their awareness that Zen practice was essential to life and should be made available for other women to practice and find freedom.

Similar hardship is sometimes still with us in the form of sexually predatory behavior toward women in Western Zen training places. Of course, compared to these earlier examples, today's Western Zen practice places are relatively safe for women. Some women have expressed that being a practitioner at a coed Western Zen center is the first time they have been in a group where they feel safe to make eye contact with men that they do not know without fear of sexual advances.

We need to do more to educate both men and women about the dynamics of vulnerability, sexuality, and power, about ways women may be seen as sexual objects, and about how women may consciously or unconsciously use seduction to appeal to male leaders within the community. While we recognize this world of predation and violence toward women as a reality, we must face it courageously and sensibly in order to change it. Our own awakening may help empower us to lessen this violence through making conscious the unconscious dynamics of attraction and fear between men and women—even those practicing Zen today— and through speaking out. I often wonder if our early Zen ancestors knew we were coming. Did they sense they were opening a path for so many of us?

Convent Nuns 6

Women Teaching Women

Women Practicing with Women

AS WE HAVE SEEN, the Zen Buddhist convent system is nonexistent in the West. Westerners do not include convents in our Zen spiritual heritage and know little about them. Yet these convent systems have existed in Asia since the time of the Buddha.

The development of coeducational practice in the West is brand new to Buddhism and exists only here. In the West, women and men practice together for better or for worse, with male and female Zen teachers teaching both men and women at their centers. There is no specific curriculum designed for Western Zen women, nor are there specific places where women can study without men.[96] For these reasons, it is important to understand what the Asian Zen convents offered women and whether traditional Zen convent roles can or should be integrated into coeducational Western practice. Understanding what the Asian convents provided Zen Buddhist women and the Buddhist community can help us assess our coeducational Zen system.

There is no evidence that the Buddha or the first founders mapped out a specific curriculum for teaching Buddhism to women, even though women had different educational levels, skills, and social roles. In convents, however, curricula and training styles were adapted to meet women's abilities and needs. Convents in different Asian traditions evolved a common approach to training women, making use of women's specific caregiving abilities and household skills and their lack of formal education. Convent training developed nuns' ability to provide social services, helped nuns maintain ties to family, and served as shelters for abused women, widows, or politically out-of-favor women.

What Was Distinctive about Zen Convents?

Zen convents, like monasteries, were established to offer training in Buddhist meditative practices, but they adapted established Zen training methods to suit the needs of women. Formal Zen practices *need* to be adapted to enhance their relevance to practitioners' specific abilities and cultural circumstances. This view contrasts with most contemporary Zen monastic practice methods, which vary as little as possible from what our Asian male founders practiced in their own home temples.

Studying the process of adaptation—maintaining the intent of practice while appropriately varying the form—can be useful for Western practitioners. For example, while most meditators face the wall or the floor in front of them, at times the nuns of Tokeiji temple practiced meditation in front of a mirror, a practice especially suitable for deconstructing a woman's attachment to her physical self-image, whether positive or negative. Addressing some of our culturally specific more stubborn Western delusions through adaptation is currently underway in the West. These adaptations, versus a rigid imitation of our Asian teachers, are an important component of our developing Western Zen practice. Studying women's adaptations may assist us in completing the transplantation of Zen to the West.

Some convent practices were specifically aimed at women's needs and attachments. Asian women were often confined within family quarters and were expected to devote themselves entirely to family and children. They had no legal rights and were prohibited from making decisions about work or leisure activities. Convents, like some contemporary all-girl schools, encouraged women to develop their initiative, independence, and spiritual potential, whereas the opposite strategy (discouraging individual initiative and power) was often a focus of Zen monasteries for training men. Since men are often conditioned and expected to be strong and decisive and to manifest leadership, one function of Zen monasteries was to reduce men's egos by depriving them of autonomy and encouraging them to follow the teacher and fit into the sangha. The opposite training goal, to encourage autonomy, may have been a force shaping convent training. The distinctive goals and varieties of practice that characterized women's Zen convents also address a serious issue in contemporary Buddhist practice—the possibility of return to full ordination for nuns in the Theravada and Tibetan traditions where nuns' ordination has ceased. Understanding the accomplishments and benefits of convents of the past for women, men and Buddhist practice could help to encourage the restoration of the nuns' order in the Tibetan and Theravada traditions.

Zen aims to expose and dissolve the ego's toxic grip of self-clinging. Self-clinging may look very different in women than it does in men. Self-clinging for women may look like dependency, a need to please others and to seek approval, a reluctance to show initiative, and a general feeling of inferior ability. Self-clinging in men more often takes the form of pride, arrogance, and a sense of power, control, or even invincibility. Convents have developed training techniques for women aimed specifically at overcoming societal conditioning that fostered obedience, docility, and servitude to their families of origin, husbands, and other institutional bodies that instilled "ladylike" behavior.

Another obstacle to be overcome was illiteracy. Women entering convent life were sometimes illiterate in the more sophisticated writing systems, relying on less sophisticated systems like *hiragana* in Japan or *nushu*[97] in China. Often they were illiterate in the Chinese characters taught to upper-class men. Consequently women in China, Japan, and Korea had difficulty studying Buddhist scriptures, which were often written in Chinese characters.

As a result, convents developed Buddhist practice based on women's actual abilities and skills. They practiced traditional crafts like sewing and the tea ceremony, and taught these arts to other women in the community. Sometimes these classes in traditional crafts became a means of financial support for the temple, as witnessed in the Soto nuns' convent in Nagoya today.

Nuns historically and currently have been responsible for giving Buddhist names to newborn babies, and convents were almost always involved in social action projects to benefit less fortunate members of society. The practice of helping families and the less fortunate began with Mahapajapati, whose very creation of the female Buddhist order rescued many widows and "pleasure girls" discarded by society. This tradition was continued by the convents of Tokeiji and Mantokuji in Japan, temples specializing in helping women restore their lives when they wished to leave a marriage at a time when women did not have legal recourse to divorce. This socially engaged aspect of convents continues to the present day. Current convent projects include caring for orphans in Japan, reclaiming and educating girls and women sold into sexual slavery in Burma and Thailand, and building hospitals for the poor in Taiwan.

The training convent for celibate nuns may have been, and may continue to be, the ideal setting in Asia for women to develop themselves spiritually. For example, in present-day Japan it is common to see men leading small temples with the support of their wives. The male priests perform the ceremonies and conduct the Buddhist classes, but their wives maintain the temple and provide pastoral care for the congregation. A nun, whether single or married, would not have a comparable support system in Asia. In most Asian countries men and women do not practice equality when it comes to household responsibilities. A married nun could not expect her husband to become the temple "wife." A single nun would not have the same resources as a married priest to support her temple. Women have needed (and may still need) to gather together, to share responsibility for maintaining the temple, and to ensure time for spiritual practice and development.

Monasteries served the community during famine (by providing food) or war (by sheltering victims and targets), but convent nuns more consistently engaged in "hands-on" practices, practices consistent with the traditional female role of caregiver. Starting with the Buddhist practitioner Empress Komyo, Japanese nuns nursed the indigent, including washing sufferers of Hansen's disease (leprosy) and providing medicine. In the preceding chapter on early Zen Dharma heirs, we saw Zhiyuan's nuns knitting leggings for their Dharma brothers suffering from the cold, and later we will learn about Eunyeong Sunim creating a barbershop and pharmacy on convent grounds for the elderly. Convent life took on some of the characteristic hands-on caregiving roles that women had previously filled in their secular life.

At different times and places we see convents addressing the needs of women and society. Geographically distinct convents shared similar techniques which trained women in ways that challenged prevailing cultural views. We will see how Mahapajapati's nuns addressed women's sensuality and how they found their freedom from the cultural demand that they be pleasure objects. Later we will see how Chinese nuns addressed the possibility of women existing and excelling independently from the family context through expressing their literary and organizational competence. Korean nuns provided an honorable profession for women in a society destroyed by war, and a way for women to help rebuild their country. Japanese nuns found a way to provide options for themselves and other women who were caught in political marriages, violent domestic arrangements, or wars between their clans of origin. Many convents also served as a refuge for orphans at some point in their history. Finally, in the development of the "divorce temple," Tokeiji, we can see the culmination of the nuns' historic role come to life in a powerful, pervasive, and innovative service for women that stood its ground for more than five hundred years despite pressures of politics and wars.

Through studying understanding and publicizing the convents' accomplishments, we can look forward to more offerings from the Tibetan, Theravada, and Zen order as ordained women's practice is further appreciated and even restored in all Buddhist traditions.

Mahapajapati's Nuns of India: Making Sense of Women's Sensuality

While many of the first Buddhist women's descriptions of awakening resemble those of the first Buddhist men, their liberation poems speak in a distinctively female voice: a release from a fascination with the body and sensuality that may be uniquely female. While there were many accomplished nuns in the time of the Buddha—accomplished teachers and speakers all—I will focus here on the most distinctive expression of their practice. Early Buddhist nuns describe their personal awakening as liberation from absorption in their own beauty and sensuality. While male accounts describe being caught by women, through their (male) sensual cravings, women describe dependence on their own beauty as a trap. Susan Murcott's *The First Buddhist Women* provides ample evidence of their practice accomplishments, their poetry of enlightenment, and how women experienced themselves at the time of the Buddha.

The women who joined the Buddha's spiritual community and became celibate nuns came from a culture that emphasized sensuality, as evidenced by vivid descriptions of female beauty in lush detail. Some women who joined the nun's order had been "pleasure girls," others had belonged to harems, while yet others were widows. Most would have known what being beautiful and sexy meant. In *Lust for Enlightenment* John Stevens describes the ideal female sexual playmate in the time of the Buddha:

> A *pleasure girl* of the Buddha's time was typically dressed in a red and gold girdle, with bracelets around her wrists and ankles. Her long, jet-black hair was adorned with flowers and ornaments. She possessed a face as lovely as the full moon, with doe eyes, a delicate nose, and red lips set off against a golden complexion. Naked above the waist, she wore necklaces and strings of pearls to grace her swelling, close-set breasts, which were shaped like golden cups, black-nippled, and rubbed with sandalwood oil.[98]

The women who joined the first female Buddhist order grew up with these images and developed an attachment to and dependence on being beautiful in this way. Their striving for beauty won them influence over their husbands and created a competitive environment and power structure in the harem. Their influence and power helped them and their offspring survive.

In the case of a harem wife or professional pleasure girl, we can understand their preoccupation with being attractive, but in the following section about a Jain nun, Nanduttara, a contemporary of the Buddha who was similarly affected, we see how pervasive the preoccupation was at the time.

Nanduttara:
The Women's Cycle of Binge and Purge

Nanduttara converted to Buddhism from Jainism during the Buddha's lifetime. In her poetry, we see a nun's attachment to beauty and sensuality and her liberation through Buddhist practice.

> I used to worship fire, the moon, the sun,
> And the gods.
> I bathed [between cliffs],
> Took many vows,

I shaved half my head,
Slept on the ground,
And did not eat after dark.

Other times
I loved makeup and jewelry,
Baths and perfumes,
Just serving my body
Obsessed with sensuality.

Then faith came.
I took up the homeless life.
Seeing the body as it really is,
Desires have been rooted out.[99]

A modern-day Nanduttara goes on a diet, works out daily, swears off
sweets, and vows to purge her guilty pleasures and renounce self-
indulgence. And yet, as studies of addiction and obsession teach, there is
the persistent rebound to indulgence that follows deprivation, and then
the return to renunciation that follows indulgence. Later, Nanduttara
finds the deep path of meditative insight that frees her from the cyclical
torment of sensual indulgence followed by renunciation. In her verses
Nanduttara describes her practice of seeing through to her true nature,
resolving her dualistic view of body and spirit. The Buddhist path affords
her peace from the cycle of binge and purge. The teachings and meditation help her see how she creates suffering when she identifies the body
as the self. This path speaks directly to contemporary women and men
who struggle with body image and the cycles of self-indulgence, remorse-
fulness, and purification through deprivation.

Ambapali:
In Love with This Beautiful Body

Ambapali was a beautiful courtesan who bore a son to King Bimbisara, a
devout Buddhist. Her son followed the Buddha, and Ambapali, who was
very wealthy, built a hermitage for the Buddha and his sangha on her land.
When the Buddha met with Ambapali, he warned his male followers to
guard themselves against her great beauty. Later in life Ambapali wrote

her own version of the Buddhist meditation on the thirty-two parts of the body.[100] Whereas the Buddha's meditation on the body starts with the hair on the head and ends with urine, Ambapali's verse in seventeen stanzas begins with the hair and ends with the feet. Each stanza starts with the beauty of her body part and ends with a humorous image of how each part has weathered aging. Here is one example of her teaching for women enamored and intoxicated with their own beauty:

> Fragrant as a scented oak
> I wore flowers in my hair.
> Now because of old age,
> It smells like dog's hair.
> This is the teaching of the one who speaks the truth.

Ambapali goes on to describe eyebrows, eyes, earlobes, teeth, voice, neck, arms, hands, breasts, thighs, and calves, all in their former radiance and now in their dilapidated states of wrinkling, withering, sagging, and yellowing. Her teaching on impermanence, directed at women's pride and sensibility, is a woman's graphic story about her most intimate possession and attachment. While a woman's body may be the currency she uses to survive in a sexist system, it is not where she should invest her life's effort. In the last verse Ambapali says:

> This is how my body was.
> Now it is dilapidated,
> the place of pain,
> an old house
> with the plaster falling off.[101]

This female practitioner of legendary beauty spoke of a woman's infatuation with the body as an object, a tool of seduction. Ambapali helps us see through this unconscious and superficial view. As long as women unconsciously and habitually rely on the power of seduction, the temptation to use this power within Zen centers, even with their Zen teacher, is very strong. Zen teachers should offer us an opportunity to see what we cling to, and to encourage us to drop our cherished certainties. The teacher's obligation to point out seduction may be forsaken if the teacher enjoys the flattery of female seductive attention. Women may attempt to regain position—their ego position—through tried and true female wiles. If male teachers allow female students to fill their need for admiration, the confluence of these two unconscious tendencies will lead to an increase in suffering and a loss of confidence in our practice places.

Vimala:
The Passive-Aggression of the Female Sexual Object

When we consider the subjugation of women as sexual objects, we don't always examine ways women may *aggressively* participate in the seduction process to gain power or use their beauty to inflict pain on admirers. As women empower themselves, they must see all sides clearly and not be blinded by a conventional view of women as helpless victims of a power imbalance. From the position of victimhood, all women can do is complain.

If we look from the perspective of what women may gain in this game of seduction, we see a subtle psychological payoff; they may gain a sense of power seeing the one seduced as their victim. The act of seduction may disguise their hostility. In psychological terms, we speak of this pay-off to the woman's ego as "secondary gain." Even though the pattern is unhealthy and even though women are victimized by it, the pattern may continue indefinitely if the victim is unknowingly hooked on this secondary gain.

Vimala describes one version of this payoff: ego gratification and perceived power plays tied to her role as seductress. She describes the unwholesome pleasure she finds in power, pride, and hate for the "victims" of her seductive powers. Vimala, a prostitute and the daughter of a prostitute, tried and failed to seduce one of the Buddha's honored monks, Mogallana. Her chilling verse describes the aggressive side of the female seductress. There is a clear-eyed view of her attachment and pride in her beauty, the hatred she experienced competing with other women for sexual prey, and the contempt she felt for the men she teased and seduced.

> Young,
> Intoxicated by my own
> Lovely skin,
> My figure,

My gorgeous looks,
And famous too,
I despised other women.
Dressed to kill
At the whorehouse door,
I was a hunter
And spread my snare for fools.

And when I stripped for them
I was the woman of their dreams;
I laughed as I teased them.

Vimala lays bare the dynamics of female aggression within sexual identity and fantasy. Her identification with the role of the hunter helps us understand the complexity of seduction, illuminating the multifaceted sexual relationships that may arise between women and spiritual leaders in, for instance, Western Zen centers.

Vimala saw through her delusionary self-image. She used her meditation practice to cut through her ego-building attachment to seducing men. With a shaved head, practicing meditation at the foot of a tree, she was healed of her ties to this unwholesome addiction.

Today,
Head shaved,
Robed,
Alms-wanderer,
I, my same self,
Sit at the tree's foot;
No thought.
All ties
Untied,
I have cut men and gods
Out of my life,
I have quenched the fires.[102]

Specific attention to women's unconscious roles as sexual objects bore fruit for these female practitioners. Women in Mahapajapati's order found deep realization when they directly addressed their primary delusion—a self designed to seduce and gratify in exchange for power and security. Released from this pattern of self-clinging, these women experienced liberation from their destructive patterns. Rarely do we witness the female self-image as an object of seduction so clearly described.

Chinese Nuns: Establishing an Authentic Lineage through Literary Sensibility, Organizational Skill, and Community

Transcending the image of woman as sexual objects was one of the contributions of the Indian nuns. Chinese nuns developed different aspects of liberation—literary excellence and the building of religious communities through organizational skill. Like the early Indian nuns, Chinese nuns sheltered society's female castoffs, but Chinese nuns also validated women's abilities by building their own communities within a culture that portrayed women as helpless and kept them invisible or hidden behind walls.

Early Chinese nuns were a striking contrast to the traditional role created for Chinese women. Although women's circumstances differed to some extent under different dynasties, in general compared to what women can expect today, women in China were hidden away, submissive and incompetent.

In China women were kept out of sight and received no formal education; their feet were bound, and they were barred from significant activity outside the family. Female infanticide, concubinage, and widow chastity resulted in the death or suicide of thousands of women.[103] The Chinese nuns' profession was a significant exception to this confined existence.

Records of the Chinese nuns emphasize an uninterrupted connection to the first Buddhist women's order in India. From the beginnings of the Chinese nuns' order in the third and fourth centuries to the present day, Chinese nuns claim to hold the only authentic, fully ordained traditional *bhikshuni* order in the world. Chinese nuns aligned themselves with their Indian predecessors, studying and enacting the same ordination requirements. And in claiming their authority through the previous women's order, they developed a meaningful profession for women, breaking ranks with a culture that commanded a singular devotion to family and spouse. The Chinese nuns exemplified women's agency and competence at diverse and varied tasks. In short, these Chinese nuns created a religious institution within which they conducted themselves as empowered subjects, not as dependent objects.

Chinese nuns' claim to an uninterrupted authentic Buddhist nuns' order has inspired many current female practitioners, Asian and Western, to seek "full" *bhikshuni* ordination in China. (Ordination in any order that does not claim uninterrupted lineal connection to the Indian orders is considered, by some, not "full ordination.") The actual survival of the "full" *bhikshuni* order in China may have been the result of a fateful historical declaration that separated the nuns' order from that of the monks. The nuns had traditionally been an order dependent on the monks for ordination, confession ceremonies, and other forms of empowerment due to the Eight Special Rules previously discussed. Because Confucianism forbade men and women mingling in activities outside the home, the first Sung emperor, Taizu (r. 960–76), overturned the enactment of these Eight Special Rules. Instead, he ruled that nuns alone should ordain nuns, and monks should no longer be involved.[104] The Chinese nuns' lineage, freed from dependence on the monks' order for ordination, survived while Buddhist nuns outside China did not. Some might argue that the order technically survived, but because it survived under conditions not proscribed by the Buddha, it did not survive intact. However, other rules for the male order changed (they could work rather than beg, for example) and no one questions that the male Buddhist order has survived.

The original Buddhist Indian nuns, remembered as the first ordained Buddhist women in the world through their poetry of awakening, set the stage for the Zen literature of the Chinese nuns. Chinese Zen nuns followed the literary example of their earlier Dharma sisters and used their privileged educational opportunities to record their Zen Buddhist experiences in poetry. While maintaining the requisite Chinese cultural value of modesty, their profession gave them an opportunity to express and record their spiritual awakening.

Early Chinese Zen nuns also established women's competence in areas other than literature. They earned the community's respect as managers and founders of convents. Working to transcend the cultural image of the passive, dependent woman hidden behind the walls of the family home, they built and preserved convents for women's Buddhist practice, and they sponsored the building of Buddhist statues and monuments for the community's welfare.

Jingchen,
"Measure of Quietude," at Bamboo Grove Convent

We have the earliest records (from about the fourth century C.E.) of the Chinese nuns and their convents, thanks to the translation of modern scholar Kathryn Tsai. In this early period we are introduced to the founder nun Jingjian and several other spirited examples of early Chinese nuns' practice. Jingjian, with the help of Sri Lankan monks and nuns, established the early *bhikshuni* order to which the later nun Jingchen belonged.

Jingchen (ca. 400) demonstrated her continuing affiliation with the nuns of India by memorizing the translation of early Indian Buddhist scriptures; she was also persistent in seeking the traditional ordination that linked her to Mahapajapati and her followers. Jingchen is remembered for her strict practice—she adhered to all the rules established for the nuns of India—and for her ability to chant more than 450,000 words of Buddhist scripture from memory.

In Tsai's translation of the record of Jingchen we meet two devoted convent women who practiced together. The story of Jingchen and her Dharma sister, Qui Wenjiang of Bamboo Grove Convent, illustrates the nuns' commitment to rigorous *bhikshuni* practice and their strength, good sense, and grasp of strategy. Both of these nuns were celebrated for their peaceful escape from the northern "barbarians" who had detained them in order to gain their teachings. Regarded as sages, they were kidnapped by foreign warriors who wanted to obtain their wisdom, and were not allowed to return to their convent home. To escape, they devised a scheme to make use of their captors' opinion of them as refined and highly developed spiritual prizes. When served delicious delicacies, they feigned bad manners, gobbling their food with greedy abandon. Their host, shocked and disappointed, lost respect for them. He released them, most likely shaking his disillusioned head in disgust at their behavior, and they were able to return to their convent. The two women who had besmirched their own reputations to escape barbarian captivity said their action had come from applying Confucian advice: "[Be] bold in action while conciliatory in speech."[105] They did not protest their capture or call attention to their plight by requesting to be released. They intuitively understood their captors, and playfully found just the right outrageous behavior to sabotage their captors' objectives.

This was the integration of Buddhist "skillful means"[106] with Confucian wisdom. They rose above the conceptual definitions of being appropriate and the practice admonitions that required ordained Buddhists to be vegetarians and made adroit use of their captors' idealized view of Buddhist practice as highly cultivated and refined. Here we see two women finding their freedom through cleverness and courage.

Jueqing:
Eloquent and Independent Spirit

In *Daughters of Emptiness* Beata Grant introduces us to the Chinese nuns' history and to the ebb and flow of these women's legal and spiritual rights within changing political conditions and Buddhist power struggles. Consider the story of Jueqing, a sixteenth-century abbess. Jueqing came from an elite and educated family but chose to find her way in a small, impoverished convent where she became abbess. During her tenure (ca. 1537), a Confucian official described himself as "highly offended" by the numerous convents within his jurisdiction—after all, their existence threatened Confucian values—and he attempted to destroy all seventy of them. He ordered the five hundred nuns in his area to marry, return to their families, or live in charity houses. Jueqing wrote a poem on her temple wall as she gathered her disciples to flee and reestablish a convent elsewhere. Through her quickly sketched poem she manifested both her devotion and her strength—breaking the law of the land to keep her Buddhist vows.

> In haste and hurry we gather up our tattered robes,
> And pack up our traveling bags: not much to take.
> Sleeves brushing white clouds, we retreat to the cave's mouth,
> Carrying the moon on our shoulders, we circle the sky's edge.
> I feel such pity for the young cranes nesting on the pine tops,
> And for abandoning the flowers I planted at the foot of the fence.

> Again and again I admonish the cats and dogs
> Not to hang around the homes of laypeople![107]

The poem, which concisely describes the situation of devout but impoverished nuns in a tattered-robes convent, offers a full range of human feelings without a trace of self-pity. The nuns did what needed to be done to preserve spiritual practice. Leaving the convent's shelter "to brush sleeves with the clouds," Jueqing describes her spiritual mission. She took responsibility for herself and her convent. She was willing to break the law of the land to help her nuns survive. "Everything changes" is an important Buddhist principle and how we adapt to these changes creates the tapestry of our life. Jueqing was able to respond skillfully and dynamically to impermanence—a change in her legal status—and maintain her Buddhist vows. Carrying the moon of enlightened practice on her shoulders, she moved her convent to safer ground. Her sadness is reserved for those left behind: birds, flowers, cats, and dogs. There is also the implication, through referencing cats and dogs, that dependence on provisions from others (the food and shelter of the laypeople or the safety of the family setting) may become the convent's undoing. We notice that far too often our human craving for security prompts us to follow our comfort and not our principles. Do we look the other way as injustice occurs when we are too comfortable? Like Jueqing we need to find and establish our own path to freedom without being seduced by a false sense of security.

Miaohui, "Ship of Compassion": Demonstrating the Community of Women

Women were often legally and physically dependent on their families for survival. Convents offered alternative means of support. Like Indian convents before them, Chinese convents provided a home for orphans, widows, and destitute women who might otherwise have perished. Additionally, there were women who fought against their family's restrictive values and joined convents to answer a spiritual calling. Both circumstances resulted in the nuns' gratitude for their new convent home and family.

Nuns often endeavored through practice communities to recreate a

new family through Dharma. Mutual care and warm relationships provided emotional support, spiritual companionship, and perhaps even a
glimpse of ultimate reality, of "no-self," through convent intimacy.

Miaohui (ca. 1600) married and was widowed at a young age. Her parents pressured her to remarry. In response she wrote an eloquent piece
that persuaded her parents to relent. She was allowed to live at home, and
when her parents died she was admitted to Prajna Hermitage, a small
convent. She became a successful Zen teacher with many disciples. This
poem describes her life in the convent and her entry into awakening
through the convent's compassionate atmosphere.

> Night rain washes the mountain cliffs,
> the dawn greens soaked through.
> Sitting, I meditate on emptiness
> as fresh breezes fill the temple.
> Words are inherently empty and yet
> still I am fond of brush and ink.
> My mind like ashes after the fire and yet
> still I am tied to the world.
> Window bamboo—empty mind;
> courtyard pine—innate purity.
> The trunk of this lofty green tree
> neither inherently form nor non-form.
> Between bell and fish-drum
> I have yet to grasp the essence of Dharma:
> Yet I get a whiff of its fragrance
> as if I were aboard the Ship of Compassion.[108]

Through Miaohui's poetry we experience the ineffable beauty of life in
her hermitage, which cradled her inner life of observing the mind. While
she grasps the conceptual tenets of Buddhism—inherent emptiness,
emptying the mind, and innate purity or buddha-nature—she does not
fully grasp the essence of Dharma, the actual experience of no-self
through the formal practices of the temple. The bell and fish-drum mark
off the ceremonial events of formal temple practice, but she finds they do
not hold the deepest meaning of Dharma; instead she begins to experience the Dharma through the convent ambience. She gets her "whiff" of

Dharma essence through her convent life "aboard the Ship of Compassion." Her experience of awakening comes through her loving relationships within convent life.

Korean Nuns Rebuild Themselves and Their Country

While the records of all early Asian nuns are scant, records of Korean nuns have been even more severely ravaged by general persecution of both male and female Korean Buddhists. Warfare in the twentieth century thinned the records even further. It is fortunate that there are currently more than ten thousand nuns practicing in Korea to give us the flavor of their tradition, a flavor that they are intent on reviving.

The current success of nuns' practice in Korea is bound up with an accident of political history and a fateful and fortuitous decision. During the Japanese occupation, monks and nuns were pressured to accept Japanese forms of practice. Specifically, celibate Korean monks were encouraged to marry and have families like the monks of Japan. Some Korean monks married, and many of the large monasteries were led by these married monks. However, Korean nuns, like Japanese nuns, were not pressured to marry, and indeed never did.

When the Japanese occupation ended in 1945, Koreans wanted to rid themselves of all of the vestiges of Japanese oppression. They sought to purge their monasteries of married monks. Not enough celibate monks were left to run all the monasteries. So the monks turned to their celibate Dharma sisters, Korean nuns, and gave them large and historically important monasteries to rebuild, inhabit, and lead. Hence the nuns' order benefited and has thrived with the respect, responsibility, and resources of the Korean Zen Buddhist community. Through hard work and commitment to rebuilding the monasteries, nuns are now respected and supported in Korea.

Korean nuns now direct large training convents, like the historically important Unmunsa,[109] manage thirty welfare projects, send disciples to university in Korea and abroad, and finance pilgrimages to India. They have created a well-managed and well-respected profession and have not only restored the women's order but have created an image of competence and independence with a true Korean identity for Korean women.

Song'yong Sunim:
A Small Nun and the Women's Way

Martine Batchelor has written about her encounters with this dedicated nun whose life is an example of finding meaning through the rebuilding of the Korean convents. Song'yong (1903–94) began her life with poverty and the loss of her family, unfortunately all too common for Koreans of the last war-torn century. Close to suicide, Song'yong experienced a strong feeling of affinity to the Buddha and decided to join a small nunnery. Like so many other Korean women of her era, she was unable to read. Her life as a nun was first marked by a lack of structure within her community. Without formal training in meditation or sutras, she taught herself to read the chants, one character at a time.

Song'yong's inability to receive proper training reveals a dark side of the convent setting and how unfortunate historical events may intervene to bring about change. Song'yong described herself as not bright, not attractive, not wellborn, and not articulate. She was a perfect embodiment of the general prejudice against women as Zen teachers: they are physically less able to model the ferocious Zen master; their teachings may not sound as profound as those of men; and they cannot command an audience or attract followers in the same way that men can. Her small size and lack of physical presence engendered prejudice within the convent, and she was assigned to be the attendant to its elder nun leader. We witness the unfortunate side of convent life through Song'yong—a form of servitude to convent elders that lacked a substantial formal spiritual training component.

Because there was no systematic system for educating nuns, Song'yong was deprived of formal training for seventeen years. Essentially a servant to her elder, she practiced by accepting her lowly position in the monastery. In 1936, when the Japanese occupation was an imminent threat, the Korean Buddhist order assigned established Korean male teachers to oversee several temples to preserve their traditional teachings. As a result, Song'yong was exposed to the great male Zen master Man'gong.[110]

Her contact with Man'gong's Dharma inspired and empowered her to leave her position as attendant to pursue formal Buddhist teachings. Perhaps seventeen years of training in letting go of self-centered concerns had prepared her to recognize the power of Man'gong's Dharma talks.

She would not be budged or dissuaded from her newly found insistence on genuine practice. Song'yong followed Man'gong back to his temple and stayed in a nearby convent. Through her practice with Man'gong and his authentically transmitted Dharma heir, the previously discussed nun Beophui Sunim, Song'yong began a meditation practice. Song'yong's practice teaches the importance of the convents in accepting and sheltering women, and the importance of male masters willing to transmit reliable teachings to the nuns. For Song'yong, encountering awakened women under Man'gong's instruction proved to her that women too could penetrate the depths of Dharma.

Throughout her life as a nun, we witness the gathering and strengthening of both her personal practice and the rebuilding of the nuns' practice. We also witness, through her eyes, the rich experience of working with enlightened teachers—both monks and nuns—and the sense of community and shelter provided by the Korean convent system. By the end of her life, Song'yong was able to see the creation of a more formal educational system for young nuns and to take her place as their teacher. She left us these teaching words:

> Outside the Zen Hall of Naewonsa
> The snow-covered world
> Is the garment of Avalokitesvara
> Expounding, like flowing water,
> The Dharma inexpressible by the body,
> Inaudible to the body,
> Invisible to the body,
> Inexpressible by, and inaudible and invisible
>   to space.
> So who is this wonderful person
> Who expresses, hears and sees it?[111]

In this poem we are treated to her awakened view of the Dharma as our own limitless and inseparable body. The teachings are represented as the world unfolding as the garment or body of the bodhisattva of compassion, Avalokiteshvara. This image of the world as the body and clothing of the Compassionate One's expression of Dharma, flowing and simultaneously teaching us, is a loving and comforting view of our spiritual home; her reference to the garment of compassion has a particularly cozy and feminine feeling.

Yet she takes us to a deeper teaching. She helps us step back and question what it is in our own personal awareness that knows, expresses, hears, and sees this Dharma teaching. Since the flow of life and the flow of Dharma are inseparable, inaudible, inexpressible, and invisible, who or what is it that can experience this Dharma teaching? She guides us to stop relying on the senses and words for the expression and comfort of the Dharma. Taking a step back, she leads us to focus awareness on its own undifferentiated flow.

Japanese Nuns: Freedom through Zen Practice and Community Service

Japanese nuns provided a vibrant counterpoint to their culture's stereotyped image of women as weak, dependent, uneducated, and submissive. They accomplished this much as their Chinese Dharma sisters did— through art and poetry and through efficient and skillful temple management. They also contributed unique social services to the needy within the wider community. Beginning with the example of the early Japanese founder Empress Komyo, Japanese Zen nuns have been involved all along in what Westerners are now calling engaged Buddhism.

Japanese nuns' charitable work seems to embody the Buddhist bodhisattva ideal. The bodhisattva is an enlightened being who postpones entry into peaceful repose until all beings are brought across to peace. The term *bodhisattva* originally referred to a person offering Buddhist teachings and practices to ease suffering in the world. However, it seems that nuns, more often than monks, understood the bodhisattva practice to mean devotion to *actual people and their everyday problems* as opposed to a *concept* of compassion. The nuns' practice helped ordinary people in their daily lives whether they were Buddhist practitioners or not. This understanding may differ from the conventional interpretation of bodhisattva practice as an effort to save people from their suffering through teaching the Buddha's words and spiritual view.

Japanese nuns engaged in bodhisattva practice in many different ways. Empress Komyo funded a pharmacy, hospitals, and bathhouses for the poor.[112] She was said to have washed leprosy victims' wounds. Hokkeji temple, founded by Empress Komyo, continues to this day to prepare Braille texts for the blind and amulets for protecting health and assuring safe childbirth. The thirteenth-century Zen nuns of Tokeiji provided a safe house for abused women when women had no legal basis for initiating divorce proceedings. Nuns of this imperial family convent used their influence to protect women who wanted to leave their homes.

The Soto nuns' convent order that followed Ekan Daishi started an orphanage after World War II, taking to heart the founder Eihei Dogen's (1200–53) words on the four virtues of a bodhisattva.[113] Perfecting one's character through selfless giving outside of the convent or monastery is yet another avenue to realizing one's buddha-nature or true self. Soto nuns' training aims to embody this understanding.

One examplar was Hori Mitsujo Roshi, a founding teacher of the modern-day Japanese Soto nuns' convent who embodied the bodhisattva way. On the day her convent was demolished by bombs in World War II, she saved the lives of all her novice nuns by instructing them to leave the air raid shelter and disperse until the bombings and fires had subsided. When the 131 novice nuns returned to their former convent garden, they found that both the convent and the air raid shelter were demolished. Hori left the convent ruins briefly to report to her Soto administrator, Takama Shudo; this is his description after that bombing raid of May 14, 1945:

> Hori Mitsujo Roshi came to report the damages. She bowed deeply with her hands together. She had just come the 6 kilometer distance in her bare feet. I invited her in, but she said she had to [return to] take care of the children [her novice nuns]. She ran back without having come in. I had tried to offer her shoes to get her 60 year old self back through the broken glass and shrapnel, but she would not accept.[114]

Hori Roshi's dedication to her community of women reminds us of Mahapajapati's walking barefoot with her assembly of women on behalf of establishing the Buddhist nuns' order. These two elderly convent leaders demonstrated selfless dedication to the well-being of their fledgling order, not as an idea but as an embodied reality of the bodhisattva's role, bringing the bodhisattva ideal to life with their own bodies.

One of the high points of Japanese convent life occurred when Zen nuns used their practice, training, and family resources on behalf of the welfare of women in dire circumstances. Tokeiji, the famous temple for refugees and divorcées, and a similar temple called Mantokuji,[115] are unique beacons of Zen Buddhist nuns' empowerment and support of women's rights.[116] Tokeiji Convent, also known as Matsugaoka, has been most recently researched in the book *Zen Sanctuary of Purple Robes* by Sachiko Kaneko Morrell and Robert E. Morrell. In thirteenth-century medieval Japan, without clear Buddhist or legal precedent, the nuns of Tokeiji established themselves as a legal remedy to marital abuse and domestic violence. They maintained this remarkable mission throughout six hundred years of shifting politics and fragile alliances.

Tokeiji's power was granted by the high-ranking births of its founders and subsequent leaders. Tokeiji served as a Zen practice place for women, as a shelter for abused women, and as a place for women to regain their dignity and independent legal status. The temple even hired bodyguards to protect their residents from angry and powerful husbands who threatened violence to get their wives back.[117]

For centuries during which divorce rights for women were hard to navigate and warlords executed entire families to maintain their clan's power, Tokeiji successfully offered women safe refuge from assassins, a way for women to leave their marriages, and a document for their graduates that allowed them to survive as single women or to remarry. Women became nuns of the temple for two or three years, husbands were not allowed to reclaim wives, and at the end of their temple stay women were free to leave as unmarried with special letters of divorce from Tokeiji temple. When Japan's laws changed in 1873 to grant women divorce rights, Tokeiji relinquished its role as divorce temple after six centuries of service.

Kakuzan Shido:
Tokeiji's Founding Abbess

The power of Tokeiji temple was established through its founder, Kakuzan Shido (1252–1305). Kakuzan's strength was formed by powerful women who served as her role models. Despite the prevailing Confucian values that claimed women were weak, whimsical, and only fit to be submissive to men, many women became powerful persons in pre-Tokugawa era Japan.[118] During the years preceding Kakuzan's birth, wives of warriors were famous for fighting to defend their families during the chaotic clan wars that devastated Japan. Kakuzan was part of that warrior class of women with a history of active engagement.

Prior to and during Kakuzan's life, samurai-class women were known for their physical and spiritual strength in surviving war and chaos. Kakuzan would have been affected by stories recounting the powerful stance of these women, who protected themselves and their children, at times fought alongside their husbands, and sometimes turned to ordination to survive and to heal the pain of war.

There was the story of Shizuka Gozen (ca. 1185), a dancer and the mistress of the famous samurai Hojo Yoshitsune (and brother to the Shogun), who took up arms against her own brother to protect her lover and his wife, Tomoe Gozen. Tomoe Gozen herself accompanied her husband onto the battlefield. The Taira clan leader's wife, Nii-dono (ca. 1185), jumped into the ocean with her eight-year-old grandson, the child emperor Antoku, believing it better to drown together than to be captured by their enemies. The mother of the boy, Tokuko (1155–1223), witnessed her son's death and so also attempted suicide at the same time, but was fished out of the water and became the nun Kenreimonin. Masako (ca. 1225), wife of the shogun Yoritomo, was called "The Nun Shogun." She wielded considerable power while living as an ordained nun. She intervened in the lethal political struggles between factions of her own family of origin and her two sons. Another example of the powerful female noblewoman, Abutsu, was ordained after an eventful life as a lover, writer, wife, and mother. She petitioned forcefully for the inheritance rights of her two sons while practicing as a nun.

In addition to the teachings of these powerful role models, it seems that Kakuzan was closely related to, and even knew, the abbess Mugai Nyodai (1223–98), mentioned in the chapter on early Zen Dharma heirs. Mugai Nyodai, although older than Kakuzan, was Kakuzan's niece (the daughter of Kakuzan's older brother). Both Kakuzan and Mugai Nyodai studied with the same teacher, Wuxue Zuyuan (1226–86), also known as Mugaku Sogen, at Engakuji Monastery. Given their familial relationship and mutual study with Engakuji's abbot, it is hard to imagine that their paths did not cross. It is easy to imagine aunt and niece engaged in discussions about Dharma practice either at Engakuji or at the Tokeiji temple that Kakuzan founded. The two temples are in close proximity and their histories were intertwined.

Kakuzan Shido founded Tokeiji Convent after the death of her husband the shogun Tokimune. Her son had inherited his father's position and sponsored the building of Tokeiji in 1285. Shortly after Kakuzan entered the temple as its founding abbess, her son ordered many members of her birth family assassinated because of his fears about their loyalty. Kakuzan established Tokeiji as a refuge for women seeking asylum. Only later did it take in women who needed to initiate divorce but had no legal means.

Her background of violent family history, coupled with the examples of the female role models of her class, contextualize Kakuzan's recorded Dharma words at the time of her *inka* ceremony. (*Inka* was awarded to practitioners who had penetrated the wisdom of the koan training system. This ceremony, and the certificate awarded, were recognized as empowerment to teach.) Conferring the seal of succession on Kakuzan in a ceremony at Engakuji in 1304, the fourth abbot, Tokei (1240–1306), allowed the attending Engakuji priests to question her. It is not surprising that, as in the case of the famous female Dharma heir Miaozong, the head monk and master of the novices challenged Kakuzan's confirmation and wished to test her understanding during her *inka* ceremony. He asked her to expound on *Record of Zen Master Linji*. Kakuzan's Dharma response is recorded to have been this:

> Nun [Kakuzan] thereupon placed a dagger before her and replied: "A Zen teacher is one familiar with the [literary flowers in the] garden of the patriarchs and his business is to mount the lectern and discourse on books. But as a woman from a military family, I indicate my spiritual direction by placing a dagger before me. What need have I for books?"[119]

Like the Chinese nuns Miaodao (chapter 7) and Miaozong (chapter 9) who both preceded her, Kakuzan essentially tells the monk to "cut the crap." She may have sensed a negative attitude, but she most pointedly was not willing to meet him on intellectual grounds. She carried the reminder of her family's roots and avoided getting caught in either a defensive or intellectual response. "Dear head monk," she seemed to say, "I do not answer to your whims. I know who I am and I will indicate the direction of the discussion. I am the master of this conversation." When the head monk continued the inquiry by asking for her understanding of her life "before her mother and father were born" (perhaps implying before she existed in a samurai family), she withdrew into meditation. While sitting silently, with eyes still closed, she asked the monk: "Do you understand?"

The monk had wisely understood her worldly reference to her family of origin as part of her teaching, and he had appropriately deepened his inquiry to that which preceded her birth and transcended death. "What is this original mind, the place that has no class or distinction?" he asked her. What is it that cannot be described by social class or function? Kakuzan manifested original mind through sitting zazen, becoming right then and there the undifferentiated state. In this action she seemed to say: I have gone beyond the knife, just as others may go beyond the books and historical records. In this place we are but one. The monk approved of Kakuzan's answer, and their exchange has been recorded as one of Tokeiji's teachings.[120]

In keeping with the need to develop practices specific to her convent's population, which included formerly married women, Kakuzan created the "mirror Zen" practice at Tokeiji to address women's interest in their physical appearance. As we have learned from the nuns of the Buddha, as well as from the popularity of contemporary cosmetic opportunities, women are often taught that physical beauty is their most precious possession and that maintaining their appearance is a primary concern. Furthermore, through using their seductive abilities, women can exercise power by seducing or influencing powerful men. Early Buddhist monks were taught to work on their sexual desire and their resistance to the reality of impermanence by meditating on a woman's body decomposing before their eyes. A corresponding practice, developed for women at Tokeiji, was mirror Zen—the encouragement to see through their feelings and attachments to physical form by meditating in front of a mirror. Instructions were to look deeply into one's nature and to ask, "Where is a single feeling, a single thought, in the mirror image in which I gaze?"[121]

Many Zen students are familiar with the teachings of the sixth ancestor Huineng's poem about the mirror.[122] Here is how Kakuzan instructed her students on Huineng's theme:

Since not a thing
Takes lodging in the mind,
It is untainted:
To speak of polishing
Is itself illusion.[123]

Kakuzan points to that which both beholds and reflects reality. Women practicing at Tokeiji are directed to go beyond shallow fixations, their own history, and their preoccupation with current dilemmas in order to find true peace during their divorce proceedings and, more important, what lies beyond. Through her description of what is untainted she reminds them of the part of themselves that is untouched by what has occurred so far in their lives. She helps them see beyond the idea of scrubbing away their previous negative self-images as abused wives. Meditation transcends purifications that are meant to repress memories and impulses, and goes beyond magical spirits with salvific powers. By identifying with what is undefiled, the women of Tokeiji, like the women of the Buddha's India before them, find release from the suffering of personal attachment and their sense of being abused in their unhappy marriages.

Kakuzan's wisdom is especially potent when considered in this context: Tokeiji's divorce-seeking nuns had to overcome societal prejudice against them as "fallen women." Tokeiji's mission was to free these women through a legally recognized divorce granted through committed spirituality. Tokeiji's function struck at the roots of Confucian ideals: women were supposed to assume a subservient place within the family structure. There was zero tolerance for women who tried to do anything other than serve their families. Even nuns had to work to avoid the negative label of not serving the family. At times, unless their practice was dedicated to the family or a lost husband, their practice was suspect.

The negative connotation of "fallen woman" is evident in a poem about Tokeiji written during the Tokugawa era, referring to Tokeiji by its alternative name *Matsugaoka*.

Should call it
"Village of Fallen Flowers"—
Matsugaoka.[124]

Stigmatization of women who had been sexually active but were not "respectably" married or part of the family structure has been a long-standing painful and harmful experience for women. Women have always needed to see through this negative stereotype, a stigma they had come to believe about themselves. Being cleansed psychologically and spiritually of their "fallen" status was almost as important as the legally divorced status conferred by the women's tenure at Tokeiji.

Becoming a nun at Tokeiji made it possible for a woman to become legally unmarried and a suitable candidate for remarriage. In this way, she was not forced to suffer mentally, socially, or financially. After serving their time as Tokeiji nuns, they could respectably reenter society. This legal status was made possible through Kakuzan's appeal to the emperor of Japan; she was a visionary Zen abbess and wielded her family's powerful sword to the great advantage of many women.

Princess Yodo:
Elevating Fallen Women

The second of the three well-known Tokeiji abbesses is the imperial princess Yodo (1318–96). Yodo was one of the less prominent offspring of Emperor Godaigo and became the fifth abbess of Tokeiji around 1336. Princess Yodo was credited with reducing the required tenure of women seeking divorce from three years to two and for introducing a change in the Tokeiji nuns' habit—purple robes. Purple robes were reserved for the imperial family and for high-ranking monks designated by the emperor. The adoption of a high-status couture was a compassionate intervention that helped to lift the negative self-image of a "fallen" woman. The wearing of the purple robe at Tokeiji was continued despite political controversy on the subject throughout Zen monasteries in Japan. The importance of the status conferred by clothing cannot be overestimated in feudal Japan, where rulers of the Tokugawa era dictated the types and colors of clothing permissible for rigidly defined classes of aristocracy, samurai, merchants, and farmers.

Yodo-ni is also remembered by two surviving teachings. One is this:

> Adorn your hearts, you who see the blossoms
> At flower-viewing hall

For the Buddha does not exist
Apart from this.[125]

While itself a beautiful teaching, invoking a vision of the flowers offered
on the Buddha altar, its context adds poignancy. Yodo-ni is speaking to the
ones regarded as "fallen flowers." She is asking these runaway and abused
wives to see that they are themselves the Buddha. It is their own broken
hearts that need to be nurtured with the same tenderness and beauty that
they bestow on the altar in the Buddha hall. Just as we offer flowers to
Shakyamuni, we need to offer the same tender regard to our own hearts.
    Yodo's other extant teaching on "mirror Zen":

Whether tainted
Or free of all tarnish,
There is [one] mind:
Whether one stands or falls,
It is with the same body.[126]

In this poem Yodo-ni transcends both worldly views about the "tainted
women" who came to Tokeiji and mundane dualistic religious striving for
purification through ceremony. She points to the oneness immediately at
hand. She underlines that we are this buddha-mind which pervades this
very body and is nowhere else.
    The key to freedom in this life is awareness of our true nature—the
true nature that is this very body. The outcome of our life's work is not
dependent on whether we are tarnished or untarnished. Our standing or
falling, no matter what happens, is dependent on knowing this one mind,
turning toward this one body of the Buddha's awakening. At a time when
Japan burned with clan wars, in the midst of love and separation, in the
midst of shame and misfortune, Yodo-ni pointed us to our own hearts to
see the Buddha we revere.

Tenshu:
Kept the Faith

Tokeiji's twentieth abbess, Tenshu (1608–45), survived the political destruction of her father Hideyori's Osaka castle. The castle was set afire in

order to bring Japan under the rule of the Tokugawa clan. While Tenshu-ni's father and mother perished in the fire, Tenshu-ni was rescued by a powerful female relative, Senhime, who was also the granddaughter of Tokugawa Ieyasu (the one who ordered that the castle be burned).[127] The condition for sparing Tenshu's life was that she reside at Tokeiji as an ordained nun for the rest of her life.

Tenshu is remembered for her simple and selfless request to the shogun Ieyasu. After he had killed her entire family, destroyed their property, and confiscated their wealth, the shogun asked Tenshu how he could repay his debt. She answered that she wanted Tokeiji temple to be forever allowed to continue its mandate providing safe haven and divorce without interference. Tenshu thus used the one wish granted her by the most powerful ruler in the history of Japan to request that Tokeiji continue in its status as a divorce- and refuge-granting temple. The temple accordingly received shogunal family support both financially and legally.

Tenshu's tenure as abbess manifested the same warrior and spiritual ancestry as Kakuzan Shido. While men who sought refuge in the powerful Shingon Buddhist temple on Mount Koya might be turned over to their enemies for assassination, Tenshu would not let this happen at Tokeiji. On one occasion, when an assassin was sent to Tokeiji to kill or kidnap the surviving family of a condemned man, Tenshu not only refused to allow the assassin to take the woman and her children, she called for help from her powerful Tokugawa relative Senhime. Senhime demanded that one perpetrator, who had hired an assassin to enter Tokeiji, be punished. In this case the offending warlord's property was confiscated. A show of such strength discouraged would-be assassins and kidnappers from entering Tokeiji to pursue women receiving asylum there. Tokeiji's hired bodyguards also offered protection from intruders.

Through Tenshu's resolve, Tokeiji maintained its status as a divorce temple and strengthened its power base for protecting those who sought asylum. However, the rare confluence of female power that led to Tokeiji's spiritual and political strength slowly declined by the end of the Tokugawa era. The custom of female abbesses coming from the ruling families faded—perhaps as Buddhist practice became more varied and diverse in Japan. The change in political winds lessened the importance of Tokeiji's sovereignty. In 1788 Tokeiji's request to become affiliated with Engakuji was granted. Administrative power over Tokeiji was given to monks of the neighboring Engakuji. Later, when the 1873 Meiji restoration legalized divorce, Tokeiji became a subtemple of Engakuji. The last abbess at Tokeiji, Junso Hoko (d. 1902), lived there with just an aged servant and a cat.

The first male abbot at Tokeiji was Furukawa Godo (1872–1961), a disciple of Shaku Soen. Shaku Soen succeeded his disciple as abbot of Tokeiji, and under a series of Engakuji monks Tokeiji was restored on a smaller scale. D. T. Suzuki, Shaku Soen's translator and a scholar famous for bringing Zen to the West, also lived at Tokeiji during his retirement. Today the temple and a small collection of its artifacts are available for viewing. Tokeiji's history remains a shining example of women's practice and resolve to provide both physical protection and awakening.

We learn from Tokeiji and other convents about women's power to change society and to transcend the role of victim. Empowered by the earliest Buddhist female role models, by strong women of their own culture, and by the liberation of Zen practice itself, women used their strength to help less fortunate women and others suffering from physical, financial, or cultural hardships. Convents provided an opportunity for women to enact bodhisattva ideals through both spiritual teaching and material support, and they educated and trained women in subjects and crafts beyond the Buddhist practice of meditation or other ritual.

Pioneering Nuns
Who Studied with Male Masters 7

THROUGHOUT ZEN'S HISTORY, there have been times when Zen teaching has flourished and times when it has dwindled or become stale; this is particularly true for the Zen nuns' order. At times the nuns' order has all but disappeared. As we've seen, there are many examples of outstanding male teachers who helped individual women, and consequently their female disciples, find authentic practice within male monasteries. These powerful teaching opportunities were offered despite official Buddhist prohibitions against men and women practicing together and seemed to reinvigorate the nuns' order.

According to the Eight Special Rules established early in Buddhism's history, women were to practice only with other women, never under the same roof as men. These rules were reestablished as part of the Zen monastic code in China, Korea, and Japan. Laywomen and nuns were sometimes allowed in monasteries for public lectures, but monastic rules mandated that they leave before dark. And yet, despite these rules, some women managed to live and train within male monasteries thanks to strong and supportive male Zen masters.

These male masters were able to uphold the spirit of practice, working around early Buddhism's limitations and prejudices. Without their help, the women's order might have perished entirely. All the women who practiced with male teachers, along with the communities that supported them, disobeyed the letter of Buddhist law while maintaining the spirit of bringing forth the Dharma. From this perspective, we can see the extent to which the survival of the women's order depended on the wisdom of these male teachers.

While most of the women discussed so far in this book were taught by male masters, the pioneering women discussed in this chapter differ from female Zen founders in two important ways. First, they neither established a system of convents that bore Dharma heirs nor ordained a continuous succession of disciples; even though some were abbesses, their formal lineages did not endure. Second, all of them left teaching records; some left records of their own teachings, some left calligraphy or poems, and some were known by their actions as recorded by gazetteers of the day. These nuns' teaching relationships with well-established male Zen masters bring their teachings to light and reveal how their teachers and peers regarded them, how they were taught, and how those teacher-student relationships provided a model for their contemporaries, and can provide one for us today.

These coeducational teaching relationships present interesting patterns. The male teachers seem to have shared a similar approach to teaching women. First and foremost, their approach was based on seeing women's potential for buddhahood. Even though some Buddhist sutras state that a woman cannot become a buddha while in a woman's body, there were Zen teachers who clearly disagreed. Second, these male teachers understood that, even with equal ability to become buddhas, the female identity of women students should nonetheless be acknowledged and supported. They taught these women as women, recognizing that female practitioners were different from men, and they acknowledged their different societal roles. One example of how they tailored their teachings for their female students is that they used stories of other women's awakenings as encouragement. Finally, these teachers understood women would reach their potential only if honest and rigorous teaching standards were maintained. So while it was clear that the students were women and not men, it was equally clear they were not to be babied or viewed according to lower standards because of their gender.

Perhaps surprisingly, the male Zen masters who taught the women introduced in this chapter shared a similar relationship to the Zen establishment of their times. They were all well known, and so their relationships with their female students were recorded in their teaching records. What's more, each of these men was the Dharma heir of an even more renowned Zen teacher. Their own male Zen masters had been recognized and honored, and their teachers had passed on to them an important temple, an empowered status, and a respected reputation. We can only conjecture about this pattern, but perhaps the first generation, that of the famous male Dharma masters, had spent considerable energy establishing their school, and these second-generation male teachers were able to build on their teachers' renown and broaden both the audience and the range of teaching that their masters had established.

We find an array of practice conditions and circumstances facing women practicing within male communities in China, Korea, and Japan. Even when women had little ability to leave home or to travel, they found ways to practice with authentic teachers. As seen in the case of Xinggang, women would initially travel back and forth between home and a small temple; perhaps only later would they train at a larger male monastery and eventually establish their own convent/hermitage. Some were married or had children, some became nuns as adolescents before marriage, and some became nuns at widowhood. For others, we know little of their life story—except that they practiced with outstanding male Zen masters.

Detailed life stories for these pioneering nuns help us envision life patterns for the countless other women whose stories remain unknown. From a selection of examples, we can extrapolate and envision patterns of life circumstances that resulted in the rare opportunity for a woman to share Dharma with an enlightened male master. We begin with the stories of Dahui's nuns.

Chinese Zen Nuns

Dahui, Yuanwu, and Their Women Disciples

In Sung dynasty China (960–1279) the number of Buddhist nuns included in the census in the year 1021 was 61,239. The number of Buddhist monks was recorded as 397,615, creating a male to female ratio of 6.5:1.[128] Yet very few nuns are remembered and, of those who are, there are even fewer teaching records. Surely out of sixty-one thousand nuns a few must have offered some deep teachings! Though some were recorded as Dharma heirs in the Transmission of the Lamp records—the official accounting of Zen masters and their disciples—particularly in the Yuanwu-Dahui lineage, the discussion of their accomplishments has not continued. Nonetheless, thanks to recent scholarly investigations, some of their names and teaching records have been recovered, notably, two who studied with the great Zen master Dahui Zongao (1089–1163).

Dahui, a widely acclaimed Zen master of this era and himself the successor of the great Sung dynasty Zen master Yuanwu (1063–1135), had several female Dharma heirs. Yuanwu, in turn, was not only well respected during his life but is remembered today for his compilation of and commentary on the *Blue Cliff Record*, one of the most important collections of koans, Zen teachings stories. Yuanwu was recognized as a National Teacher and received purple robes from two emperors. Dahui came to study with Yuanwu after broad exposure to various styles and schools of Zen. Dahui's understanding blossomed under Yuanwu's training, becoming so profound that Yuanwu fully shared his teaching responsibilities with him. Dahui was sometimes compared to old Master Linji himself. Dahui learned to teach koans from Yuanwu, and he also learned to work with female students. Yuanwu had several female Dharma heirs and was a strong supporter of women's practice. Unfortunately, while we know their names, the records of Yuanwu's nuns and their teaching words are not extant.

Like Yuanwu, Dahui also designated female Dharma heirs when he began to function as an independent teacher. We have the good fortune to know something of their life history, providing us with a view of how they came to practice, their teaching relationship with Dahui, and their subsequent teaching ability. In particular, the nun Miaodao (discussed in the next section) was Dahui's very first Dharma heir, female or male, and the first person to experience awakening under his guidance.

The teaching relationship between Miaodao and Dahui had a significant impact on him and the teaching style he used throughout his lifetime. Through his teaching relationship with Miaodao and her subsequent awakening, Dahui gained confidence in his methods. He recounted teaching Miaodao and how her awakening unfolded through their interactions. Dahui's other famous female Dharma heir, Miaozong (see chapter 9), was memorialized by one of Dahui's head monks after she bested him in "Dharma combat," a debate-like brief exposition of Zen understanding that unfolds between two Zen practitioners.

The nuns Miaodao and Miaozong have been remembered and honored by the many female practitioners who followed in China and in Japan. Beata Grant in a recent paper describes how women Zen masters in the Ming dynasty (1368–1644) celebrated their dual lineages—the lineage they inherited from their male teachers and the lineage of the female Zen masters before them.[129] Miaodao and Miaozong were among the most highly celebrated members of their female lineage. Later, in Kamakura Japan, the story of Miaozong and Dahui's head monk was used as a training koan.

Miaodao with Dahui

Miaodao was a Zen prodigy who fulfilled the promise of her ability by training with the great Master Dahui. According to Miriam Levering's account of her life,[130] she was born into an influential and politically successful family, and her father's position most likely helped Miaodao gain access to training with well-known teachers at Zen monasteries. Her father was both intelligent and extremely practical; he agreed to Miaodao's Zen training only after he had carefully observed the seriousness of her calling. As a child, she lost interest in worldly pleasures and would sit quietly contemplating, seemingly forgetting herself. Her father carefully observed her remarks and actions to see if there was the slightest contradiction between her words and her actions. He seems not have found any, and when she reached the age of twenty Miaodao was allowed to ordain and receive the nun's ordination robe.[131]

After ordination Miaodao practiced actively at several Zen temples before meeting Dahui. Her most significant early Zen relationship was with Qingliao. Qingliao was an elder Dharma brother of Hongzhi, the teacher who became an inspiration for the Japanese founder, Eihei Dogen. Qingliao served as *shuso* (head monk) under Hongzhi's abbacy of Changlu Monastery around 1123. Both Hongzhi and Qingliao were proponents of the Silent Illumination method of meditation that later became Soto Zen in Japan. Miaodao studied with Qingliao at Chungsheng Monastery on Mt. Xuefeng. Miaodao probably met Dahui in 1134 when he gave a guest lecture at Chungsheng during a practice period.

Miaodao broke her commitment to the three-month intensive practice period to follow Dahui to Kuangyin Monastery, where he was guest instructor. Dahui later said about his teaching relationship with Miaodao that "Miaodao's awakening (in 1134) and the subsequent awakenings of thirteen others the following year shaped my approach to teaching from then on."[132] Their relationship was recorded in the *Lien teng huiyao* (Outline of linked flames),[133] one of the Zen genealogical records that purports to document the transmission of the buddha-mind from one Zen teacher to the next authenticated student. These genealogical records attempt to map the various branches of Zen and include the earlier teachers tracing their alleged connections to the Buddha himself.[134]

Miaodao seems to have experienced doubt and worry as she transferred her study from the gradual school of Zen, Silent Illumination (Caodong in China, which would be called Soto in Japan), to the school of Sudden Awakening with Dahui (in the Linji, or Rinzai, lineage).[135] This doubt, and a personal sense of betraying her former teacher by leaving the practice period, can be seen in her request for repentance through the sponsorship of Dahui's lecture in 1134. Her request and repentance were recorded the year she arrived to study with Dahui. In his words,

> Recently the senior nun Miaodao came from Xuefeng and asked three times to enter my chamber [for instruction], saying it is because "death follows life and with terrible speed, and the samsaric cycle of birth and death is a matter of great urgency. I am not yet clear about myself and therefore I wish to beg for instruction."[136]

From this dialogue and his later response, we learn details of the intimate inquiry and relationship between student and teacher. Dahui accepts her request and puts her worry in perspective—telling the community that it is not a bad thing to wish to acknowledge our wrongdoings; this itself is a sign of a student's strong intention. Moreover, her desire that others be awakened before she herself has been carried to the shore of enlightenment is the aspiration of a bodhisattva.

We can only imagine Miaodao's turmoil when she decided to change boats in midstream. A senior and committed practitioner, she left her teacher, broke her commitment to the practice period, and set out to follow this newer, less-established teacher, Dahui.[137] Many practitioners know firsthand how doubt and distraction may arise upon entering a silent retreat, but for Miaodao there was additional uncertainty in changing meditation methods.

For many meditators, the cacophony of thoughts and feelings that arise in the midst of a meditation retreat can seem overwhelming despite a deep commitment to settle the mind. We are often surprised, having come to the retreat to deepen practice, how the monkey mind tries to assert itself. Miaodao was suffering guilt and regret as well as anxious anticipation of her new training. Her teacher acknowledged her suffering and gave her a larger context within which to view her angst.

Dahui offered an important lesson for Miaodao, and for all who enter strenuous training. When we attempt to find the mind of awakening through intensive practice, our doubts and fears may emerge, quickly take hold, and multiply. We naively believe we enter a peaceful sanctuary from worldly concerns when we enter retreat. We quickly discover that our internal life appears as a collection of our worst nightmares. This was also the case for ancestors who preceded us on this path. Dahui instructed Miaodao to practice with all of the noise, or "demonic obstacles," arising in her mind. Contemporary practitioners can also make use of his explicit meditation instruction.

In the passage quoted below we witness the extent of Dahui's support for and confidence in Miaodao; he both acknowledged and reframed her concerns about being swamped with delusions. Obstacles are not such a problem, he explained. The important thing is that you have noticed these obstacles and are redirecting your mind back to the Way. No matter how many times the mind wanders or rears up to disrupt meditation, you are to direct the mind back to the object of the meditative focus— whether it is the breath or a koan.

Dahui helped Miaodao see the Way-seeking mind within the morass of her personal resistance. He underlined and focused the importance of bodhichitta, her aspiration to practice unselfishly. He helped her to see through her fear and highlight her strength. She had bodhichitta, and bodhichitta itself was her strength in her journey, something upon which she could rely. We can feel his strong faith in her aspiration just as she surely did.

Dahui's extremely relevant and timeless practice instructions, offered on behalf of Miaodao, can guide us today through the rough waves of our mind:

Today the senior nun Miaodao has put forth a thought that she wants to obtain directly the peerless buddha fruit, bodhi. As soon as one raises this aspiration, all the wrong acts that one has committed are like dry grasses piled as high as Mount Sumeru, and the aspiration itself is like a mustard-seed-sized spark—they all can be burned up completely without any remainder.[138]

A beautiful rendition and reminder that aspiration for the mind of awakening is buddha-heart itself and that its very arising turns us away from our negative karma. Aspiration to practice is the complete manifestation of the lifeblood of the buddhas and all ancestors who have offered their lives to the Dharma. This aspiration is the living nondual Buddha that we have been seeking outside of ourselves; it is right here; it is our heart's desire!

Dahui instructs Miaodao and all of us not to create separate categories called delusion and awakening. When we release our attachment to these categories, and we stop using the mind to either grasp or to avert, the natural function of the mind arises—lucid and vast. The light that shines forth within this very person at this time illuminates the absolute truth of the interconnected, undifferentiated nature of beings. This profound view of our true nature undoubtedly guided Dahui's decision to teach women and his choice of teaching methods—all of us are made of this light, with no difference related to gender. All of us long to experience this light.

Dahui later trained Miaodao in koan meditation. Here is his instruction to Miaodao on working with the "turning phrase" in koan practice.

I raised [Master] Mazu's "It's not mind, it is not Buddha, it is not a thing" and instructed her to take a look at it. Moreover, I gave her an explanation: "(1) You must not take it as a statement of truth. (2) You must not take it as something you do not need to do anything about. (3) Do not take it as a flint-struck spark or a lightning flash. (4) Do not try to divine the meaning of it. (5) Do not try to figure it out from the context in which I brought it up. 'It is not the mind, it is not the Buddha, it is not a thing; after all, what is it?'"[139]

Dahui recorded his explicit instructions to Miaodao as his first awakened student. Is he more explicit with her because she is a woman, or is it simply because she is one of his first students? These instructions, later offered to all of his students, remain classic guidelines for koan practice. Does her vulnerability inspire more explicit support and guidance from her teacher? Does he give her more complete instruction to inspire confidence that even in a woman's body she can attain enlightenment? Dahui has complete faith in the gender-free essence of the awakening of Bodhi mind, but he must also be aware that Miaodao has few women role models to follow. Clearly, he addressed her doubts and supported her potential before he tested and strengthened her realization with his obstructions.

Dahui used Miaodao's training as an encouragement to both his male and female students, as if to say to men: "You see, even this woman, a being whose ability you might question, can find her way using this method. The mind of the Buddha is found in every person." For women students, he is clearly proclaiming: "She can do it and so can you!"

Dahui's own enlightenment experiences helped him to sense Miaodao's approach to her own awakening, but he could also sense that she was still not there. With a loud yell, he startled her into seeing there was more depth to uncover. Later Dahui described to Miaodao how another woman training with his teacher had broken through.

> Further, I told her that in Szechwan there was a [woman] Jishou Daojen who studied with the old monk [Yuanwu].... He instructed her to look at "It is not mind, it is not Buddha, it is not a thing—what is it?" This went on for a number of years without an entrance. One day she told the old monk: "I have looked at this saying and have not yet an entrance. Do you have another expedient means?" The old monk said: "When I ask you, 'What is it?' make a comment." He then picked up the whisk and showed it to her, saying: "It is not mind, it is not Buddha, it is not a thing," leaving off the clause "what is it?" She suddenly understood.
>
> After a while she [Miaodao] came again, bowed, and said: "I really do have an entrance." You could say that I coddled her like a beloved child. I stopped blocking her path and opened up a path in front of her, I asked her: "It is not mind, it is not Bud-

dha, it is not a thing. How do you understand this?" [She] said: "I only understand this way." Before the sound of her words had died out, I said: "You added in an extra 'only understand this way.'" She suddenly understood. In the several years since I became head seat and took up teaching, she was the first to succeed in investigating Chan.[140]

From Dahui's description of his conscious interventions with Miaodao, we see that he pushes her to go deeper, that he is tough with her, and that he demands that she experience a more profound awakening.

From Miaodao's side we get a glimpse of how important it is for the student to trust and persevere in the teacher's path. Because of their supportive relationship and Dahui's encouragement, she trusted his demand that she push harder. It is difficult for a woman who has experienced gender discrimination from her teacher to trust his intentions. A teacher who has treated a woman unfairly, or shown symptoms of prejudice toward female students, may find that his female student balks at his demands or harshness. Judging from Dahui's description, Miaodao confidently accepted his guidance. We also see the moment of awakening as a shared moment. The opening occurred as Dahui shared his understanding with his student, but she was required to meet him on his level. Together they were aware of the great reality.

Miaodao's Teachings

After her awakening, Miaodao was certified as a teacher by Dahui, and we can follow her teaching career through several chapters. She became abbess of a nunnery in her hometown, and later she moved to two other convents, finally settling in Jingzhu nunnery where she died. Technically, no Dharma heirs are listed for her, although Jingzhu was recognized for its Chan women's lineage, and Dahui mentioned a number of women who trained with her.

Several of Miaodao's lectures are recorded in the *Lien teng huiyao*. The first one presented here is a portion of the sermon on the occasion of her becoming abbess. At these empowerment events, students and dignitaries ask questions to test the new abbot's or abbess's understanding. We begin with such a question and her response:

A monk asked: "When words neither extend to the matter nor connect with the hearer, what then?" The teacher [Miaodao] said: "Before you have defecated, you have fallen into the hole."

[Miaodao] continued: "Do not ask too many questions. Even if it were true that you are very fluent at arguing and that you have wit enough to overturn mountains, within the gates of the sangha you will have no use for such [skills]. Before the Buddha appeared, there was originally nothing whatsoever to be done."[141]

Well known for her literary skill, Miaodao, when confronted by a challenging monk's wordy conundrum, didn't fall into the trap of explaining. She addressed the monk personally and directly. "What are you doing, falling into the shit-hole, before you even produce anything worthwhile?" She implied that some questions are difficult, and at times the answers show us our blind spots. But this was a question that was itself as "covered with shit" as the asker, a question designed specifically to trick or befuddle the one who was to answer through use of the intellect. There was no substance to be found in the question.

Her further advice has a wicked edge: "Even if it were true that you are very fluent at arguing..." She is implying the opposite; it is not true that this monk, who thinks himself so clever, is even fluent at arguing. He is a "legend in his own mind." Without insulting him directly, she quickly jabs and adds her wisdom. Even *if* you had great verbal skill, we don't need that within the sangha. What we want to bring forth for the benefit of the sangha is true mind, the mind that preceded Buddha's coming and going. Miaodao had developed the confidence to stand on her own practice and on her own two feet when challenged by men or women, confidence developed through her relationship to Dahui, his support, and his tough standards.

Miaodao's second sermon also reflects her articulate style—both grounded and poetic at the same time.

If what we are talking about is a meeting between the original endowment of two people, then there is no need [for me] to ascend this high seat. But dharmas do not arise singly; their arising depends on causes and conditions. And since today the balance scale [of authority] is in my hand, I respond to whatever changes occur in the moment, grasping tight and letting loose, rolling up and rolling out, doing this with great freedom....

Moreover each person is complete in every way, each thing is perfect, and [that which is totally complete and perfect] covers the earth and reaches to heaven. Eyes are horizontal and noses are vertical. Spring courses among the ten thousand plants; the moon is reflected on a thousand waves. There is no lack and no excess.[142]

Miaodao, at ease with her authority, lucidly describes her teaching process. How do we come together, dependent on the specific conditions of our life, to bring forth the Dharma? What exists even before two people meet? How do we bring it forth and let it flow between us? Miaodao has come to use the methods that Dahui described when he helped her deepen her understanding. There is the blocking—no passageway—and there is the opening when it is time for the student to move through. She is using Dahui's methods by inhabiting the strength and wisdom herself—not by deferentially quoting his words. Clearly her teaching style has been formed through her time with him.

Miaodao also differentiates between the immediacy of understanding and unending intellectual investigation. She illustrates this difference when speaking of the innate perfection in all life creation—what need for comparison or analysis? Of particular interest is her expression "Eyes are horizontal and noses are vertical." These same words were spoken one hundred years later by Master Dogen. Miaodao's sermon provides an interesting historical context for the oft-quoted remark Dogen made when he returned to Japan from China: Not having visited too many Chan monasteries, but having studied under the late Master Juching and plainly realizing eyes are horizontal and the nose is vertical.... I come home empty-handed."[143]

We don't know where and when Dogen heard the expression. Was it in use before Miaodao? Did Dogen learn it from someone quoting Miaodao? It is wonderful to see Dharma communicated clearly and identically by male and female ancestors, century after century.

Korean Zen Nuns

Korean nuns have a long and rich history, but the vicissitudes of support for Buddhism in Korea and many premodern and modern wars have ravaged the records of all Korean Zen (Son) activity. Fortunately, the Korean scholar Young Mi Kim has begun recovering women's records, particularly information on two Buddhist nuns of the Koryo period (918–1392), Yoyeon and Wangdoin, and their teaching relationship with National Preceptor Hyesim (1178–1234).

Additionally, through Samu Sunim's *Spring Wind* publication, we can celebrate, in English, the story of female Zen master Manseong Sunim. Manseong Sunim's life is a classic story of a Korean woman's journey and development under a great male Zen master, in Manseong's case Man'gong Sunim (1871–1946). Her early widowhood, subsequent physical hardship, and her emerging sincerity and strong leadership weave a classic and timeless example of women's Zen practice. While Manseong could have been included in chapter 4 on female Zen founders, her relationship with her male teacher is unique and worthy of exploration. All three of these Korean female Zen practitioners—Wangdoin, Yoyeon, and Manseong—were students of a well-recognized Zen master who articulated his position on teaching women.

Hyesim and His Disciples — the Nuns **Yoyeon** *and* **Wangdoin**

Hyesim was the successor to the great Korean teacher Chinul (1158–1210). According to Robert Buswell in *The Korean Approach to Zen*, Chinul established his school and built a monastery to unite the doctrinal and the Zen approaches, but the school really blossomed under Hyesim's leadership. Chinul and Hyesim were both influenced by their study of the records of Dahui, which were available in Korea. Dahui had refined the use of koans for the practice of sudden awakening, and Chinul and Hyesim developed Dahui's method in Korea. Chinul believed koans were useful only for people of a certain ability, but Hyesim seemed to support the use of koans for everyone, including women, and is remembered for compiling more than seventeen hundred koans in a collection called the *Seonmun Yeomsung*.

Hyesim believed that enlightenment was not related to conditions such as gender, social status, or even ordination. When women wrote to him of their Zen aspirations and their inability to escape their family responsibilities, he encouraged them to practice throughout the day with a koan. He encouraged both laywomen and his own nuns to practice with the understanding that women could attain enlightenment in this present body—they had no need to await rebirth in the body of a man, as was commonly preached in his time.

Like Dahui, Hyesim taught his nuns with stories about other women's accomplishments. One of his nuns was named Yoyeon. *Yoyeon* is the literal Korean translation of the Chinese characters that spell the name *Moshan* (discussed above in "Zen's Women"). Hyesim related the story of Moshan and the upstart monk who challenged and is bested by her. He then said to Yoyeon, "Since the Yoyeon of the old days did like that, what will this Yoyeon do?"[144] Again we notice how a skillful Zen master helped guide a woman by using another woman's accomplishment as an example.

Wangdoin, another of Hyesim's nuns, became a nun when she was widowed in 1219. The daughter of King Kangjong,[145] she was married to a man named Choi Chung Heon, who opposed the king. She was caught in the middle of this terrible conflict and corresponded with Hyesim about her desire to practice and attain enlightenment in the midst of her turbulent life. She felt her karma prevented her from participating in formal practice and asked Hyesim for guidance. Hyesim responded with sympathy and clarity: "It is clear that you are fervent,...thank goodness there are the teachings of the sages of ancient times. It will suit you if you use an old *kongan* [koan]." Hyesim then gave her the koan Mu Zhaozhou's dog.[146] He advised her to continue meditating on this koan "for a long, long time in [the midst of] your ordinary life."

Unlike Korean Zen teachers before and after him, Hyesim supported women's practice, taught women students, and allowed women to participate in summer meditation retreats. While records are scant, it is clear that he trained women rigorously using the same traditional methods he used for training monks.

The Nun Manseong and Her Teacher Man'gong

Manseong Sunim (1897–1975), born Unja Kim, was an only daughter who married when she came of age. Her husband died just a few years after the marriage, leaving her deeply distressed. Her grief was so extreme that she sought a "spiritual reunion" (a séance) with her late husband through Zen Master Hanam (1876–1951). In the Korean culture of her day, a spiritual meeting with a deceased loved one was not thought unusual. Zen Master Hanam promised her she would meet her husband once again if she renounced the world and became a nun. While Unja was hoping for a supernatural ceremony, she was comforted by Hanam's words, although she neither understood nor agreed with his instructions and their meaning. She didn't ordain immediately, but years later in dreams she saw herself dressed in nun's garments and began to consider ordination. At this point her grief had abated. When she heard that Master Man'gong (1871–1946) was teaching nearby, she went to meet him.

Master Man'gong, considered one of the foremost Zen teachers of his day, was a strong force for preserving and revitalizing Korean Zen during and after the Japanese occupation (1910–45). Japanese Buddhist missionaries and bureaucrats had taken advantage of their occupation by attempting to destroy Korean Zen traditions and replacing them with Japanese Zen practices. Man'gong was a powerful force in restoring the Korean Zen traditions that had suffered during the occupation. Manseong sought his guidance.

Man'gong knew he was forbidden to ordain a nun, but he believed that Manseong's aspiration to become ordained was sincere. Their relationship illustrates how an enlightened male Zen master creatively fostered a woman's practice. When Man'gong ordained Manseong, he used a funeral tablet, the memorial marker from his own late mother's funeral, as a substitute for a senior female nun, one empowered to ordain. In those war-torn times it was difficult to come face to face with a fully empowered female nun to ordain Manseong. Perhaps there were no female Zen masters to represent the community of ordained women in Manseong's ceremony. Man'gong followed an old ordination tradition of the nuns' community by invoking his dead mother, Uiseon Sunim, during the ceremony—a type of ordination (called in Korean *wip'ae sangjwa*) that allowed a disciple-teacher relationship to be formed between a new student and someone who, deceased, had been a monk or nun in life (like Man'gong's mother), with a priest (like Man'gong) acting as the intermediary. In this way Man'gong connected Manseong to her female roots, honored his mother's practice, and allowed the nuns' order to resume its ancient authenticity under his guidance.[147]

Manseong began formal Zen training studying koans under Man'gong at his retreat site on a small island. She alternated seated meditation with walking meditation, but she never lay down. After several weeks of intense effort, she began to break down physically. She developed "zazen sickness" (Korean: *sanggi*),[148] which according to Chinese medicine is the rising of heat and energy to the head, but she persisted in her practice. Man'gong instructed her to do abdominal breathing while walking slowly. She also did one hundred days of chanting to clear her mind.

Manseong took five years to complete her Zen study under Man'gong. After Man'gong's death in 1946, she went on pilgrimage to test herself and mature her practice. One recorded incident during this time tells of how she approached one Zen master, put her foot on top of his, and asked, "Whose foot is this?" Her question reveals her understanding and her confidence in nondual awareness developed through koan practice. Can you tell me something about this foot that goes beyond the superficial naming of yours and mine? It is a decisive and bold exposition of her understanding and at the same time a test of the teacher she meets. We should also note that she is clearly not intimidated by direct physical contact and is confident enough to challenge a male master directly and strongly—how will he respond in this moment? Courageous and direct, she intended to teach or be taught.

Manseong's Teaching

Manseong survived the Korean War that broke out in 1950, and she finally settled at Taeseong Convent near Pusan in 1955. During her years of teaching she attracted many nuns from across Korea, serving as a living example of Dharma. She kept her temple unheated and advised her students not to use bedding at night. She believed in the strictest Zen as the best method for enlightenment. Korea was impoverished and supplies were scarce. It is hard to know whether Manseong's strictness was an enactment of "macho Zen" or a response to difficult times. Her stern manner earned her the nickname Gnarled Stick. But though her teaching methods were strict, she was known for her compassionate care for her nuns and her convent; there was not a square inch of her temple that she had not touched with her own hands. While her temple had previously been poorly funded, her strong teaching eventually attracted ample financial support.

Manseong was known for her simple and direct teaching during formal lectures and work practice. One day a nun asked, "How do I cultivate the Way of the Buddha?" "No cultivation," answered Manseong Sunim curtly. The nun persevered, "What about obtaining release from the cycle of birth and death?" "Who chains your birth and death?" she was asked in return.[149]

In this exchange we can experience Manseong's resistance to turning Dharma practice into a to-do list. While there is awakening, we cannot self-consciously follow a map or a list of the right steps; we need to be completely present and let go of categories. The to-do list tends to pervert our practice into an idea of gain: "if I do this, this, and this, then I'll get a *big* awakening." This way of thinking chains us to desire. In asking the question "Who chains your birth and death?" Manseong again points to that which creates and sustains a sense of imprisonment within the cycle of life and death. What is it that chains you in this cycle? You need to realize the answer for yourself. Look closely inside yourself. Can you find the chains that bind you? Your specific chains? Your beliefs, anger, disappointment, longing?

On another occasion a nun asked, "How long does it take for a sentient being to become a buddha?" "There is no sentient being and no need to become a buddha," answered Manseong Sunim. The nun looked puzzled and tried to ask another question when she suddenly heard a thundering shout from Manseong Sunim. The poor nun suffered a shock. Nevertheless, when she recovered moments later she "glowed" with an instant understanding and made a deep bow.[150]

In this exchange a nun, operating on a conceptual level, proposes categorical differences: there are buddhas, there are sentient beings, and there is time. With a powerful shout Manseong moves the student to break through conceptual thinking.

One day Manseong Sunim showed up where several nuns were grinding soybeans to make tofu and demanded, "Is it your hand or the millstone that is turning?"[151] Manseong was helping the nuns wake up in the midst of their daily lives. When you are grinding soybeans, are you making concepts and deepening your delusions through attachment to ideas of separation in conventional reality? Can you see through these conceptualizations in the midst of soybeans just as you can in the midst of your meditation? The exchange harks back to our earlier discussion of Miaoxin. "Your mind doesn't move, the flag doesn't move, the wind doesn't move." What moves what?

Manseong's last wishes were to be thrown into the ocean, and that thereafter her name never be spoken again. She was teaching even with her own death—there is nothing to hold on to; find your own truth. And yet her disciples violated her commands and cremated her body after a formal funeral service—expressing their respect for her and her teachings, even as they disobeyed the letter of her request. We can see this as an actual empowerment, a beginning of trust in their own authority and inner wisdom.

Manseong Sunim's development under the chaotic conditions following the end of World War II would not have been possible without the support of Man'gong. He insisted on rigorous training standards, giving her a koan that sapped all of her strength. But when she faltered, Man'gong taught her how to work through her physical problems and push on to complete her journey to awakening. We see Man'gong's skill; he recognized both her ability and her need to follow the nun's path. Man'gong was both strict and personally supportive of Manseong. His direction was invaluable for her development as a teacher.

Japan's Great *Abbess* Ryonen Genso and Her Teacher Obaku Hakuo

Ryonen Genso (1646–1711) was a well-known Japanese female Zen teacher of exceptional ability who studied with a male Zen master. Her relationship with her teacher illustrates how a male master broke the rules to enable a promising female student to develop. In Ryonen's case we can also see how the example of an earlier female Zen master, Mugai Nyodai, may have guided her successful entry into a male monastery.

Ryonen was born Fusa in 1646 just outside the gates of Sen'yuji, an imperial temple in Kyoto. Both of Ryonen's parents were accomplished in the culture of the imperial court.[152] Her father was a cultivated layman active in the Rinzai Zen sect; her mother served the emperor's wife, Tofukumonin; and her maternal grandmother was the wet-nurse to

Emperor Gomizuno'o. When Tofukumonin was left with an eight-year-old granddaughter, Yoshi no Kimi (1643–76), to raise when the child's mother died young, the young Ryonen, then called Fusa, was brought to court (around 1652) to be the child's playmate until the princess was married some ten years later.

Between the age of six and sixteen Ryonen was steeped in the Zen culture of the imperial family. Both Empress Tofukumonin and Emperor Gomizuno'o were devout Buddhists.[153] Prior to Ryonen's arrival as the companion for eight-year-old Yoshi no Kimi, the emperor had resigned his position over conflict stemming from his support for the Zen masters of Daitokuji and Myoshinji.[154] Yoshi no Kimi's grandmother, the Empress Tofukumonin, also left the position of empress and took the tonsure as a Zen nun.

In addition to hearing lectures by many outstanding Zen masters of the day, the young Fusa was also steeped in the support for women's practice that prevailed in the imperial family. Eight of the emperor Gomizuno'o's thirteen daughters and thirteen of his granddaughters became abbesses.[155] Besides attending to his own spiritual development, Gomizuno'o wholeheartedly supported Zen practice for both genders. Ryonen clearly benefited from Gomizuno'o's enlightened stance and the imperial family's interest in Zen.

During Ryonen's lifetime the rigid class system of the Tokugawa era (1615–1867) controlled occupational activity, educational opportunities, marriage choices, and even clothing options. The specific expectations of Ryonen's family and the demands of the Tokugawa-era class structure were aligned in direct opposition to Ryonen's desire for formal Zen training. Because she served as a playmate to the grandchildren of the imperial wife,[156] whom Ryonen's mother had previously served, Ryonen was expected to take up her mother's position at court. After her imperial court service, Ryonen was to enter a class-appropriate arranged marriage with a nobleman from a suitable family. She would be expected to produce children and to stay within the confines of her home. She would be allowed to write poetry and perhaps to practice the tea ceremony and calligraphy. For these purposes alone, Ryonen was skillfully tutored in the arts that were meant to shape the course of her life. These and only these activities were allowed.

Ryonen was sixteen years old when she married in 1662. She had at least one son with her husband, who also fathered children with his "second wife," a concubine. Ryonen left the marriage after ten years; biographers suggest that there had been some kind of a prior arrangement to do so. Her child or children were left to the care of the concubine. Ryonen is one of the few women whose home leaving echoed that of the Buddha; she left home, husband, and children to pursue Buddhist practice. We do not know how her relationship with her children continued; we know that it did continue. (Ryonen's home leaving will be explored further in the next chapter.)

Ryonen, still called Fusa, returned to the imperial temple Hokyoji around 1672. Four years later, when her childhood friend the imperial princess Yoshi no Kimi died, Fusa, now age thirty, was tonsured and given the Dharma name Ryonen Genso (Comprehension Simmering, Original Entirety) by the Rinzai abbess Richu-ni of Hokyoji. Richu-ni was Gomizuno'o's daughter. Ryonen formally entered the imperial convent Hokyoji as a nun and spent two more years there.

Imperial convents were only an option for the daughters of the emperor and the nobility. These convents provided some opportunity for religious practice apart from worldly life but did not necessarily provide either rigorous Zen training or the specific opportunity to work closely with an enlightened master. After practicing at Hokyoji for six years, Ryonen, dissatisfied with the "women's temple" practice, left the safety of the temple to find a more suitable practice place in Edo (Tokyo). Maybe she had compared notes about training with her two Zen priest brothers and decided Hokyoji wasn't satisfactory. Regardless, she left the security of the known to pursue an unknown path; she relinquished the shelter of women's practice to find an enlightened Zen master.

Ryonen had thus far obeyed the rules for women—in pursuing practice at the imperial convent she had followed the predictable course of a noblewoman's life. She now abandoned the well-traveled conventional path and began to explore unknown territory. Her home leaving and her desire to enter the male monastery raise the question of what caused Ryonen to transform her life of submission into this self-directed activity. She explained her turn toward Zen practice in this way: "When I was young I served Yoshi no Kimi the granddaughter of Tofukumonin, a disciple of the Imperial temple Hokyoji. Recently she passed away; although I know that this is the law of nature, the transience of the world struck me deeply and I became a nun."[157] Nothing, not even imperial status, offered protection from life's impermanence. No status or position gave advance notice of one's allotted time on this earth. Ryonen's understanding of the nature of life and death, revealed through the death of her companion, transformed her consciousness. At the time of this profound experience of impermanence, Ryonen developed a deep resolve to explore the meaning of this transient life, and this is when she began applying to male monasteries for entrance to practice with a Zen master.

For the most part, recognized Zen masters were only found in all-male monasteries. Ryonen had already given up the security of her family life with no guarantee that she would find what she was looking for in convent life. Now, in leaving the convent life, she was giving up the only practice opportunity that was actually available to her. She had no guarantee that she would be accepted into a male monastery. No historical evidence suggested that women were allowed to enter male monasteries during Ryonen's lifetime, the fact of which she presumably knew. So what gave her confidence that a teacher would break the rules and allow entry during an era of rigidly observed rules? Even though the authentic practice of Zen guides all beings to their liberation, Tokugawa-era women were excluded from Zen monastic training. No authority or law would intervene on her behalf. There was neither a women's liberation movement nor an equal employment opportunity office that would prosecute cases of gender discrimination and intervene on her behalf. However, it is likely that while Ryonen lived at Hokyoji she found encouragement in the teaching and life story of Mugai Nyodai, the founder of the imperial convents (including Hokyoji).

Since Mugai Nyodai was the acknowledged founder of Hokyoji where Ryonen studied, undoubtedly Nyodai's teachings were in evidence during Ryonen's stay at Hokyoji. As we saw earlier, Mugai Nyodai's training at Tofukuji brought up two recurrent themes for early Zen women: their exclusion from the male monasteries based on potential impropriety, and their quietly but dramatically enacted battles for monastic inclusion.

Legends at the imperial convents refer to Mugai Nyodai's encounter with the famous founder of Tofukuji, Enni Benen.[158] At first, Zen Master Enni Benen had permitted Mugai Nyodai to train at his monastery, but when male disciples protested, the offer of training was withdrawn. Mugai Nyodai, who was in fact from a wealthy family, offered to sponsor the construction of a convent within the grounds of Tofukuji as an enticement, but the offer did not pacify the monks. When Enni Benen withdrew the opportunity for Mugai Nyodai to train with the monks at Tofukuji, she scarred her face with a hot iron to gain entrance.[159] Her self-mutilation, perhaps inflicted because she sensed the unexpressed objection that her female presence would distract the monks training at the temple, was a declaration of her sincerity and her lack of interest in using seductive wiles. She was granted entry.

Ryonen, in studying Mugai Nyodai's history at Hokyoji, may have concluded that a woman had the right to train with a teacher of her choosing, and that a woman had powerful options for displaying her sincerity to her teacher—*if* she truly valued practice above all else. Thus Ryonen was likely inspired by Nyodai's powerful aspiration to practice, the circumstances she faced, and what she had accomplished by facing those obstacles and persevering. Ryonen needed not only to find a true teacher but also to convince this teacher that she was a worthy student. This meeting of master and disciple, described in Zen folklore as two arrows meeting in midair, ideally transcends cultural, familial, and legal constraints and is the inevitable destiny of our deepest spiritual intention. We have no detailed historical account of Ryonen's thoughts or plans, but her actions speak clearly and offer one of her deepest teachings, which I would express as: "No life circumstances will keep me from my intention to practice Zen."

Ryonen pursued a teacher from the Obaku School of Zen just as Nyodai had, signaling her high standards and thorough knowledge of the Zen community of her day. Obaku Zen, founded by immigrant Chinese priests,[160] was thriving during Ryonen's lifetime. And Obaku, in contrast to the Rinzai and Soto schools of Zen in seventeenth century Japan, had not deteriorated into mere intellectual exercise. Obaku offered an alternative to the stylized Zen practice that had infected other Zen schools. While Ryonen's father had practiced at a Rinzai temple, both of her brothers studied with Obaku teachers, and she had encountered Obaku teachers while serving the imperial family. The emperor Gomizuno'o himself became an Obaku devotee and an Obaku-line Dharma heir. No doubt Ryonen understood the distinctions of the various schools of Zen and wanted to study with the strongest one.

In particular, Ryonen sought out teachers who were the spiritual descendants of the Obaku master Mokuan (1611–84). Mokuan was an influential teacher who did much to propagate Obaku Zen. Mokuan's fierce demeanor in medieval Japan had inspired his nickname Daruma-san, after the very famous first Chinese Zen patriarch, Bodhidharma. Ryonen first approached the renowned Obaku Tetsugyu (1628–1700) at Kofukuji temple in Kamakura, but he refused her entry. Undeterred, she then sought permission to study with the less well-known Hakuo Dotai (d. 1682) at the smaller Zen hermitage Daikyu-an.

It should be noted that Ryonen is the only nun presented in this book who is better known to history than the master who taught her. As Mokuan's Dharma heir, Hakuo had impeccable credentials, and his father had served at Taiunji temple. Buddhist practice was part of his family life. However, Hakuo is best known for his teaching relationship to Ryonen Genso.

Picture Ryonen, thirty-two years old (around 1678), making her Obaku pilgrimage, her head shaved, wearing the black robes of a Zen nun. She had already been practicing for six years at Hokyoji, the imperial convent in Kyoto, when she first encountered Hakuo. "I cut my hair and dyed my robes black and went on pilgrimage to Edo," she writes. "There I had an audience with the monk Hakuo of the Obaku Zen sect. I recounted such things as my deep devotion to Buddhism since childhood, but Hakuo replied that although he could see my sincere intentions, I could not escape my womanly appearance."[161]

Ryonen's interview with Hakuo inspired something in her. After listening and acknowledging her sincerity, Hakuo honestly told her what the problem was. He did not quote Buddhist scripture to her; he just described the situation, namely, that her "womanly appearance" would create problems in his temple. She knew he saw her ability, but he was dissuaded from admitting her, fearing her beauty would disrupt the monks' practice.

Hakuo is to be commended for sympathizing, for being honest about his reservations, and for exposing his high standards. We have seen previously that this is the right combination of strengths for a Zen teacher to use with his female students. Support without honesty offers no solution; honesty and rigor without compassion offers no hope. Ryonen sensed his recognition of her sincerity. She had something to work with; she could address his expressed misgivings.

Imagine Hakuo's refusal from Ryonen's perspective. She had given up children, husband, home, and her training temple to make this journey. She was now thirty-two years old, and this was a time when living fifty years was a remarkable accomplishment. Standing in Ryonen's shoes and facing Hakuo's rejection, we uncover the real-life, essential question that Zen practice addresses. The modern-day Zen teacher Hisamatsu calls it the single fundamental koan: "When nothing will do, what will you do?"[162] How do we keep our balance in the face of this adversity that we call our life? We seem to get stuck in situations that are unfair, that block our growth and saddle us with unpleasant choices. In Ryonen's place, what would you do?

The essential Zen koan of our life, overwhelming constraints blocking our spiritual development, can only be solved with sincere practice; Zen teaches transcendence through accepting the unacceptable. Only once you accept what is actually so, even in the most unfair situation, can you see if there is anything that you can do *about your own ego* to express the truth. The question emerges, even in an unjust situation, "What is my part in this obstruction, and where is my freedom?"

In this dark moment Ryonen returned to the essence of Zen practice, and to the example of Mugai Nyodai. Let us conjecture what she thought as she examined her remaining attachments. Looking deeply into her own heart, could she say she was completely free of her need to be attractive? As a thirty-two-year-old noblewoman, who had spent her life cultivating refinement, was she entirely liberated from attachment to her own beauty? It was impossible to discard her female gender, but it was not impossible to discard her *attachment* to her gender. She could discard her continuing desire to be attractive. And thus Ryonen, like Mugai Nyodai before her, burned her face to show her sincerity to practice when words could not do the job.

Some women are lucky enough to release their attachment to physical appearance during the aging process. Some women are vain until the moment of their death. Ryonen released herself in an instant. Ryonen's teacher had told her that she could not escape her womanly appearance, but she believed that she could escape her attachment to her womanly appearance—and therefore she heated an iron and held it against her face.

Through this action she declared that she was not weak, indecisive, vain, or seductive. She declared that Zen was the only path for her. She threw away the option of returning to her former life as a noblewoman. Keeping a return ticket to her former life, through her feminine appearance, was a luxury she could not afford in her urgent search for Zen training and the freedom it holds out. She threw away her beauty as a tool for persuasion in any future endeavor. She found her wordless voice and declared her Zen aspiration.

How can we make sense of Ryonen's action psychologically, historically, and spiritually—was it indeed transcendence or merely self-mutilation? If Ryonen had been physically self-destructive we might have seen the signs of this kind of disturbance manifest in her life both before and after this event. But we see nothing of the sort. We see a determined woman pursuing her practice, one trying circumstance after another. If we voiced Ryonen's action it might say, "Even though you see a woman in this body, I do not cling to womanhood. I will not forsake my opportunity to practice Zen in this lifetime."

In addition to Ryonen and Mugai Nyodai, there are other historical examples of women disfiguring themselves to enter practice. There is the Chinese Taoist practitioner Sun Bu-er (b. 1124).[163] Sun Bu-er's teacher believed that his beautiful student's path as a hermit would be obstructed by rape and kidnapping. Rather than lose her opportunity for hermitic practice (essential in Taoism), Sun Bu-er headed straight for her kitchen and splashed hot oil on her face to spoil her beauty. Her teacher was delighted, and Sun Bu-er is remembered for her attainment of great spiritual enlightenment. Indeed, this very account of a Taoist master's dedication to spiritual training may have been included in Ryonen's classical education.

The scholar William Bodiford writes about the nun Eshun (ca. 1370), who burned her face with tongs to convince the abbot of Saijoji to allow her to enter the temple.[164] The abbot was none other than Eshun's brother, Ryoan Emyo (1337–1411), and he was both sympathetic and honest with Eshun. After Eshun entered the temple, she faced some sexual harassment by her fellow monks. It is possible that Ryonen knew of Eshun as well.

The Zen tradition, originating with the legend of Bodhidharma bringing the teaching from India to China, is based on renunciation. The most powerful place for renunciation is in relationship to one's own body. According to early Chinese legend, Bodhidharma's first disciple, Huike, cut his arm off to convince his teacher that he was sincerely applying for discipleship. Apparently, the severed arm allowed Huike entrance to Bodhidharma's cave. And there are other stories of monks who had a finger cut off and a leg broken—though none of the monks disfigured their faces as the nuns did.

This sacrifice of limbs, versus scarring of the face, helps to emphasize the different delusions that dominate the male and female psyche. Monks need to cast off their attachment to competence and physical power, while nuns cast off their attachment to their lovely physical appearance. Joshin-san, who maimed herself through cutting off part of her little finger, was careful not to interfere with her ability to cook or sew.

It is important to recognize not only the oneness of all beings but the *differences* in beings as well. Zen teachers must help each student, male or female, understand and transcend his or her own individual style of self-clinging without encouraging that student to resort to historical examples of self-harm. In the past women needed to invent extreme actions to demonstrate their sincere desire to practice. Just leaving home, or leaving a position of power, was not seen as sufficiently convincing. However, taking attachment to body literally, and acting out the cutting off of attachment, would seem to be a destructive and impulsive way to express this point. Let us hope that these methods do not find a home in the West.

Ryonen chose a small but potent act of self-harm to make a big point. Consider this poem of Ryonen's:

> Formerly to amuse myself at court I would burn incense;
> Now to enter the Zen life I burn my own face.
> The four seasons pass by naturally like this,
> But I don't know who I am amidst the change.[165]

Ryonen's deepening awareness taught her that she could live her life without her beauty but not without meaning. She does not condemn the system that excluded her. She does not blame others for her difficulties. She does not protest the unfairness of the Zen establishment. Instead she exposes the inquiry beneath her motivation to practice Zen. The question behind the act of scarring her face is revealed in the last line of the poem: "But I don't know who I am amidst the change."

When Ryonen showed her disfigured face to Zen Abbot Hakuo he was shocked, but he immediately allowed her to enter the all-male temple, Daikyu-an. She soon became one of his leading students. Her act of letting go of worldly identity is among the few records of her life. Much of her published work, including the poems she wrote after her Zen training, has been lost. Piecing together her story we find a few remaining expressions of her awakening.

Initially, Ryonen leaned toward rejection of the phenomenal world.

In this living world
the body I give up and burn
would be wretched
if I thought of myself as
anything but firewood.[166]

Ryonen actively engaged in the letting go of all attachments to the phenomenal world. At this stage, she is leaning into emptiness, pushing away phenomena. She is actively rejecting form, including her own human form. Later poems and calligraphy suggest that her Zen training with Hakuo bore fruit; she expressed her understanding through the beauty of the phenomenal world, not just through rejection of it.

One of Ryonen's remaining calligraphy pieces references the thirty-seventh case of the Mumonkan.[167] In this case a monk asks Zhaozhou: "What is the meaning of Bodhidharma's coming from the West? Why did the Zen teachers travel here with this practice?" Zhaozhou answered, "The oak tree in the garden." Ryonen's calligraphy is written in the *kana*,[168] the ordinary women's script, and is described by the art historian Stephen Addiss as modest but skilled and confident.[169] The question of why Bodhidharma came from the West is a question about the meaning of Zen practice. This answer points to natural function and form of life as part of the Zen way; nothing is left out. Teachers come and the Dharma flows just as seeds take root and grow. This is how life expresses itself. Ryonen's choice of "the oak tree in the garden" expresses her recognition of the enlightened nature of the familiar and ordinary in our own yard, right here in front of us.

Ryonen's examination of "What is the meaning of Bodhidharma's coming from the West" is all the more poignant as we study her life. What is the meaning of Ryonen's leaving her children to enter Hokyoji? Why did Ryonen leave the women's temple to go to Edo? Why did Ryonen burn her face to enter the temple? What was the meaning of Ryonen's long journey? Her answer and the answer for Bodhidharma express all of this single-minded effort unfolding naturally in practice—"the oak tree in the garden." This one tree, growing its own way in this very garden, manifests the wisdom of the entire universe. Can you see what her life of practice saw in that tree?

Her realization and investigation blossomed through formal practice with her teacher. Her Zen mind found expression in her art. Her life of hardship, investigation, and cutting off of attachment became balanced with realization, naturalness, and appreciation of the phenomenal world. Hakuo fully acknowledged Ryonen's practice through giving her a certificate of enlightenment in 1682, the same year that he died. Through her severe practice Ryonen was reborn to bring her unique human gifts to fruition.

Ryonen had abandoned the care of her home and family in order to practice Zen, but later, through her role as Zen abbot, she was able to contribute to the well-being of her temple community. She skillfully founded a temple at a time when the building of new temples was opposed by the shogunate. She then expanded the temple to a full-scale monastery, Taiunji. The temple was dedicated to her late teacher, Hakuo, and the name of the monastery referred to the temple where Hakuo's father had served. At Taiunji there are memorial stones for both her teacher Hakuo and for her deceased ex-husband.[170] Even though she had ended her marriage, she honored her ex-husband's life and his role in hers. Ryonen also recognized her teacher's sympathetic honesty throughout her life.

Ryonen was well known in the Taiunji's area for both her good deeds and her scholarship. Her work in the local area to help the community is remembered. She sponsored the building of a bridge and used her own educational skills to enable Taiunji to become a center of Obaku learning. Children from surrounding villages were educated at her temple. Though she was well known for her poetry, calligraphy, and her painting, she was remembered by one of her contemporaries not only for her act of nonattachment to her body but for her presence as a "wise heart in the temple," the respected abbess she had become.

Body discarded
For the road to buddhahood—
The evening bell
Sends its resounding peal to
The wise heart in the temple[171]

Ryonen's painful life, courageous investigation, and deep awakening are integrated in her own death poem.

In the autumn of my sixty-sixth year, I've already lived a long time—
The intense moonlight is bright upon my face.
There's no need to discuss the principles of koan study;
Just listen carefully to the wind outside the pines and cedars.[172]

Here Ryonen expresses a sense that her life has been long enough. As she describes the "intense moonlight bright upon my face," we can sense her healing and the intensity of her self-illumination. The scarred face and the sacrifices are now all shining in the bright light of the moon, the full moon, a symbol for enlightenment. In this way her enlightenment, the light of realization, and her sacrifices come together as one, awakening in her body. There is no mark or distinction in this bright shining. Her personhood takes its proper place in the illumination. It is neither discarded nor distinctive in any way. The illumination and her own face, in that very moment, together express the full embodiment of Zen practice. The formal pursuit of Zen words, "the principles of koan study," is no longer needed. Instead, life expresses itself wordlessly, naturally, through her illuminated presence. She requests that we answer our own koan through attentiveness to nature's voice, "the wind outside the pines and cedars."

Ryonen's life of courageous action is both surprising and disturbing. She experienced a full life with its change in seasons. From a hidden source she found the strength and tenacity to investigate the truth, no matter what. When there was no path, she made one. She used her faith in Zen practice as a compass to guide her through uncharted territory. When she confronted difficulty, she was relentless in her pursuit of truth and in her willingness to sever her attachments. The radical and violent action that opened the gate for her formal Zen training left scars that were softened over the years. Her courage and determination resulted in an awakening that sustained her and gave birth to kindness and teachings that nurtured her community.

Western Zen's Sewing Ancestor

Kasai Joshin

Kasai Joshin (1914–84), called Joshin-san by her American students (and in this book), was an inspirational Japanese nun who had a profound effect on contemporary Western practice. As mentioned earlier, nuns were often trained by a number of teachers that often included male masters. Joshin-san's complex lineage relationships are well illustrated by the chart on p.148 created by contemporary Zen sewing teacher, Jean Selkirk, of the Berkeley Zen Center.[173] In tracing the history of how Westerners took up the devotional practice of hand-sewing Buddhist robes, a practice that had become nearly extinct in Japan, Selkirk shows the web of relationships that linked two nuns, Yoshida Eshun Roshi (1907–82) and Kasai Joshin-san (1914–84), to their intertwined Japanese roots and to their subsequent relationships with Western male founding teachers. Joshin-san is discussed here with her primary male teacher, Sawaki Kodo Roshi. Clearly, actual teacher-student relationships and transmission are far more complex than has been portrayed in the traditional charts of patriarchs' lineages, and women's lineage relationships are even more complex.

Joshin-san was invited to San Francisco Zen Center (SFZC) to teach traditional Buddhist sewing and trained SFZC Zenkei Blanche Hartman Roshi (1926–) in the art of sewing Buddha's robes. Zenkei Roshi became abbess of SFZC and has since trained many Western sewing teachers, instilling in them a love and devotion to this profound and ancient practice. Hand-sewn priest robes (*okesa* for priests and *rakusu* for laypeople), while a rarity in contemporary Japan, have now become an important part of training at Western Zen centers. The revival of the hand-stitched priest's robe is attributed to Joshin-san and another nun, Yoshida Eshun Roshi (1907–82), through the lineage of Hashimoto Eko Roshi (1890–1965).[174] Joshin-san was ordained by Hashimoto Eko Roshi and also trained at Yoshida Eshun Roshi's temple. This is where she learned the style of hand-sewn robes (called *nyohoe*)[175] that was also used

Legacy of Sewing Buddha's Robe and its Transmission to the Suzuki Roshi Lineage

Two nuns in Jiun lineage from Koki-ji travel to Horyu-ji (Yogacara temple at Nara built in the 6th century).

Jiun Onko (1718–1804), Shingon Risshu (Vajrayana and Vinaya schools) master at Koki-ji temple in 1700's; also studied and taught Soto Zen style meditation. Studied Sanskrit and reconstructed/documented most authentic *okesa* sewing style from *The Mahavagga* texts.

Kodo Sawaki Roshi (1880–1965), 6th abbot of Antaiji, professor at Komazawa University. Studied Dogen's *Kesakudoku* and also the *Vinaya* (as had earlier scholars). He visits Horyu-ji and sees "two beautiful nuns" wearing *Nyoho-e* (True Dharma Robe). They are like traditional robes he's seen on statues, or of Jiun's, or worn by his teacher, Fueoka. Visits Koki-ji regularly (walking half-a-day each way) to borrow robes to study *okesa* construction. These pre-date Soto Zen robes worn in Japan, adopted when the Obaku School came from China in the Edo Period (1600's).

Shunryu Suzuki Roshi (1904–1971), who first ordains priests in the U.S.A. in 1963. He brings Katagiri Roshi to San Francisco Zen Center and knew Yoshida Roshi. Teacher of both Sojun Mel Weitsman (b. 1929) and Zenkei Blanche Hartman, who becomes a dharma heir of Sojun Roshi's.

Sawaki Roshi meets fellow student Hashimoto, sharing *Nyoho-e* sewing studies with him.

Sotan Oka Roshi (1860–1921), Dogen scholar, studied texts on the robe, founded Antaiji in 1923, teacher of . . .

Ian Kishizawa Roshi (1865–1955), 3rd abbot of Antaiji, a teacher of . . .

Joshin Kasai (1914–1984), who studied first with Yoshida Roshi, learns sewing from Sawaki Roshi. Joshin-san visits San Francisco Zen Center (SFZC) and Tassajara over 1973–1974, returning often until 1984 to teach & sew Buddha's Robe.

Eko Hashimoto Roshi (1890–1965), who teaches sewing to Yoshida Roshi and also teacher of Katagiri Roshi.

Dainin Katagiri Roshi (1928–1990), attendant of Hashimoto Roshi and translator for Yoshida Roshi at SFZC. Encourages start of sewing practice.

Eshun Yoshida Roshi (1907–1982). Visits SFZC in 1970 and 1971. She teaches Joshin-san, Tomoe Katagiri (b. 1932), and Zenkei Blanche Hartman.

San Francisco Zen Center

Shohaku Okumura (b. 1948) meets Joshin-san at Antaiji in 1969 while practicing and ordaining with Kosho Uchiyama Roshi (d. 1998) who succeeds Sawaki Roshi as Abbot. Okumura studies English with Graham Petchey (Suzuki Roshi student). Later, he translates SFZC's *rakusu* sewing instructions for Joshin-san to affirm.

Zenkei Blanche Hartman (b. 1926), former abbess of SFZC, to whom Joshin-san transmitted sewing Buddha's Robe, says that this line from the *Genjokoan* describes what is special to her about Joshin-san: "Doing one thing is practicing completely." "Joshin-san was totally devoted to *Nyoho-e* sewing. That total devotion made her happy."

Reprinted and adapted with permission from: *Buddha's Robe Is Sewn: The Tradition of Sewing Practice in the Shunryu Suzuki Roshi American Lineage.* www.BuddhasRobeIsSewn.org © 2006 Jean Selkirk

in the lineage of Sawaki Kodo Roshi, to whom Joshin-san later transferred her discipleship from her original teacher, Hashimoto Eko Roshi.
Joshin-san's transfer of discipleship spoke volumes to the rigor underlying her gentle and easy-going exterior. When she decided to change her
teacher from Hashimoto Eko Roshi to one of Hashimoto Eko Roshi's
peers, Sawaki Kodo Roshi, she could not obtain approval from Hashimoto Eko Roshi or encouragement to go forward from Sawaki Kodo
Roshi either. Certain that she wanted to make the change, but uncertain
as to how to accomplish it while showing adequate respect and sincerity
in her practice, she decided to cut off part of her little finger. As legend
reports this incident, rather than a quick cut, Joshin-san spent most of one
night removing the finger joint since she did not have a sharp knife. Her
story is told below by a priest she knew at Antaiji, Sano Kenko.

The Story of the Nun Joshin-san,
by Sano Kenko[176]

Kasai Joshin-san (1914–84), given name Kikue, was born in
Mine-gun, Yamaguchi prefecture, the second girl of four siblings. Her father was a doctor who committed suicide when
she was just a baby. She was told that her father was a man with
a keen sense of justice. Kikue's mother died at age 46, so she
was raised by her grandfather. Kikue was described as a child
with a hot temper.

Kikue was married in her early twenties to a clothing store
owner; they had been introduced by a friend. Kikue soon
learned that her husband had the dissipating habit of visiting
geishas,[177] so she left and divorced him after [approximately] six
months [of marriage] and moved in with her paternal aunt,
Soko, in Tokyo.

Her aunt was a student of Harada Sogaku Roshi,[178] and was
helping him with his *zazenkai*.[179] Joshin-san joined her there,
participating in the *zazenkai*. After a while, she was ordained by
Hashimoto Eko-roshi and practiced *okesa* sewing, *zazen*, and
takuhatsu[180] at Kaizenji,[181] a nun's temple of Hashimoto Roshi's
disciple [Yosida Eshun Roshi] in Aichi prefecture. A few years
later, she started to have doubts about her way as a nun. She

was scolded by her siblings: "Isn't this what you chose for your-self without listening to our cautions?" Once again she went to stay with her aunt Soko in Tokyo. Around this time she first heard Sawaki Roshi's *teisho* [teaching] at his *zazenkai*, and she aspired to become his disciple. It was not easy to change one's teacher, but since Hashimoto Roshi and Sawaki Roshi knew each other, it was not impossible. People around Hashimoto Roshi didn't accept or encourage her aspiration to change her teacher. Sawaki Roshi didn't say yes, either.

Thus the cutting off of her [little] finger happened. [Joshin-san said] "I wanted to be Sawaki Roshi's disciple so much that I became desperate. I don't know why I did such a thing...." Her words sounded heavy [to me].

In 1982, it was getting more difficult for her to live in Antaiji through winter, during which time the temple is covered in deep snow. She moved to her older sister's house in Tokyo. I learned her location from a friend and started to visit her there. She was very glad to see me, and I was able to ask her about her life, and about the extraordinary Sawaki Roshi, whom I had never met. [This is what I learned from her.]

Joshin-san said, "After I became Sawaki Roshi's disciple, I never had any doubt and served him in peace. Sawaki Roshi found a temple in Kobe for me to live with another nun. But I couldn't get along with her, and it suited me better to live like Ryokan-san[182] without being constrained by a temple so I moved out. [Sawaki Roshi] said [ruefully], 'Oh well, there's nothing to be done for it! It can't be helped.' He was disap-pointed, but put up with me [my temperament and my deci-sion]. Later in Sawaki Roshi's life, he was worried about me and offered to adopt me.[183] He had so many disciples, and I was content to be just one of them. [I was concerned that] the adoption might also hurt his reputation, so I declined."

"After my death there is to be no funeral. Bury my ashes at Antaiji. My belongings should go to Narita Shuyu Roshi, Sawaki Roshi's first disciple in Akita. My okesa and koromo go to Myogenji in Nagoya. Thank my sister."

She was in the hospital for about six months, and deceased

on May 29th, 1984. After her long illness and time in the hospital, her hair had grown out, so I shaved her head in preparation for her [nun's funeral]. Hearing the rough sound of it, I imagined Joshin-san saying, "Ouch, you're clumsy!"[184] I had a gathering with her sister's family to say farewell.

I kept her ashes for a while in Jizo-an in Akagi, where I was living at that time. Then I asked Sakai Tokugen Roshi [a Sawaki Roshi disciple] to take care of them. He told me that someone from Myogenji would be kind enough to take her ashes to Antaiji, so I handed Joshin-san's remains to this person on the platform for the Super Express at Tokyo station. I then delivered her belongings to Akita and Nagoya. Her older sister said, "Joshin must be happy for she lived out her life in the way she wished."

Six years later, my son and I visited Hamasaka, the town where Antaiji is located, for the occasion of her 7th memorial service. Her gravestone was behind Sawaki Roshi's, and from there, it looked like she could watch the view with ease. I peacefully chanted a sutra for her.

Joshin-san was passionate about her practice and about sewing Buddha's robes. Her delight in sewing and teaching sewing practice was an inspiration to Zenkei Roshi here in America. Sewing has become one of her main teaching venues, and she was moved to this practice, despite her doubts about sewing as women's work, through her relationship with Joshin-san. Through Joshin-san's passion and devotion she transformed the practice of Zen in America, where most priest robes (*okesa*) and lay robes (called *rakusu*) are now sewn by hand. Suzuki Shunryu Roshi, the founder of San Francisco Zen Center, was not familiar with or disposed toward sewing the robes; initially, the robes were purchased. He was persuaded to endorse the sewing practice by Katagiri Dainin, who had also been a student of Hashimoto Eko Roshi and knew Yoshida Roshi. Yoshida Roshi became the first sewing teacher at SFZC, but she could not continue her teaching because she was ill. Joshin-san, who was described to Zenkei Blanche Hartman Roshi as a genius with the *okesa*, was enlisted. Joshin-san first visited SFZC in 1974, after Suzuki Roshi's death, but it is generally believed that they had met at Antaiji when Suzuki Roshi was fundraising in Japan for Tassajara, the first Zen monastery to be built on American soil.

Joshin-san taught her students that the hand-sewn robe represented the complete body of the Buddha, and that every robe started must be finished to the last stitch. Her entire body of teaching was in her sewing; she never gave Dharma talks. Like the previously discussed Korean founder Beophui, Joshin-san had suffered early and repeated losses of loved ones. Her practice, like that of many other nuns, was devotional, and it was accomplished through her own hands. Given that she taught with her body, it is not a surprise that she chose to make her statement about her change of discipleship with her own body and her own hands rather than through words. Following the Japanese tradition of expressing regret for a dishonor to one's clan by cutting off a finger joint, Joshin-san simultaneously expressed to her teachers her seriousness, her regret, her respect, and her inability to excuse her mistake by the act of cutting off her finger.

Joshin-san spent her mature years serving as cook for long *sesshin* (meditation retreats) at the Antaiji temple when it was located in Kyoto. Tiny as she was, she carried huge pots of rice during *sesshin* there, and was also known for standing her ground with the tough head monk Koho,[185] who intimidated everyone but Joshin-san with his ferocious ways.

Joshin-san's relationship with Sawaki Kodo Roshi was both strict and caring. He let her find her own way to become his disciple, but he also offered support by placing her in a nun's temple and was even willing to adopt her if necessary. This teaching formula—strict standards combined with expressed affection—was consistently employed by male Zen masters known for their ability to instruct and empower female disciples.

What We Learn from the Relationship between Women and Their Male Zen Teachers

This creative relationship between women and their male teachers reveals several common patterns. Most Zen women who are known to us today studied with male Zen masters. Dharma heirs of female Zen masters are not as well remembered. Mysteriously, the female lineage, once started, does not seem able to sustain and continue itself. Perhaps this is due to a changing social climate that would alternately allow and then disallow women's participation. Perhaps the loss of the female lineage has to do with the financial hardships or the lower status that were established in early Buddhism by the Eight Special Rules. Male Zen masters' willingness to teach women was clearly essential to the survival of the female Zen tradition.

Another pattern in the relationship between male teacher and female disciple was the combination of rigor and support. On the supportive side, male teachers consistently gave their female disciples koans that other women had answered, or used stories of other women's awakenings to encourage their female students. Male teachers understood that their female disciples were coping in an unfamiliar and unfriendly environment with training techniques that were developed for men, and they found ways to bring in other women's experience to acknowledge the hardship.

Male teachers may have wondered if their female students could experience awakening through the same methods as their Dharma brothers. Given the different lives and roles women played in the cultures of their day, these would not have been unrealistic concerns. On the side of rigor, the teachers were firm and strict with their female disciples; this helped the women train to their full capacity. We note Hakuo refusing Ryonen entrance to his temple until she had demonstrated her seriousness. Dahui relays how many times he sent Miaodao away, even when she felt she had a breakthrough with her koan. He was tough; he sensed she could have a deeper understanding and he pushed her into it. We hear the rigor in Hyesim's advice to Wangdoin and to his other nuns, "Work with this koan all the time, in your everyday life, for a long time. Don't expect this to be easy!" At the same time, all of the teachers gave their female students the same clear messages—"You can do this!" and "Other women have done this."

We can also see a surprising similarity among many of the male Zen teachers who taught these renowned female disciples. As we have seen, most of the male Zen teachers in this section were successors of a great Zen master who was even better known and more venerated: Dahui was the successor of Yuanwu. Yuanwu was more highly thought of in his own lifetime and better known today than Dahui. Man'gong was the disciple of the great master Hyo Bong, who revitalized modern Zen in Korea and served as the archbishop of Korean Buddhism. Hyesim was the disciple of Chinul, one of the most important Korean Zen masters of all time. Hakuo, of whom we know little, was the disciple of the very well known Mokuan. What can we speculate about this interesting similarity?

Men who taught women were part of a well-respected lineage. No one doubted their credentials and understanding. Women would have known about them through the lineage these men represented. For the male teacher's part, they could break rules because they were already recognized as part of Zen's establishment. As a successor to a great Zen master, they had nothing to prove. They could work on expanding the venue and the scope of their teaching. They had been taught by a truly enlightened teacher; the Zen they received from their teacher transcended rules and constraints. They enjoyed the use of this Zen freely; by training women they explored new territory. An exception to this pattern was Sawaki Kodo, the teacher of Joshin-san, who was by nature a free-thinking teacher but did not inherit his legitimacy from a more famous Zen master.

Women needed to have supportive teachers who broke the rules to admit them to an all-male monastery but who maintained their rigor with them. The teacher also needed to have the time to work personally with these women; if the teacher's monastery was too large or his reputation too great, women might not have access to the personal relationship so necessary for Zen transmission. Finally, if the teacher's accomplishments greatly overshadowed his students, we might never have learned of these women and their accomplishments.

Nuns and Family Practice 8

THE BUDDHA ENCOURAGED his monastic followers to find freedom beyond conditions by abandoning family life—a long-standing Indian spiritual tradition of home leaving. His suggestions proscribing family life for his renunciate followers can be summarized in three categories: first, abandon the responsibilities of family life—elderly parents, wife, and children; second, avoid the entanglements of man-woman or husband-wife relationships; and third, do not engage in intercourse (and thereby avoid having children).

On the other hand, Bhikkhu Basnagoda Rahula shows in *The Buddha's Teaching on Prosperity* that the Buddha gave extensive instructions to his lay followers regarding how to choose a wife, what it meant to be a good husband or wife, and how to raise children, among other topics. Sadly, over time Buddha's instructions for monks have dominated the translations offered in English, so these lay-oriented instructions have not been disseminated. Even though the Buddha described four types of practitioners—monks, nuns, laymen, and laywomen—ordained nuns have at times looked like a hybrid of a nun and laywomen, enjoying the formal practice of a nun but living with family as a laywoman.

The purpose of this chapter is first to examine the Buddha's recommendations to his ordained community for home-leaving practice and then to consider the ways female Zen Buddhists practiced with family life. The key point here is that Western Buddhists—whether ordained or lay—often live like the female Zen ancestors and follow a hybrid model.

Rather than living at home, many ordained Western Buddhists have brought their families into the monastery or have sought to find practice within home and family life. These innovators may gain some insight into possible ways to blend family practice with monastic life by studying how female Buddhists have practiced with a monastic-family hybrid in the past.

Leaving the Family

The Buddha's view of home leaving is summarized in these words: "Household life is crowded and dusty; life gone forth is wide open. It is not easy, while living in a home, to lead the holy life."[186] In the midst of the family environment, how indeed could it be "easy" to lead a holy life? All of those messy people, dusty conditions, and mundane responsibilities get in the way. In this way the Buddha differentiates between what is holy and what is otherwise. The "otherwise," he suggests, is what gets in the way of training the mind to recognize reality. This "otherwise," messy as it is, could be most essential to Western practice.

The Buddha himself abandoned his wife (or wives), child, mother, and father in pursuit of spiritual awakening. He advised his (male) followers to do the same. The Buddha's recommendations supported the establishment of a monastic order. Monks who left home were in a position to devote themselves to their practice and establish a practice environment without consideration of the needs of families left behind. Simply put, the new monks' resources of time and effort could focus entirely on supporting, validating, and realizing the benefits of the Buddha's teaching.

The Buddha did allow for the creation of a female Buddhist nuns' order. During his lifetime in India, there was an order of nuns who also had left their homes. But as Buddhism continued to migrate, most women who attempted to follow the Buddha's teaching across the centuries and across the Asian continent found that abandoning family (as the monks did) was not a viable, or sometimes not even a *legal*, option. Through Confucian and other belief systems, women were seen as the property of their families—subject to the commands of father, husband, and, later, their own sons.

For better or for worse, women who wished to practice Buddhism needed to find ways to do so while living with their family, or after their family responsibilities lessened. As a result, we find examples of Buddhist practice integrated with family life. We also find evidence, in the female ancestors' writing, of genuine feelings usually associated with close personal relationships: expressions of vulnerability, human love, and affection occurring within Buddhist practice. These female Zen teachings offer a contrasting view to the teachings of Indian and Chinese monastic patriarchs (and later of the Japanese samurai). Early patriarchal teachings were composed with stark Dharma words of nonattachment and often evinced a preference for the realm of the absolute, sometimes a disconnection from the realm of human feelings—except for monks' feelings of well-being about themselves and their monasteries—a shadow side of the monastic path that needs watching as we develop Western Buddhist monastic institutions.

As we develop a Western Zen practice, we need to regard the Buddha's first teaching about "life gone forth" carefully; we need to be careful about cutting off both human feelings and relationships. Practicing *nonattachment* is not the same as practicing *detachment*. The former practice addresses the human selfishness we bring to all of our relationships and is guided by the relinquishing of self-clinging to reactions that arise. The latter is repressive and disconnected and seeks to keep our delusional self-centeredness intact by avoiding intimate relational contact and feelings.

Furthermore, the description of family life as "crowded and dusty" might encourage some to think that holiness is found elsewhere than that dustiness. Somewhere, other than right where we are, there is an ideal practice life that is dustless. Somewhere there exists a life pure and elevated from the dust of human family relations. Imagining this to be true is a serious mistake, and sadly not an uncommon one. While each of us needs to find quiet time to reflect on our true nature, it is important to see buddha-nature reflected even in our most annoying family members, relatives, and associates. If we cannot do this, our practice develops a puritanical, precious, detached, and heartless quality.

As Western practitioners, we need to hear the voice that expresses our relationship to the absolute *and* to our messy humanity. Because we have not lived in the richly textured Buddhist culture that practices letting go within a community context, there is a danger in establishing a Western Buddhist order resembling a cult that only imitates a theoretical approach to practice.

Male-Female Magnetism and Sexual Attraction

The Buddha's second instruction to his monks concerned the dangers of sexual attraction. In a discourse in the Anguttara Nikaya, he says:

> Monks, a woman, even when going along, will stop to ensnare the heart of a man: whether standing, sitting, or lying down, laughing, talking, or singing, weeping, stricken, or dying, a woman will stop to ensnare the heart of a man.[187]

The context for this sermon is that the Buddha had just been informed of an incestuous mother-son relationship within the sangha. As a response, the Buddha chose to lecture on the sexual power of women rather than on these particularly unwholesome family dynamics. The implication here is that the ensnaring woman functions as an outside force to steal a monk's heart/mind and turn him away from his devotion to practice. Through this teaching the view of women as dangerous objects is reinforced, and monks learn to stereotype women and avoid them, rather than to reflect on what arises within themselves during their encounters and relationships with women. Is it only the case that women ensnare men, or do men too have a longing to belong to, to be part of, the union of male and female energies? The answer is obvious, but the scripture has nonetheless continued to form the basis for some of our Buddhist practices and institutions.

In this one-sided early Buddhist view of male-female magnetism we see once again instructions to steel ourselves against emotions and to avoid and repress feelings. Rather than strengthening the monk's training to observe the arising of desire and primitive impulses, there is an attempt to control the monk's behavior and emotional vulnerability by creating a dangerous object or projection. This projection labels women as a danger to practice, something to be eliminated. Instead of eliminating contact with or feeling for women, wouldn't it be more in keeping with true mindfulness practice to experience the sensation, the feeling of longing for intimacy and union with the feminine? This seems like a deep and healthy practice of mindfulness for men and women. The scripturally based practice seems much less so.

The importance of clarifying the Buddha's early teaching on women was obvious to Ananda, the Buddha's faithful follower. Ananda persisted in questioning the Buddha even when the Buddha was passing away (as chronicled in the Mahaparinibbana Sutta). Ananda asked the Buddha how the monks should act toward women. The Buddha responded at first with his policy of avoiding women and repressing the whole experience of meeting the feminine: "Don't see them, Ananda." Ananda continued to probe: "But if we see them, how should we behave, Lord?" The Buddha advises further rejection: "Do not speak to them, Ananda." And finally Ananda asked the Buddha what to do if all previous avoidance has failed to repel the woman: "But if they speak to us, how should we behave, Lord?" Only after this third inquiry does the Buddha allude to a practice for engaged and sexual human beings: "Practice mindfulness, Ananda."[188]

In this passage we see Ananda working to clarify the Buddha's teaching on relating to women before the Buddha is gone, before his earlier repressive injunctions become the de facto records. Ananda seems rightly to be concerned about instructions that will guide followers in the millennia to come. He seems to have realized that a policy of avoidance and revulsion is both inadequate and inconsistent with the mindfulness practice the Buddha taught. Perhaps on the most advanced practice level the Buddha is saying that we don't need to see women and men as differentiated sexual objects. But even so, what about the arising of human feelings, and what about women's need to be taught, spoken to, and included in practice? What then, Buddha? Ananda's questioning helped the Buddha clarify his teaching that meeting the feminine or the object of desire with mindful attention is the essence of understanding and releasing attachments.

Shunryu Suzuki Roshi noted in the 1960s that American Zen practitioners were neither priest nor lay. He encouraged us to continue to clarify just what Western practice would be for us. This was not something he could do for us; it is our work—to bring the practice to life in our world. In order to develop a sustainable Western Buddhism, we need to incorporate the Buddha's teaching for laypeople along with Suzuki Roshi's instructions for monastic practice.

It's interesting to note that in most Western Zen centers the head teachers are married rather than celibate. We need to study explicitly how to practice within relationship, since this is what most Western practitioners are actually doing. Applying the Buddha's rules for monks' home leaving does not help us to establish a relevant Western practice. We need to understand just how effectively practice can be developed within the family context, and how family life affects training in a monastery. While we will need to explore this topic as Western Buddhists in our own innovative practice environments, female ancestors faced this dilemma and developed their own solutions. The teachings that resulted from their blend of family and formal practice offer us further instruction in bringing our practice to meet our everyday life.

Back and Forth: Between Family and Practice

In reviewing historical Zen women we find numerous ways that social and familial barriers have made it difficult for women to commit to formal practice. Most Asian cultures placed greater pressure on women to focus exclusively on their families, and women have therefore struggled in their spiritual paths. Acknowledging this history is an important teaching for Western practitioners. We need to recognize that practicing in the midst of family is not a second-rate practice but a legitimate alternative to monastic practice. And we must recognize that others have in fact become fully awakened while living with family. There has been tremendous variety to Zen Buddhist practice—it did not come to us only through monastic training.

While the female Zen masters we will examine in this chapter may not have explicitly taught how to integrate the practice and family life, the fact that they managed to stay connected to family while practicing deeply can be a source of encouragement to Western Zen. Serious and enlightened practitioners struggled, just as we do, to find their true nature in the midst of family life, refusing to use family responsibilities as a way to avoid asking difficult questions about the meaning of life and death.

For women, being in a family may create a sense of self-worth dependent on serving others; the risk is that women may come to see their worth only in that context. Women may struggle with a compulsion or tendency to gratify and please others to validate their own meaning. Women practitioners and their teachers need to see this style of self-clinging clearly. Women may successfully disguise their need to serve and be needed as selflessness, when in fact this need is an unwholesome dependency on the approval of others. Currently women "hide out" in the Zen sangha, seemingly serving family and sangha selflessly but all the while building and strengthening their ego as the "good girl."

In the sections that follow we will see several alternative examples to home leaving: women teachers who practiced after raising families, nuns who maintained family ties while practicing, nuns who created convents to shelter family members, and nuns who expressed love and longing for their lost husbands. These female Zen teachers demonstrate that family relationships, sexual relationships, and loving words all have a rightful place in an authentic Zen practice. There was, and will continue to be, an enormous variety in practice situations and an enormous appetite for practice despite abundant obstacles and difficult choices.

Zhiyuan Xinggang:
Treating the Sangha as Family

We have already touched on two important Zen abbesses in different contexts who began practicing Zen but stayed with their families until they were released from family contracts: Zhiyuan Xinggang was discussed in chapter 5 as an early Zen Dharma heir, and Ryonen Genso was encountered in the previous chapter. In this section we will look at their family lives.

The Ming dynasty nun Xinggang was required by her male Dharma teacher to stay home until both of her parents died, even though he had not fulfilled this filial requirement himself. During that time she worked on her koan practice and offered her devotional practice to the Buddha while living at home—meditating and chanting prayers at her home altar. Occasionally she visited a teacher. After both parents died she devoted herself to monastic practice. She established her own temple after being designated a Dharma heir.

Xinggang's gentle, down-to-earth, and no-nonsense approach is expressed in the following poem:

> In the gates and hall of the elders, the work of the lineage flourishes.
> Knowing my own lazy ignorance, I've hidden away in order
>   to be still.

Esoteric methods, blows and shouts—
I'm giving them all a rest.[189]

In this poem Xinggang reveals her flaw—laziness. It is a wonderful and refreshing admission by a Zen master, and perhaps exposing this flaw is part of her more familial, softer approach as contrasted with the traditional male masters. While remaining true to her lineage, she maintains that the practice can flourish, even as she admits to letting go of the traditional harsh Rinzai methods. Perhaps the blows and shouts were tempered by the day-to-day working out of difficulties within the family context. *Reminds me of Reading Lolita in Tehran!*

Also, her students and Dharma heirs had particularly intimate and companionable relationships both with her and with each other. Resolving needs within the family context has much to offer Dharma teachers training in developing sangha relationships. Xinggang's long relationship with parents who loved her dearly must have taught her something of the value of human affection and the way it might be used to encourage commitment and harmony in the community.

Ryonen Genso:
Leaving Her Family for Practice

Recall that Ryonen began her practice as a girl when she served as a playmate to the emperor's daughter. Later, at the insistence of her family, she married and had a son. There were four children in her household, but several of them may have been children of her husband and his concubine (who could also be called a second wife or mistress). When her son was ten years old, she was able to leave home and begin formal practice with her palace childhood friend Yoshi no Kimi. Upon the early death of the emperor's daughter, Ryonen decided to pursue a more intense serious practice at a male monastery under the guidance of Obaku Hakuo.

Ryonen is remembered mostly today in connection with the act of burning her face, but who can say whether the loss of her children may not have been the greater hardship? Perhaps her decision to leave home and children in the hands of her husband's second wife reflected a realistic grasp of what was best for the family, given her unconventional need to practice Zen. There was a stepmother in the home who cared for the children, her husband's concubine. This (unnamed) woman seems to have been satisfied with her role as wife and mother. Ryonen's son apparently adjusted to his family life and social position. He became a successful bureaucrat, following in his father's footsteps.

We learn more explicitly about Ryonen's relationship to her children through a poem she wrote to her daughter, Momosenko.[190] While the context of the poem is unknown, its content indicates that Ryonen and several Obaku monks offered greetings and encouragement to Momosenko. The poem suggests that Ryonen's daughter might herself have had some affinity for Buddhist life and practice. Ryonen offers her daughter some possibility of peaceful resolution to what might have been a wrenching separation between them. Perhaps Momosenko rejoined her mother in the pursuit of a spiritual practice. Ryonen wrote:

> Still surroundings, with few people the birds are slow to arise.
> Even the bamboo and moss relax while propping up our
> elbows.
> Good fortune to encounter a pure world from which I leisurely
> enjoy the remains of old age.
> For this reason, desirelessness gives birth to a low tune.
> High on a pillow, in front of the steps I watch the wild deer.
> The farmer, shouldering his tools, stops to talk outside the door.
> If on this side you think you can come question me,
> The purity of mountains, rivers and branches will answer you
> with my poem.[191]

Ryonen provides her daughter a glimpse of the tranquillity of a life of practice. We sense her easy connection to this natural setting. She also refers to the pure world from which she found peace and enjoyment in her old age. The sense of shared peace with her daughter tends to affirm that their separation did not result in complete estrangement. Clearly they had not lost touch with each other.

Perhaps Ryonen invited her daughter's questioning, now that she had found her peace of mind through practice. She promised that the harmonious growth of the natural universe would answer her daughter's questions. The truth of life's unfolding might say what words could not.

Her own life force could only follow its own true nature. What mountains, rivers, and trees express through natural movement, Ryonen expresses through Zen practice and poems.

In addition to her children, Ryonen had maintained contact with her family of origin. Correspondence between Ryonen and her brother indicate that she maintained a loving relationship with him as well. He wrote to her:

> The mountain blossoms spread their brocade, the orioles tune [the seven strings of their zither], and I sit myself at the window with a view of the pines. Suddenly I am brought your precious missive; I jump up and respectfully read it out.... Humbly I consider that the land of Japan for nearly three hundred years has gone without a woman of wisdom. Now that you have taken on this weighty position, it can be said to be like a lotus blossoming in the midst of fire, or a unicorn or phoenix appearing in this world.[192]

Her brother acknowledges his delight in receiving a letter from her. One senses the warmth of their relationship. At the same time he voices respect for Ryonen's role as abbess. She had become celebrated for her Zen teaching, poetry, calligraphy, and painting. He tactfully acknowledges her hardship. Referring to the lotus in the fire, he gently comforts the one who was burned, acknowledging the blossoming that appeared because of the fire.

His reference to the three hundred years that have passed in Japan without a woman of Dharma wisdom most likely evokes the Japanese abbess Mugai Nyodai, whom we've already met. He does not name Mugai Nyodai, but he could be referring only to her—a woman whose history would have been familiar to Ryonen through her training at Hokyoji, the temple Nyodai founded. Both Ryonen and Mugai were spiritual heirs to immigrant Chinese teachers, and both were recognized as outstanding nuns within their lifetimes. Both had been married women who followed their passion to practice. Both of them left the family environment to practice under the skill, "the hammer and tongs," of a great teacher. Perhaps their ability to thrive in an all-male teaching environment and their sensible, balanced approach to leading their communities were augmented by skills acquired through managing a household of complex relationships.

Laymen Practicing with Family

Before we discuss the nuns' family practice, it is important to clarify that there were also a few well-known enlightened men who practiced within the family context. In contrast to the example of the Buddha who left his wife, newborn son, and parents, we have the example of the Buddha's disciple Vimalakirti, who insisted that he could practice as a wealthy householder—and did so. Vimalakirti, who lived during the Buddha's lifetime, attained an unsurpassed enlightenment that was acknowledged by all of the Buddha's early disciples. Later on, in Zen's Chinese history, Layman Pang (740–808) refused ordination and practiced with his family and challenged established monastic leaders to test the understanding he had developed as a householder. Layman Pang not only refuted the necessity of monastic lifestyle for himself, but he also affirmed the awakening of his family members and their family practice.

> I've a boy who has no bride,
> I've a girl who has no groom;
> Forming a happy family circle,
> We speak about the birthless.[193]

Pang was not only dismissing the necessity of monastic training, but he was also refuting the Confucian values that required sons and daughters to marry. His daughter, Lingzhao (or Ling-chao), is discussed in one of the following sections.

As Zen Buddhism became institutionalized, however, these outstanding examples of family practice were neglected; authentic teaching was reported only from the monastic perspective. The practice of nonattachment in the Zen tradition became associated with home leaving.

The virtue associated with abandoning home and family is illustrated in the story of Chinese Zen Abbot Dongshan (807–69), founder of the Caodong (Soto) school. In order to practice, Dongshan abandoned his elderly mother,[194] who then followed him to his monastery begging for food and shelter. We are told that his strong resolve to practice resulted in his command that his own aging mother be put outside the monastery gate. He refused to take care of her, and this action was supposed to be an example of his clear and unattached Zen mind. After her death, it was announced in his temple that she had found peace in paradise because of the purity of her son's Buddhist practice.

Many Western practitioners have questioned whether this aspect of Dongshan's practice represents a healthy model for today's practitioners. One of my own teachers, Shunryu Suzuki Roshi, taught us to set up our practice right where we were, right in the midst of our lives, including our family responsibilities. He performed my own wedding ceremony in 1968 after considering the match "appropriate." His teaching meant that we are not to look for perfect practice circumstances; we need to begin to be present and continue that practice wherever we are.

So how do we understand Dongshan's act? Was it lack of compassion? Perhaps we can attribute Dongshan's abandonment of his old mother to the inflexible view that home leaving is *de rigeur* for monks. Or did it stem from his own particular relationship with his mother? It is a puzzling action in a practice that advocates compassion as a core value. His action makes sense only as a Zen Buddhist monk's choosing of Zen monastic values over Confucian filial duty, in a culture laden with Confucian obligations. Dongshan's act might have been recorded by monastic followers to celebrate Zen practice uprooting burdensome and traditional Confucian demands.

Since Layman Pang and Vimalakirti were able to practice deeply while residing at home with their families, Dongshan's rejection of his mother is perplexing. Did Dongshan and his monastic community perhaps lack an integrated view of practicing with family? Perhaps Dongshan's seeming lack of compassion was in trying to follow too literally the Buddha's home-leaving instructions for monks. Suzuki Roshi instructed Westerners to integrate our practice in our actual life, not to try to create an ideal practice situation. The examples of Zen's female ancestors provide more flexible practice options that can help us find our own way.

Convent Nuns and Family Relationships

Buddhist nuns seem to have steered a course between the Buddha's instructions for monks to leave home and his instructions for laypersons to provide for their family. An unusual example of an early nun who made a choice between ordained practice and family life was Prasannasila (ca. 300). Prasannasila, an ordained nun, felt the need to return to family life to further the Dharma.[195] According to a recent discussion led by the Tibetan teacher Khempo Tsultrim Rinpoche, Prasannasila concluded that since her participation in the Dharma was limited by her gender, she would make a larger contribution by having sons and raising them to be monks. She gave birth to three sons, fathered by scholars or Buddhist monks, whom she raised to be Buddhist monks (like their fathers) as her unique body-to-body contribution to the Buddhadharma. Two of her sons played a powerful role in the formation of the Mahayana tradition—Asanga and Vasubandhu.[196] Prasannasila benefited the Buddha's teaching by leaving the nuns' order and going home rather than leaving home to be ordained, finding her own way to deliver her wisdom for the benefit of Buddhist practice. Like other female ancestors her path was her own; she traveled in the direction opposite to what the Buddha had taught in order to benefit others. To uphold the spirit of practice, she disobeyed the letter of the law.

Nuns formally continued their family relationships after ordination in two usual ways. The first was through a temple life devoted to prayers for their family and ancestors. This was the practice of widows, imperial daughters, and other nuns whose temples were specifically designated to pray for imperial and shogunal families. The second way was through the creation of small convents that took in the nun's family members that had been displaced by wars or political persecution. We'll now look at these both in detail.

The very earliest Buddhist convents in Japan were, like early Chinese monasteries, dedicated to the welfare of the emperor and the continued well-being of the state. These temples were financed by the government and held ceremonies to protect the governing powers. This practice also evolved from the earliest Shinto practices in Japan, where women were often Shinto shamans who entered into special psychic states to influence the gods and spirits on behalf of the ruling family. Within the tradition of temples honoring loved ones or family, we have the example of Empress Komyo, who took the tonsure after the death of her husband, Emperor Shomu, to pray for his soul. Another family prayer temple is Kodaiji,[197] established in 1605 by the noblewoman Kita no Mandokoro in memory of her late husband, Toyotomi Hideyoshi (1536–98). Following the custom among noblewomen of her time, she became a Buddhist nun after the death of her husband, adopting the religious name Kogestu-ni. Kita no Mandokoro, known as Nene while wife of Hideyoshi, was also accorded the honorary name of Kodai-in. It is from the latter the still existent Kodaiji Temple derived its name.

A special category of family-oriented convents, *amamonzeki*, flourished in Japan under four imperial reigns from 1571 to 1732, when 70 percent of the imperial daughters became Buddhist nuns. This was especially true during the reign of Emperor Gomizuno'o (1596–1680), when eight of his thirteen daughters and thirteen of his granddaughters became nuns.[198] Some of them were taught by the same Zen masters who taught the emperor himself. The proliferation of opportunity for these women was due in part to the emperor's strong Buddhist practice coupled with his belief that the bodhisattva path was open to both genders. These temples were populated by daughters of the royal families who were dedicated to prayers and rituals to protect their families. While these nuns took the tonsure and renounced married life, they were neither cloistered nor impoverished. These well-educated imperial princesses often remained actively engaged in court life and at the same time made significant contributions to Buddhism through their art and poetry.

If we read between the lines, we find from the Buddha's time, starting with his stepmother Mahapajapati's ordination, to contemporary Japan where temples pass from father to son, there are many vibrant examples of family practice. What follows are examples of women who practiced in a family context, more flexibly integrating lay and monastic life.

Lingzhao
and Pang Family Practice

Lingzhao (early ninth century C.E.) was the daughter of Layman Pang and helped to support the family financially by selling baskets. A part of the Pang family practice consisted of ongoing Dharma conversation and debate as evidenced by this exchange:

> The Layman [P'ang] was sitting in his thatched cottage one day. "Difficult, difficult, difficult," he suddenly exclaimed, "[like trying] to scatter ten measures of sesame seed all over a tree!"

"Easy, easy, easy," returned Mrs. P'ang, "just like touching your feet to the ground when you get out of bed."

"Neither difficult nor easy," said Ling-chao. "On the hundred grass-tips, the Patriarchs' meaning."[199]

We witness both the family's training method and the lack of traditional Confucian boundaries as daughter challenges both her mother and her father's understanding of how realization unfolds through Buddhist practice.

Her father starts by asserting that realizing one's original nature is as difficult as putting sesame seeds back on the plant from which they'd come. Her mother answers that it is easy to find one's way, it occurs as naturally as finding the ground beneath your feet when you awaken in your bed. Lingzhao corrects, integrates, and expands both statements, asserting that the way to realize the Buddhist path is not defined by either difficult or easy, but depends on the correct view. Lingzhao teaches her parents that since we are surrounded by true realization, our awakening is dependent on seeing wisdom on each tip of grass. It is neither difficult nor easy, we just need to maintain the effort to keep returning to the practice, looking for the teaching fully manifest in every situation.

Lingzhao's nontraditional relationship with her father is also illustrated in an exchange where she playfully challenges his willingness to practice publicly. Her father has flouted convention in favor of acting out Zen mind, but when she does the same, he expresses a little embarrassment:

The Layman was once selling bamboo baskets. Coming down off a bridge he stumbled and fell. When Ling-chao saw this she ran to her father's side and threw herself down.

"What are you doing!" cried the Layman.

"I saw Papa fall to the ground, so I am helping," replied Ling-chao.

"Luckily no one was looking," remarked the Layman.[200]

In this Dharma play Lingzhao enacts the hapless tactics of all of us who remain stuck in the world of suffering. We see our loved one's suffering, and we quickly react by throwing ourselves into their situation at the same emotional level, bemoaning life's unfairness and trying to comfort them from the same perspective that is causing the problem. Rather than maintain our footing on stable ground, we plunge into the very view that created the problem in the first place. Buddhism teaches us to find our own way to clarity and stability even as we try to help another out of his/her mess. Lingzhao acts this teaching out playfully with her father, who hopes that no one has seen how far she has moved from conventional behavior.

Zen teaches that each disciple must surpass his/her teacher to express his/her own understanding and to validate the teacher's effectiveness. Lingzhao repeatedly does this with her father who is also her teacher. Her final trick on her father expresses the level of skill attained in her practice.

> The Layman was about to die. He spoke to Ling-chao, saying: "See how high the sun is, and report to me when it's noon."
>
> Ling-chao quickly reported: "The sun has already reached the zenith, and there's an eclipse."
>
> While the Layman went to the door to look out, Ling-chao seated herself in her father's chair, and, putting her palms together reverently, passed away.
>
> The Layman smiled and said: "My daughter has anticipated me."
>
> He postponed [his going] for seven days.[201]

Maybe the Layman was right, perhaps she did take her Zen teaching too far. While Lingzhao was able to express her spiritual accomplishment and manifest the deepest nonattachment to her body, one might wonder if her relationship to her father/teacher was entirely healthy. She chose to end her life through a final one-upsmanship with her father/teacher. We are left wondering about their relationship. Why didn't she choose to go on living and teaching without him, and why didn't she return home to her still living brother and mother?

Lingzhao is a fascinating example of spiritual accomplishment within a family context, at a time when women often did not have access to the opportunity to study or teach Buddhism.

Shenyi:
Basing Her Convent on Her Family

A particularly poignant family-based convent was established in eighteenth-century China by the nun Shenyi (d. 1722) and her female followers, a sister-in-law, Zaisheng, and a cousin, Jingwei. All three of the women were widowed. Shenyi was ordained after the culturally required year-long mourning period. Due to persecution based on her family's political affiliations, her family home was reduced to rubble and her father subsequently committed suicide. As an ordained nun she fled the chaos and built a hermitage on the banks of the river. Shortly thereafter she was joined by some members of her immediate family and her husband's family as well. When her father-in-law was arrested for treason, her mother-in-law drowned herself in the river. Shenyi retrieved her mother-in-law's body from the river to give her a proper burial ceremony. Later Shenyi was joined by her sister-in-law and her cousin, and then this attracted other practitioners.

The women set up a kind of a "family hermitage," initially opened to shelter family members whose mourning became Dharma practice, that was joined by non-family. Shenyi had a large number of disciples and left a discourse record, which was assembled by Jingwei. To get a sense of her style, consider the following poem Shenyi sent to her disciple Zaisheng:

> Human life consists of meetings and partings,
> In the end but froth and foam.
> Gazing back at the vast expanse, I am moved
> By thoughts of our past excursion.
> The morning dew had not yet dried, the
> Blossoms were plentiful and firm,
> The noon shade was about to settle, the songs
> Of the birds were hidden away.
> Inhaling the fragrance around the little bench,
> We were oblivious to the dusty world,
> Walking in the moonlight our pure talk swept
> Away all the old sorrows.

The slanting shadow of the plum blossom
Looked just like a painting;
Who will gather up the tattered blossoms
Strewn upon the ground?[202]

In this poem Shenyi expresses affection for nuns' shared intimacies. Family closeness, while impermanent, was enhanced by their pure intention to resolve their pain through Buddhist practice rather than through material security. Their close practice relationship provided the healing needed for the violence and loss they had all suffered. In the last lines Shenyi looks for an answer to the chaotic circumstances that had torn them from their families: Who will care for all these tattered blossoms strewn upon the ground? How can we develop the means to repair what war and loss have torn apart?

We can offer each other spiritual practice, but there is still the breakage, still the homeless ones. The convent system across Asia and throughout history has often taken up this task—providing shelter and care for the tattered, fallen blossoms, even those from our own family tree. The poem provides a contrast to the male Zen masters' family renunciation in its abundant inclusion of loving relationships, memories, and tender feelings as Zen teachings.

Shozan Genyo:
Finding Zen through Family Practice

One particularly talented imperial princess who became a nun, Shozan Genyo (1634–1727), studied Zen throughout her life alongside her father, Emperor Gomizuno'o, whom she persuaded to support the Chinese priest Ingen (Yinyuan Lungji) and the founding of the Obaku sect of Japanese Zen. She became ordained when her father died, when she was forty-seven years old, and converted the imperial villa Shugakuin into an imperial convent called Rinkyuji in 1682. Her life was dedicated to creating beautiful images of Kannon that can be found today in many Kyoto temples. Her death poem is inscribed on one of her self-portraits:

Old, but not yet decrepit,
Facing death is not difficult

Work accomplished, vows fulfilled,
My remaining years I entrust to fate.[203]

Although Genyo began her practice as part of the imperial family's activities, her death poem suggests that Zen affected her deeply. We sense a resolution of the meaning of her life and death. It is also clear that when she wrote the poem she still had some time left to live and practice; she was not yet "decrepit." Work done within this spirit of nonattachment has a particularly liberated quality.

Because of her devotion to the Lotus Sutra and its instructions for repetition and copying of the sutra as a means to enlightenment, Genyo completely devoted herself to chanting and producing images of the bodhisattva Kannon, which she dedicated to the salvation of her deceased parents. Brought to Buddhist practice through her family, she then fittingly expressed her practice through her devotion to her family.

Sangha as Family, Family as Sangha

Some nuns viewed their sangha as a surrogate family. As we saw in chapter 6, the Japanese abbess Hori Mitsujo Roshi referred to the young nuns under her care as her "children." Contemporary Soto nuns have also sheltered and raised orphans as part of their bodhisattva practice, and perhaps also as a way to enjoy child rearing while following the nun's vocation. I sensed this need when I visited the Soto nuns' convent in Nagoya in 1992 with a group of twelve American women who had come to practice Zen in Japan. Some of us were ordained, some were lay practitioners, but all of us had made a big commitment to Western Zen practice. The Soto nuns' first question for us was: "Could we Western women have children and still follow our vocation and commitment to Zen?"

While not having a husband and not living with her family of origin may be a significant sacrifice for a nun, not raising children may loom even larger in the female psyche. Male Zen priests in Japan may marry and raise children, but their family temples are supported by the almost slavish work of their temple wives. Married nuns could not find that counterpart—a supportive husband or helpmate—in current Japanese society. Instead of finding a husband who would help her manage the temple, a married nun would fear being bound by the Japanese wife's duties to serve her husband as well as her temple.

Despite the sacrifices, each year 70 percent of Japanese Soto Zen nuns vote in favor of maintaining a celibate and unmarried order, whether they miss having children or not. Nuns' activities include raising orphans, teaching children in temple schools, and being involved in naming the newborn babies of their congregation (a special tradition for nuns)— activities that perhaps reflect their need for a surrogate family.

Asian customs have not allowed for a married nun to fulfill the functions both of a dutiful wife and a temple priest. Unlike our new attempt at equality in Western relationships, where men and women share household duties and child care, the role of the "good" wife was strictly defined in terms of serving her husband and family. A practicing female Zen teacher would almost certainly not have had her husband's support when devoting herself to the temple. Dedicating herself to her sangha at the expense of caring for her husband would have been viewed as too radical a departure from the appropriate female role.

There were laywomen who attempted to practice within households, but they left no record of their experience. On the other hand, we can glean reflections about love and practice from the writings of female Zen masters who had been married. Through their writings we catch a glimpse of how their teaching may have been affected by their love for their husbands, or how personal love was viewed within a life dedicated to Zen practice.

Tachibana no Someko:
A Concubine's Awakening with Her Husband's Guidance

Tachibana no Someko (1667–1705) was a woman whose children's deaths left her depressed and without the will to live, and whose husband then encouraged her to practice Zen. She wrote a short autobiographical account of her Zen awakening titled (in translation) *Wastepaper Record*.[204] She is also credited with a commentary on the Mumonkan, "The Bird's False Cry," which has not yet been translated into English. She was the concubine—or consort—of the samurai lord Yanagisawa Yoshiasu (1658–1714), who served the shogun Tokugawa Tsunayoshi (r. 1680–1709). One version of how she came to serve Yoshiasu became part of a Japanese tel-

evision docudrama. Her father was a samurai who had lost his supporting clan, and her mother may have served Yoshiasu's family prior to her
birth. A rumor has also coupled her with the shogun Tsunayoshi who was
said to have visited her many times.

Someko had been raised in the Pure Land tradition to chant the name
Amida Butsu and read the scriptures, and converted to Zen practice after
the death of three of her four children. Yoshiasu found her musing on the
meaninglessness of life after her fourth child, a three-year-old daughter,
died. He gave her a poem to contemplate as an entry into Zen. He further
instructed her to stop chanting the name of the Buddha, to stop reading
the sutras, and to "enter straight into buddhahood with a single step."

When Someko expressed surprise that her husband had never introduced her to Zen practice before, her husband explained that previously
she had been "attached to worldly Dharma." He predicted that she was
now ready to seek the buddha of no form and suggested that she begin
studying the teaching of Bassui's Enzan Kanahogo.[205]

> If you intend to escape from the suffering of samsara, you
> must know the way to directly realize buddhahood. The way
> to realize buddhahood is to know your own mind. Your own
> mind is that which has not changed from before you existed
> and from before your parents were born, up to now. This is
> called the "original face" because it is the original nature of all
> sentient beings.[206]

Someko's husband discouraged her previous practice of dependence
on prayers promising divine intervention. After all, if the divine could
intervene, why couldn't it save her child? He offered her teachings that
pointed to her own ability to find peace, a method that would help her
realize the true nature of mind. When Someko protested to her husband
that she lacked the formal education for such practice, he quoted the wise
Chinese teacher Zen Master Dahui, who had pointed out that the written
word has been a hindrance to students of the Way.

Someko's husband, Yoshiasu, encouraged her practice and introduced
her to Zen Master Ungan of Ryukoji, from whom she received a koan:
"Shakyamuni and Maitreya are no more than his servants. Tell me, who
is he?"[207] During the course of her meditation on this koan she was

supported by the encouragement and teaching instructions of her husband. She said of her husband's support:

> Whenever the Lord General [Yoshiasu] left the Shogun's palace and had some time free from affairs of state he instructed me in a variety of ways, using both direct pointing and skillful means. The benefits I received from him—even if all the bamboo on the southern mountains were cut and made into writing brushes and all the waves of the western bays were made into a rushing torrent to moisten the inkstone, it would be impossible to describe even two or three parts out of a million of all the benefits I received from him.[208]

In this passage and elsewhere in *Wastepaper Record* Someko expressed admiration and gratitude for her husband's support—though we get no clear impression that she necessarily loved him in a way that transcended admiration and gratitude. Yet clearly, he was very fond of her; even while remaining her lord and master, as was the custom of the time, he offered her the benefits of spiritual companionship and guidance as a Dharma companion. He also preserved her writing.

Finally with the guidance of her husband and her teacher Ungan, Someko had an awakening. Of this she wrote:

> The Great Question that I have borne for so many years is now, all at once, completely crushed. The Original Face is just this. Truly, holding all the Buddhas of the three worlds in my two hands, we simultaneously look at each other and understand. In all the vexed and contorted words of the 1700 koans, there is not the tiniest point of true meaning that I do not understand. I return them as a great pile of wastepaper.[209]

Someko had reached the place where she was no longer constricted by her own thinking, questioning, or concepts about buddhahood. She directly experienced buddha-nature. Her understanding poured forth in the moment, and she felt freed of her need to read or study the ancients' words. Someko's awakening was verified by her teacher, who later gave her the Buddhist ordainee's robe, the *kesa*. Conferring the *kesa* was a creative way for Ungan Roshi to give Someko an ordination ceremony. Obviously, as a married and sexually active woman, she was not eligible for nun's ordination according to the official standards of Japanese Zen. Nonetheless this enlightened Zen master found a way to grant ordination to empower and nourish a woman's practice despite prevailing customs and opinions.

Her ordination and awakening are noteworthy for a laywoman; the record of her practice is unique. We learn from her that neither sexual relations, married status, nor lack of formal education need derail one's ability to realize buddha-nature.

Other women had to wait until their husbands' deaths to devote themselves to practice. We have already discussed several such women: Empress Komyo, Kakuzan Shido, and Manseong Sunim. Manseong was so devoted to her husband that the first request she made to a Zen teacher was for a meeting with her deceased husband through a séance.

While these women apparently had been closely coupled, and while they dedicated the merit of their temples to their deceased husbands,[210] it is only from the nun Rengetsu, whom we will meet in a later chapter, that we have Zen love poems written to a husband.

Satsu:
A Laywoman Who Became a Dharma Heir

Satsu (ca. 1700) was a teenager when her father introduced her to Zen master Hakuin.[211] Her father was concerned about her irreverent and unconventional behavior and hoped that Hakuin, a Zen master known as a man of the people, would provide guidance on controlling his willful daughter. The story starts with fifteen-year-old Satsu's parents instructing her to pray to Kannon, the bodhisattva of compassion, for help in attracting a husband. Satsu's father becomes concerned when he finds her sitting upon the Kannon sutra book. Satsu answers his rebuke for her disrespect with this: "The priest of Shoinji [Hakuin] says that everything has Buddha-nature, so how can there be a difference between my rear end and a sutra book?"[212] Hakuin found some merit in Satsu's statement and encouraged him to bring her to study with him. She proved to be quite a handful even for Hakuin, reportedly asking for an explanation and walking out as soon as he began to use words to answer. She was known for her direct approach and independent mind. When a monk who tried to bully her asked: "Within a rubbish heap a white rock is smashed. What is the principle of this?" Without a moment's hesitation, Satsu immediately smashed the monk's teacup to bits, and he beat a hasty retreat.[213]

Satsu began practicing Zen meditation fulltime at Hakuin's temple and refused to marry. Hakuin advised Satsu to take her practice off of the cushion—specifically, to marry and raise a family.

> You comprehend Zen well, but you need to put it into practice. It is best for you to marry, acting in accordance with the natural pairing of male and female. Spirit and form, enlightenment and actualization must be harmonized with the realities of everyday life.[214]

Hakuin repeatedly taught that enlightenment in action was more powerful than enlightenment in stillness—awakening needs to be taken off the cushion into everyday life to fully ripen.

Satsu eventually did marry, and went on to have children and many grandchildren. At the death of one of her grandchildren, she was witnessed weeping profusely by her neighbor. The neighbor, believing authentic enlightenment meant that Satsu should no longer experience such emotion, questioned Satsu's reaction:

> "I heard that you received a certificate of enlightenment from Hakuin himself, so why are you carrying on so?"
>
> "Idiot!" Satsu shot back. "My tears are a better memorial than a hundred priests chanting lugubriously. The tears commemorate every child that has died. That is exactly how I feel at this moment!"[215]

Satsu lived her life as her teacher instructed—fully engaged on the cushion and off the cushion as well. True to her teacher, she expressed heartfelt emotion appropriately in an emotional situation. She did not try to live up to someone else's ideals about how Zen should express or not express itself. True to herself, she offered the same ferocious answer as a grandmother that she was known for as a teenager. After years of training she still served a slap, but she also offered a teaching along with it.

While practice may transform our experience, we retain our individuality. Satsu, an example of an awakened lay woman, is an inspiring example of Zen practice alive and well in family life.

Teishin:
A Nun Who Loved Her Teacher

Teishin (1798–1872) was born the daughter of a samurai in the town of Nagaoka. She was married around the age of eighteen. Within a few years, when she was widowed, she decided to become a Buddhist nun. Traveling around begging for food, she heard that the Zen monk Ryokan (1758–1831), known for his simple but authentic practice, lived nearby. Teishin stopped by his hut for coaching with her poetry writing, and soon became romantically enamored of him as well as drawn to his Zen teaching. She formally applied to become his disciple in 1826. When they met she was twenty-nine years old and he was seventy.

Ryokan offered her training in Zen and in writing poetry. Their remarkable relationship was preserved in poetry that expressed the deep, romantic, and emotional love between them. Teishin collected and published Ryokan's poetry as *Dewdrops on a Lotus Leaf.* Many of their poems have been translated into English in multiple versions. Consider this poem, written from Teishin to Ryokan after their first meeting:

> Wondering if it's a dream,
> I'm filled with joy,
> Never awaken me, if it's a dream.
> Leave me, please, in this joy forever.[216]

Teishin is clearly infatuated with her teacher. She refers to the dreamlike quality of emotional attachments, but wishes to continue experiencing this amazing and joyous fulfillment. While we usually ask our Zen teacher to help us wake up from our delusions, Teishin's request is more complicated. She is asking that, even if their relationship and the joy she has experienced is delusional, he allow this attachment to continue and that their relationship continue to extend into the personal realm of love and affection.

Ryokan answers her request by putting their relationship in the context of eternity. Zen masters teach us to see arising phenomena within the context of impermanence and to see also that which is unarising and unceasing. Ryokan gave Teishin instructions: Do not see this love from a dualistic, personalized perspective; instead let it be, let it float in the vast and eternal space of awareness. In other words, let love exist without clinging to it. Ryokan replies,

> Slumbering in the dream land,
> Talking about the dream.
> Why not float our dream
> On the stream of eternity.[217]

Their relationship, though believed by scholars to be nonsexual, was correctly perceived by others to be a love affair. At one point, when Ryokan asks Teishin why she hasn't come to visit him, she answers:

> Disturbed
> By rootless rumor,
> I am imprisoned
> Against the desire of my heart.[218]

Teishin knows she is in love but struggles with the nuns' vows and propriety. While (presumably) she does not have sex with her teacher, she knows that she loves him emotionally, not just in a spiritual sense.

Ryokan's poem in answer to her conflict stresses the ultimate purity that will illuminate them both if her practice deepens.

> So pure is the light of the moon,
> It shines out all of the earth.[219]

Ryokan clarifies his instruction to Teishin in this way: "Falsehood and truth, darkness and light, will become clear when the thin clouds over the peaks disappear."[220] In other words, whatever wisps of delusions are troubling you will be cleared away when you break through to the moon of enlightenment in your meditation practice.

Teishin takes his instructions to heart and responds with a poem of her awakening:

Darkness as well as light has gone,
Only the bright moon
At dawn![221]

Teishin apparently freed herself of doubts and worry about gossip and propriety. Squarely facing her truest intention, she broke through and found her freedom. Through her meditation and practice as a nun, her life became illuminated. It became clear to her that their relationship was about transcendence and that, in spite of gossip or judgments by others, she needed to follow her own experience. After this poem and the realization she expressed, she resumed visiting the teacher she loved.

Ryokan continued to encourage her practice and her love for him. He reminded her to never forget her vows to the Buddha, and she assured him that she would not. As they continued to stay together in his hut and exchange poetry, the nature and boundary of their relationship was clarified. When she suggested that he take her with him on a trip, he teased that they would be called lovebirds. She answered that they were just what they were, so what could be wrong with that? Her confidence in her practice strengthened; she no longer seemed bothered by potential gossip.

When Ryokan was nearing death, Teishin came to stay by his bedside. Her poem to him revealed her struggle to accept her deeply felt loss within the Buddhist context.

We monastics are said
To overcome the realm
Of life and death—
Yet I cannot bear the
Sorrow of our parting.[222]

This poem of Teishin's from the time of Ryokan's terminal illness expresses her human vulnerability and her emotional struggle as practice. Understanding that practice transcends life, death, and personal loss, she remains true to her human feelings. It cannot be helped; the heart will open and then break, the tears will fall, and the practice will continue. Teishin does not claim to have "mastered" her human emotions; feelings arise and she surrenders to them as the scenery of oneness. She is humbled by life's ebb and flow, by its beauty and its loss. In the ocean of life, she is completely drenched and yet not submerged. Teishin expresses no pride in monastic accomplishment, just acceptance of what is.

Deep acceptance of human vulnerability is another side of Zen wisdom—a wisdom that does not exclude human love. Ryokan's teachings illustrate that love is not entirely absent from the teachings of the male Zen masters. But love is loud and clear in the teachings of Zen's female ancestors. Accepting love and also accepting our undoing when losing love, we truly transcend the sufferings of birth and death. We transcend because life and death, and love and loss, are thoroughly accepted, not because we have avoided feelings or loving relationships. Teishin expressed feelings and transcended them through her accepting perspective. This is a great teaching that illustrates how to practice Zen and honor our loving relationships—an essential teaching for Westerners who, for the most part, practice within committed relationships and families.

Gyokusen Kogai and Nantembo

Resembling the linked poetry created by Teishin and Ryokan is the art of the nun Gyokusen Kogai (1853–1928) created in the style of her teacher Nakahara Nantembo (1839–1925). It is interesting to compare Gyokusen's work to Nantembo's. While they share the theme of *rempatsu* (monks or nuns on their begging rounds), we see that in her paintings Gyokusen pays more attention to the details of monks' and nuns' robes. When I found this art in a Kyoto shop, the art dealer acknowledged that Gyokusen Kogai was Nantembo's disciple, but he intimated that she was "maybe his girlfriend," using the English word and tilting his head as if to imply the two were more than "maybe" lovers. Was their close relationship subject to rumors, as in the case of Teishin and Ryokan, or were they known to have a romantic relationship? We cannot know. Like other nuns, Gyokusen did not write her own Zen words on her paintings, but had them inscribed by her teacher or left them blank.

The Complicated Matter of Loving the Teacher

What do we make of the emotional involvement of Ryokan and Teishin, or more broadly of a disciple's involvement with a teacher? Clearly, this is a tricky business, given the many wrenching stories and scandals in contemporary Western Zen centers. A number of Western women have fallen in love and have had sexual affairs with their teachers, resulting in the downfall of several Zen centers and the suffering of many sangha members, and often the teacher and his lover.

But as for this couple, Ryokan lived outside of a monastery, and perhaps Teishin was Ryokan's only student, removing the complication of other sangha members' jealousy. It seems likely that Ryokan's own emotional needs were being met by Teishin's adoration, but he seems to have maintained integrity around sexual boundaries. To Ryokan's credit, we believe there was not a series of devoted and loving female students—just Teishin. Teishin's love and emotional involvement with Ryokan helped her to deepen her understanding. And indeed he encouraged her to keep her vows and to deepen her practice. Perhaps Teishin's attachment and devotion to Ryokan limited her interest in studying with other teachers or her ability to rely on her own understanding. On the other hand, the quality and the depth of the teaching she received from him was evidently profound, and did in fact guide her toward a deeper understanding. The beauty and clarity of her poetry seems to cut to the deepest heart of this matter, showing that even persistent and very personal delusions can be transformed into deeper awareness. Teishin seemed to have an enlightenment experience while struggling with the meaning of their attachment. It would seem that neither of them was aware of the subtle dynamics that might have resulted in Teishin feeling forever dependent and inferior to her teacher.

Yet harm may have been done to Teishin's practice even as it deepened. Currently we understand through institutional experience and psychological expertise that there can be a shadow side to overly attached spiritual relationships. It is now considered wise to train Buddhist teachers about how their own emotional needs can affect their students' training. For women who may mistake the meaning of Teishin and Ryokan's love as justification for a love affair with a teacher—look again more deeply. There was no sex involved, there was no marriage being compromised, and there were no sangha dynamics to sort out around the teacher's personal love for this one student. The blurry boundary between spiritual oneness and an emotional connection, and the damaging dynamic of romantically intimate teacher-student relationships in contemporary Western Zen practice, will be further discussed in the final section of this book.

Nuns and Sexuality 9

The Buddha's Teaching on Sexuality

THE BUDDHA TAUGHT laypeople about how to have successful sexual and familial relationships, but as we have already seen, he taught his monks to avoid all contact with women. He taught monks one way, and laypeople another, but his monks mostly recorded his teaching to the ordained. More specifically, he instructed his monks to avoid at all costs the impurity of sexual intercourse. The purpose of this chapter is first to examine some Buddhist teachings on the importance of avoiding intercourse, and then to meet non-celibate female practitioners and explore their implicit and explicit teachings on sexuality.

Regarding the Buddha's—or the early Buddhists'—proscription on the impurity of sexual intercourse, we cannot say definitively whether the Buddha made these statements, but these words were attributed to him and remain part of the Buddhist canon even today. According to the Buddhist scriptures, the Buddha advised his monks to abstain from the "vulgar practice of sexual intercourse,"[223] in order to abide in purity. In the story that follows, the vehemence with which the need to abstain from sexual intercourse is expressed may shock our modern sensibilities.

Sudinna, previously a married man, had lapsed in his practice of celibacy and confessed this fact to the Buddha. Sudinna had engaged in sex, to impregnate his ex-wife to assuage her grief over her loss of her husband (himself) to the Buddhist order. Sudinna tried to emphasize the selflessness of this sexual act with his ex-wife and his sense of repulsion toward her; his sense of family duty conflicted with the Buddha's command that he sever ties to his family. The Buddha rebuked Sudinna over this defeat, this failure in his practice.

> It would have been better, confused man, had you put your male organ inside the mouth of a terrible poisonous snake than inside the vagina of a woman. It would have been better, confused man, had you put your male organ inside the mouth of a black snake than inside the vagina of a woman. It would have been better, confused man, had you put your male organ inside a blazing hot charcoal pit than inside the vagina of a woman.[224]

Thus, it seems that according to the Buddha (or later Buddhist editorial additions) a woman's vagina and sexual intercourse are more dangerous to a monk's practice than the harm caused by a poisonous snake or a burning charcoal pit. While it is not so hard to understand the Buddha's warning against sexual pursuits, this admonition carries quite a charge. Far from manifesting a cool, dispassionate, and mindful approach, the Buddha's admonition sounds almost hysterical.

In discussing this passage at various Buddhist centers, conflicting responses have arisen about how to make sense of these words attributed to the Buddha. Four distinctive positions have emerged and were presented in chapter 1. To summarize, we may believe the Buddha's words are beyond reproach; we may believe that the scriptures recorded were not the Buddha's words but still are beyond reproach; we may believe that the scriptures, rewritten later, include questionable material; or we may hold the Buddha responsible for these remarks as a human being who still struggled with karma and his own reactivity.

Clearly our response to these issues and other issues surfacing in the Buddhist canon depends on whether we see the Buddha as a manifestation of perfect realization or as a human being, and whether we take the Buddhist sutras at their word or see them as writings that have weathered many edits. The Buddha himself suggested (in the Kalama Sutta) that we would do well not to just accept what is taught, but to examine and experiment with teachings to see whether following them brought wholesome results.

If, in our evolving Western Buddhism, we subscribe to either of the first two positions, we will follow only what is written. But if we consider the scriptures from the last two possibilities, that these sutras contain negative or unwholesome material worthy of investigation—whether spoken by the Buddha or not—we may analyze these views on sexuality from a contemporary psychological perspective. We could argue that the vehemence of the Buddha's response to Sudinna indicates that either the Buddha or Buddhist followers had, in today's language, some "issues" with women and sexuality.

If these words were extrapolated from the Buddha's teachings, we might see him as a man who was passionate about spiritual practice and fearful about the power of women and sexuality to subvert his followers. If these were the Buddha's actual words, we might also analyze them from a psychological perspective. We might consider that the Buddha's possibly oversexed early life may have led to a sexual addiction, and recovery from this addiction may have given birth to a vehement and puritanical approach to the dangers of sexuality.

Remember that the Buddha's father, upon hearing the prophecy that the Buddha would be either a great worldly leader or a great spiritual leader, greatly preferred that his son stay in the worldly realm and succeed his rule. One method he may have used to tie the Buddha to his family's wealth and privilege was supplying him with his own private pleasure room and his own harem of concubines. It seems that the Buddha had such a pleasure room and a harem as well as two wives. It would almost seem that his parents knew about the power of sexual pleasures and perhaps even the dynamics of sexual addiction, and how hard it would be for the Buddha to give up palace life and entirely abstain from sexuality (after such excessive indulgences) in order to practice an ascetic and spiritual life.

Viewing the Buddha as a human being, as someone subject to the psychological forces that all human beings endure, may help us to understand the urgency with which he cast off his sexual longing and advocated his distorted view of women as sexual objects. He saw women through his own early experiences—those of a prince surrounded by women hired to seduce him.

Unfortunately, the demonization of sexuality—and specifically a woman's genitalia—became embedded in the early Buddhist teachings. If we combine the stereotype of a woman's "ensnaring" ways with the purportedly horrific effects of her vagina, she appears to be a formidable demon indeed. Western Buddhist practitioners need to find a way to examine and clarify these women- and vagina-hating sections of the Buddhist canon. We will see how one Chinese nun, Miaozong, acknowledged, embodied, and challenged this traditional Buddhism's demonization of the vagina.

According to later records the Buddha taught that even while living a non-celibate life, his followers (both male and female) could become accomplished in his methods of awakening.²²⁵ But neither he nor his male followers sufficiently elaborated on the practices that may facilitate awakening under these conditions. Zen Buddhist practice has been developed by ancestors living in monasteries following (or claiming to follow) the Buddha's requirements for home leaving and celibacy.

As mentioned previously, nuns often came to practice after being widowed or, if they had suffered the death of children, even while being married. For this reason nuns, more than monks, practiced Zen having already had a long experience of lay life, often as married. Their practice therefore is one that combines the Buddha's teachings for nuns with his teachings for laypersons. This section explores how female practitioners experienced and taught awakening in the midst of sexuality, and it addresses the all-pervading buddha-nature, the inherent purity, of the vagina and sexuality through the teachings of female Zen ancestors.

Including Sexuality within the Realm of Zen

Miaozong Vindicates the Vagina

Miaozong's (1095–1170) bold behavior and quick wit have endeared her to practitioners from her own era through contemporary Western Zen. From Sung and Ming dynasty China through Kamakura Japan, she has been venerated by nuns who learned of her encounter with Wanan, the head monk at Dahui's monastery. In her most famous teaching encounter she vindicates the vagina: she extracts it from the Buddha's "blazing hot charcoal pit" and "mouth of a poisonous black snake" and transforms it into the passageway and birthplace of all Buddhas and practitioners. We can appreciate Miaozong's originality when we learn a little of her life circumstances— her training as a daughter and wife of an upper-class family.

Born to an educated and politically successful family, the young Miao-zong had a natural awakening as a teenager. While quietly contemplating the "Great Matter," the meaning of human life destined to death, she had a profound insight. She had no idea that her experience was out of the ordinary; she just assumed that her understanding was universally known.

Miaozong's famous encounter with Wanan, wherein she "vindicates the vagina," was first discovered and translated by Miriam Levering; subsequently Ding-hwa Evelyn Hsieh suggested that Miaozong's elder sister-in-law, the nun Zhidong (d. 1124), may have helped her get acquainted with Zen studies.[226] Zhidong, discussed in the next chapter, had been married but returned home to request permission to become ordained. When Zhidong's father refused to allow her to enter the nun's order, she practiced Zen at home. After Zhidong's parents died, she traveled and met many Zen masters. She experienced enlightenment with a Linji master and was well respected for her understanding by Yuanwu. She was eventually ordained as the nun Weiju and attracted many followers. Zhidong's success may have helped Miaozong's family appreciate the benefits of Zen practice for a woman—benefits to be enjoyed later in life.

Miaozong studied with various Zen masters while young. On an early foray into Zen she met with Master Yuan for a Zen interview.

[Master] Yuan said: "A well-brought-up [privileged] lady from a wealthy family, how can you be prepared for the business of a great [male] hero?"

Miaozong replied: "Does the buddhadharma distinguish between male and female forms?"

Yuan questioned her further. He said: "What is the Buddha? This mind is the Buddha. What about you?"

Miaozong replied: "I've heard of you for a long time. I'm disappointed to find that you still say that kind of thing."[227]

Without much formal Zen instruction, she was ready to rumble, to challenge authority. "How dare you say that buddhadharma discriminates worthy and unworthy among male and female practitioners?" Miaozong had, without doubt, previously encountered the patriarchal attitude Yuan expressed so concisely, and her answer was immediate. She puts herself squarely in the tradition of Mahapajapati, who was admitted to the Buddhist order after Ananda skillfully asked the Buddha, "Can women attain enlightenment or not?" Miaozong's question, "Does the Buddhadharma distinguish between male and female forms?" suggests she had an intimate understanding of Buddhism and knew of the Buddha's (implicit) response to Ananda that women could equally attain enlightenment. Buddhadharma and enlightenment are blind to gender.

Besides referring to early Buddhist teaching, Miaozong's answer challenges Master Yuan's understanding. "What is it that discriminates based on outward appearances? What kind of Buddhism is that? And by the way, what kind of understanding do you have?" Her response is also reminiscent of the well-known earlier exchange between the preeminent Zen patriarch Huineng (638–713) and his teacher the fifth ancestor of Zen in China, Hongren (601–74). When the fifth ancestor asked how an uncivilized man of southern China came to study Zen, Huineng responded, "As far as people are concerned there are north and south, but how could that apply to the buddha-nature?"[228] Miaozong's answer expressed clear understanding and emerged in her own voice: "As far as people are concerned, there are men and women, but what does that have to do with buddha-nature?"

Rebuking Master Yuan, she invited him back to this moment: "With all of your renown, you still can't rely on your own words! What a disappointment to hear you, a reputable teacher, using stock Zen phrases in real-life discussions!" In a Zen encounter, she insisted, you need to stand on your own truth. What does someone else's expression have to do with our discussion? What about right here, right now, you and me? Despite being early in her Zen training, Miaozong answered Yuan's question appropriately, using the right words and the correct understanding. She directly engaged his delusions. However, her encounters with misogynistic attitudes didn't end because her understanding was clear; indeed, her encounters with negative attitudes toward female Zen students continued under other circumstances. She must have encountered disapproval repeatedly as she disobeyed the Chinese customs of her day, which recommended secluding females behind a wall in the women's quarters. Most likely both men and women criticized her unusual and unwomanly pursuit of Zen training. Miaozong's opportunity to seek the Dharma later at Dahui's monastery may have come as a result of being widowed;

otherwise it is hard to imagine a woman of Miaozong's era and social class functioning independently as she did in her Zen studies with Dahui at his male monastery.

Miaozong, married to a bureaucrat, had the opportunity to travel and attend Zen lectures with her husband; this is how she first met Dahui, the teacher from whom she eventually received Dharma transmission. First encountering Dahui at a public talk, she walked up to him, bowed silently, turned away, and left.

Dahui said to the monk with him, "That woman, who just came, she has seen something. But she has not yet encountered the hammer and tongs, the forge and bellows of a real master. She is just like a thousand-ton ship in a closed-off harbor—she still cannot move." The monk said, "How can you say that so easily?" Dahui replied, "If she turns her head back this way, I will have to make a finer discrimination."[229]

Dahui recognized and acknowledged Miaozong's spiritual potential and expected to verify his intuition through another meeting. After his Dharma talk, Miaozong returned to meet Dahui, and he gave her the name Wuzhuo—"No Attachment"—ironic and perhaps fitting for a married woman struggling with the conventional attachments of her day to pursue Zen practice. The naming occasioned the beginning of their teacher-student relationship.

In the Zen tradition, studying in close proximity to a teacher is essential; at that time, access to a teacher's mind and guidance occurred through residential life in convents or monasteries. Women could sometimes attend public lectures and ceremonies, but they were not allowed to stay in (all-male) monasteries after dark; they were allowed entrance only for formal occasions. Miaozong had found a teacher, but her teacher headed a monastery that didn't permit her residence.

Zen monastic life meant living in tight quarters, up close and personal. In fact, the monks might use the meditation hall for dormitory-style sleeping quarters. In Zen style, sitting meditation and sleep occurred in the same space. The abbot had separate quarters where monks might come for private instruction, as Dogen recounted regarding his teacher Rujing.[230] The abbot's quarters might include guest rooms, and this is where Miaozong was housed. She neither disturbed the monk's dormitory, nor was she subject to the rough-and-tumble lack of privacy the men endured. Putting aside the monastic rules forbidding women's entrance, her residing in the abbot's quarters made sense, but Dahui's head monk still didn't approve.

Miaozong is most commonly remembered for the unabashed way she defended her right to practice with her teacher, and her refusal to accept the Buddhist view of woman as temptress. The head monk, Wanan, leader of the temple's monastic practices,[231] repeatedly questioned Miaozong's womanly presence within the monastic setting. Wanan's objection fit the charter of his position. He questioned Dahui: Why are you breaking the monastic rules? As senior monk he had distinguished himself at the monastery, and he was appropriately setting standards for other monks. To say that Wanan, unlike the enlightened teacher Dahui, had a bad attitude toward women practicing Zen would be superficial and miss some of his legitimate points. Miaozong's stay in the temple was against monastic rules, and Dahui's own teacher, Yuanwu, the famous compiler of the Zen classic Blue Cliff Record, had not just broken these rules by training women in Zen (he had at least three female Dharma heirs), he had also taken lovers at his temple.[232] Let's hope that the students and the lovers were not one and the same. We have no records clarifying these relationships, but we do have one of Yuanwu's love poems. Wanan most likely knew, at the time he confronted Miaozong and Dahui, the murmurings regarding Yuanwu's amorous private life. Yuanwu's private life was saved for the record centuries later, and referred to in the writings of Ikkyu Sojun (1394–1481). Ikkyu was publicly quite the ladies' man himself, and had a great admiration for Yuanwu and his Zen teachings as well as their shared human foibles.[233] What we know centuries later about Yuanwu and his amorous adventures is Yuanwu's concise and graphic response to his lover, suggesting a tryst at Yuanwu's temple after a long separation.

Thirty years ago we were of one heart,
Single-mindedly spending the nights in elegant dalliance.
Since then I've turned old and useless;
Yours too wide, mine too weak![234]

Here Yuanwu first acknowledges the delightful sex shared thirty years earlier. He quickly adds the sad but true physiological facts in his own blunt and poetic way. He suggests that age has taken away the keen edge of sexual pleasure they used to share. He confesses that, alas, his male member is limp, and he guesses that his partner's genitals must now be flaccid too.

Yuanwu's sexual dalliances were not just limited to his youth. His poem suggests a long life of sexuality at various ages with many partners also of various ages. Given Yuanwu's behavior, perhaps Wanan had good reason to suspect that Dahui might be following his teacher's example, having a sexual affair with a woman at his temple. If sexuality was the basis of Dahui's relationship with Miaozong, the head monk deserved to know. Wanan persisted in questioning Miaozong's presence at the monastery, and finally Dahui suggested that Wanan visit Miaozong and interview her himself. The following passage, discovered by Miriam Levering under the record of Wanan, describes his interview with Miaozong and what led up to it.

> [Wanan] relied on Dahui, and served as his Senior Monk (the head monk of the Sangha Hall in which the monks in Chan training lived and studied) at Dahui's monastery on Ching-shan.
>
> Before Wuzhuo [i.e., Miaozong] had become a nun Dahui lodged her in the abbot's quarters. The head monk Wanan always made disapproving noises. Dahui said to him, "Even though she is a woman, she has strengths." Wanan still did not approve. Dahui then insisted that he should interview her. Wanan reluctantly sent a message that he would go.
>
> Wuzhuo said, "Will you make it a Dharma interview or a worldly interview?"
>
> The head monk replied: "A Dharma interview."
>
> Wuzhuo said: "Then let your attendants depart." [She went in first, and then called to him,] "Please come in."
>
> When he came past the curtain he saw Wuzhuo lying face upward on the bed without anything on at all. He pointed at her [genitals] and said, "What kind of place is this?"
>
> Wuzhuo replied: "All of the buddhas of the three worlds and the six patriarchs and all the great monks everywhere—they all come out from within this."
>
> Wanan said: "And would you let me enter, or not?"
>
> Wuzhuo replied: "It allows horses to cross; it does not allow asses to cross."

Wanan said nothing, and Wuzhuo declared: "The interview with the Senior Monk is ended." She then turned over and faced the inside.

Wanan became embarrassed and left.

Dahui said, "It is certainly not the case that the old beast does not have any insight." Wanan was ashamed.[235]

Miaozong had received a message through monastery channels that Wanan would be coming to conduct an interview. Before he could open his mouth, she stripped naked to encounter him. What was that about? Miaozong was a sexually experienced woman when this encounter took place. She must have sensed Wanan's critical attitude about her, his suspicions about her role as a seductress in the celibate Zen monastery. She chose to confront the attitude directly—after all, her right to practice was at stake, and perhaps other women's as well. How many enlightened Zen masters in her day would allow women to train in their monasteries? Perhaps only this one—Dahui. She may have taken on this exchange as her spiritual life-or-death struggle on behalf of herself and women to come. Faithful to her teacher's spirit, she held nothing back—in true Zen Dharma combat style.

In this encounter Miaozong suspected that Wanan was coming to challenge her presence. His arriving with attendants broadcast his need for formality, his need for a witnessed meeting. The Buddha had long ago established that monks were never to be alone in a woman's room. The need for the chaperones was obvious on that count. Attendants also signaled their status.

Miaozong, a master of strategy, taking control of the meeting before it even started, asked, "Will you make this a Dharma interview or a worldly interview?" When Wanan asserted this was to be a Dharma interview, Miaozong suggested he dismiss his attendants, and that she would dismiss hers too. Her request, consistent with understanding that communicating Dharma is intimate, required that he engage directly and remove all conventional armor and status symbols. Without attendants or position, the Dharma flows unimpeded by baggage.

Miaozong's call for a clarification of purpose—Dharma or worldly—is the Dharmic version of a duel. Choose your weapons and proceed at your own risk. A Dharma interview is no ordinary discussion. Everyday conventions of politeness, propriety, and half-truths are thrown out the window. A Dharma interview's sole purpose is to make clear the whole truth, in this very moment, through the most direct, pertinent, and simple expression possible. Ultimate truth and this particular moment appear in one seamless response. Cut to the chase: no need to talk about the weather, make chitchat, or engage in conversational ploys assuring the other person that we like them.

Miaozong saved Wanan the time and trouble of stating the problem that he had with her presence at the monastery. She presented the problem as directly as possible by exposing her utterly naked body, in spread-eagle fashion. Without speaking a single word she said: "It's this isn't it, it's my actual female body right here in your male monastery. Isn't that the heart of your objection? I give you my arms, legs, belly, breasts, and my vagina. Nothing is hidden, nothing is wrapped in conventions or clothing. How do you wish to engage the problematic existence of these female body parts in your monastery? What about this body will you point to, which part is the direct cause of your disapproval?" Wanan, to his credit, did not faint or back down at the outrageously unconventional behavior of this well-bred lady from a respectable family. Her behavior went way beyond the conventions of Sung dynasty China, which sequestered women behind walls. Even worse, her behavior was in direct opposition to the explicit Buddhist rules against a woman being alone with a monk in monastery. Being naked with a monk in her room even goes way beyond our own liberated and sometimes far-fetched twenty-first-century student responses in Dharma interviews. Unless a student is interested in seducing her teacher, who among us has awakened so fully that exposure of our naked body is no problem?

This may have been the first time in his adult life that the celibate monk Wanan was in the presence of a nude woman. Wanan held his own by asking, "What kind of a place is this?" while pointing to her genitals. He got right to the point, and we can imagine his unspoken words: "What the hell do you think you're doing with that thing, missy, here in this monastery? Of everything you have shown me, what is the meaning of that particular place, your sex organs? Why do you bring that thing, that place, into our monastic setting? How will you make sense of that place in Zen practice?"

Aha! Now Wanan has clarified his disapproval; he has directly pointed to the problem between himself and Miaozong. The problem is the fleshy entryway between her legs. Miaozong made it easy for him to choose the exact problem. Quickly and silently she processed the nature of his objection to her participation in the monastery: "Oh, it's this, my female sexuality, right here in my body. This is the crux of your problem! I brought my female sex organs right into your holy monastery! This isn't about my personality, my physical appearance, my ability, or my marital status, is it? Hey you, enlightened head monk, it's this little place, my vagina, which is bothering you and your deep understanding of the Buddhadharma."

What an accomplishment. Everything is now out in the open. Without missing a beat, without repressing, bemoaning, or defending Wanan's disapproval, without rationalizing or apologizing for any inconvenience or hardship her vagina had caused by accompanying her inside the monastery, without acting out hurt feelings or imagining what the problem was, the issue could now be addressed with Zen mind.

Both participants were openly and honestly showing themselves. We can guess that by this point in her Zen career Miaozong was tired of explaining or defending her right to practice, tired of saying that the Buddhadharma has nothing to do with male or female, tired of worrying about disturbing the holy male monk's composure with her female appearance, and tired of arguing about the necessity of bringing her female genitalia into the male monastery.

Right then, out loud, Miaozong answered Wanan and the entire Buddhist history that condemns women and their vaginas as sexual traps for aspiring monks: "This is the place through which all buddhas and patriarchs and all monks everywhere come out." We hear her unstated meaning: "Hey monk, if you have a problem with my vagina, tell me where will you get the buddhas and monks you need for your beloved Zen practice? This female place right here, this is the source of your entire Zen lineage and all of your practice, so now tell me where's the problem? Why is the source of all buddhas, including yourself, something to be kept outside of the Buddhist monastery? In the Zen practice of nondiscrimination, why is this particular little place such a big unholy problem?"

Miaozong demonstrated and taught Wanan that freedom from attachment is found in squarely facing its pull, without repudiating longing and without embracing it. This is why she did not beat around the bush; she presented it directly. Let's not talk about it, let's face up to it right here and now. As Dongshan said, "Turning away and touching are both wrong, for it is like a massive fire."[236] Let's embody the problem of human desire and simultaneously transcend it by neither acting out our desire nor condemning it.

Now, it's important to note that Wanan was not a ladies' man, but we surmise that he appeared to have some lively interest in the outcome of this encounter. For a celibate monk, irritated with the presence of a woman in his holy Zen monastery, it didn't take long for him to express a somewhat primitive interest in the function of Miaozong's particular entryway. He voiced the question: "And would you let me enter (this place) or not?" Well, at least he wasn't a prude.

Wanan asked that Miaozong clarify her intention: "Since you are naked, Ms. No Attachment to Propriety, is it your intention to have sex with me or not? What is your meaning, the extent of your nonattachment? Since you are willing to show it, will you also share it in the usual way with me, right here and right now?" Again, the monk Wanan is to be credited for bringing the situation back to the here and now. Perhaps Wanan had forgotten, in the excitement of the moment, that this was to be a Dharma interview, not a worldly one? Or was he truly testing Miaozong's nonduality, her ability to put it out there but not engage it in the conventional sense?

Miaozong's next answer turned Zen tradition on its ear one more time by both using and reversing an expression of the great Zen master Zhaozhou (778–897). Zhaozhou, in referring to his own ability as a bridge to enlightenment, once answered a challenging smart aleck who was referring to him as the "Great Bridge of Zhaozhou." The smart aleck questioned the greatness of the bridge, and Zhaozhou responded: "Horses can pass over (this great bridge of Zhaozhou) and asses can too."[237] Zhaozhou meant that his teaching was strong enough to carry even an ass, like the smart aleck, across to enlightenment. In her reference to the wisdom of Zhaozhou, Miaozong answered by recreating Zhaozhou's wise remark to fit her present occasion. Regarding the gate Wanan asked about entering, she replied: "Horses cross, asses don't."

Miaozong and Zhaozhou showed their teaching skill as they both reflected the small minds of inquiring monks in their own mirror mind. Zhaozhou helped the smart aleck see himself reflected in the unruffled great teacher's eyes; Miaozong helped Wanan see his deluded attitude toward her vagina. With a judicious and recognizable Zen reference, which she altered instantaneously to fit her own circumstances, Miaozong asked Wanan to consider his view and its consequences. The account of their interview, written by Wanan himself, described his exiting the interview with a red face. Miaozong helped this head monk to reflect on his attitudes. Perhaps he had learned how to enter each situation with humility and an open mind—a good lesson for each of us. Beata Grant observes that in Ming dynasty China abbesses quoted Miaozong and considered themselves part of her (female) lineage even though they were not her direct Dharma descendants;[238] and in fourteenth-century Japan women of Tokeiji temple studied the words that Miaozong exchanged with Wanan as a koan in formal meditation practice.

When Miaozong referred to her genitals as the place where "all of the buddhas of the three worlds and the six patriarchs and all the great monks everywhere...come out from," she was also integrating another level of wisdom about temple geomancy—the science of orienting buildings in harmony with the universe. The monastery buildings are laid out in the shape of a human body; designed thus, the temple itself becomes the communal body for the monks.

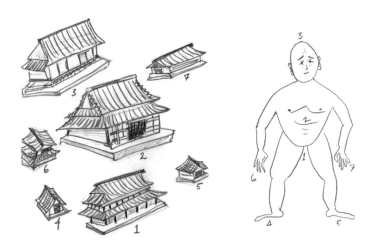

The seven main buildings of the temple are:
1. The Mountain Gate, main temple gate or entrance; 2. The Buddha Hall;
3. The Dharma Hall; 4. The Toilets; 5. The Bathhouse; 6. The Monks' Hall;
7. The Kitchen   Credit: Peter Schireson[239]

The arrangement of the Chinese Zen temple buildings was established in Tang dynasty China and was later copied in Japanese temples. The architecture incorporated seven monastic buildings in the shape of a human body. While we might imagine that the design would arrange the buildings according to human functionality, that is not the case. For example, the latrine is not associated with the anus or urinary tract; instead it forms the right foot of the human body. We might correctly predict that the head of the body is the Dharma hall, where the teachings are discussed. The genital area is represented as the Mountain Gate, the first building.

Therefore, the main temple entrance is in actuality the place through which "all of the buddhas of the three worlds and the six patriarchs and all the great monks everywhere…come." In order to practice, all monks must enter the path, must find their entrance to systematic investigation within a community of monks or nuns. All monks and nuns enter the temple through this Mountain Gate. Often there are maxims inscribed on the Mountain Gate to alert entering students of the seriousness of their entry into the practice place. Traditionally, passing through the Mountain Gate meant releasing the hold of both desires and conceptual thinking. Furthermore, I learned that my teacher in Japan, Fukushima Keido Roshi of Tofukuji, was in Dahui's lineage. If Miaozong had not persisted at entering and succeeding at Dahui's temple, I wonder if I would have been allowed to stay in the abbot's quarters at Tofukuji?

In order to be born and in order to practice at a monastery, one must pass through this communal body part, the genitals/Mountain Gate. A monk or nun must squarely face human desire and must pass directly through. We cannot enter monastic practice by avoiding this place. There is no other entrance to practice; we must acknowledge our relationship to this place of human desire and human connectedness. Realization—the understanding that entering the gate to the temple requires resolving, not avoiding, one's relationship to sexuality—manifests as the continued unfolding of the Buddha's teaching.

Kim Ilyop:
A Bold Korean Nun

As modernity dawned in colonial Korea, during the Japanese occupation, Kim Ilyop (1896–1971) found her voice as a feminist, radical writer, and poet. Born as Kim Won-joo and educated as a Christian, she was converted to Buddhism in her twenties through association with the Buddhist publishing company Pulgyosa. Won-joo was given the pen name Ilyop (also spelled Ilyob and Iryop), "One Leaf," by her "one true love," Yi Kwangsu, who is called the father of modern Korean literature. He ended their affair by becoming a Buddhist monk. Before her Buddhist conversion, she was an advocate for women's rights through her magazine, *Sinyoja* (New Woman).[240] In particular, she had strong beliefs that women, like men, needed to be free to have sexual relationships outside of marriage, just as men did as part of their developing liberty. It is well known through her writing that she had many sexual affairs, and it is believed that she gave birth to a son out of wedlock who himself became a Buddhist monk, Kim T'aesin, and wrote an autobiography describing their relationship, *Rahula ui sa'mo'gok* (Songs of Rahula Yearning for His Mother).[241] The transformation of the radical, outspoken, and sexually liberated Won-joo Kim to the Zen master Ilyop is unique within the history of female Zen masters, particularly since she continued to write about her love affairs after her ordination.

Some have suggested that she was seeking solace from misery over the loss of her only true love by becoming a nun, but Ilyop's own words tell a different story. Her ordination followed his "entering the mountain."[242] Her poem "My Song" declares her intention for Zen Buddhist nun's practice:

> I'd like to sing a song freely,
> Completely free of even the beautiful musical melodies and
>   beats....
> It's not a song of love, it's not a song of sorrow, it's not even a song
>   of inspiration.
> I would simply like to sing the mysterious verse of complete
>   ecstasy.
> Then even the decomposed soil and dried up tree barks would be
>   moved.[243]

Here Ilyop expresses the possibility of experiencing an all-pervading ecstasy. Previously she had found this ecstasy through love and freedom of expression; now she recognizes the possibility of knowing and expressing the fundamental ecstasy permeating the essential nature of existence.

Ilyop's poetry suggests an overlap between her longing for her lost lover and her longing for liberation and profound realization:

> Things cast shadows,
> My approaching lover makes a rustle.
> Peach blossoms smile silently
> But in the winter mountain, plum blossoms bloom,
> Who would deny that spring and winter are one?[244]

One senses the electric and sensual anticipation of erotic love, and yet there is silent serenity and the beginning sense of oneness. Ilyop is moving from her romantic yearnings for individual love to a love for awakening and a sense of oneness.

Ilyop had three aspirations for her own Zen Buddhist practice and for her writings as a nun. She wished to help end her own suffering, she wanted to know the true meaning of this life and her true nature, and she wished to participate in helping others find freedom from suffering through Buddhist practice. To that end she published several best-selling books in the 1960s as a nun, including *O'nu sudoin ui hoesang* (Memoir of a Practitioner), *Ch'ongch'un ul pulsaru'go* (Having Burned Out My Youth), and *Haeng pohaeng ui kalp'i eso* (In between Happiness and Unhappiness). After having been a nun for more than thirty years, Ilyop created quite a stir by including her letters to her lovers in the first two books. In her third book she included advice to those seeking happiness through romantic love. Her books are credited with converting many women to Buddhist practice through the subject of love and relationships.

In her writing, Ilyop places her search for romantic love in a larger context—the search for freedom, meaning, truth in relationship, and lasting passion, living fully present, in this life. Prior to her becoming a nun, she wrote her 1927 newspaper article "Na ui chongjogwan" (My View on Chastity) repudiating the Korean double standard, by which society demands a woman be faithful to one man and avoid sexual relationships before she is married, but a man is free to engage sexually before marriage and to take lovers after marriage.

> In the traditional concept of chastity, chastity was materialized and thus a woman with a past has been treated as if she was

stale and had no freshness. In other words, when a woman had a sexual relationship with a man, she was treated as if her chastity had been lost. Chastity in this case was viewed as a broken container made of jewels.

However chastity is not such a static entity....

Even when a person had affairs with several lovers in the past, if the person possesses a healthy mind, is able to completely clean up from the memory [of] whatever has happened in the past, and is capable of creating a new life by fully devoting herself/himself to the new lover, such a man or woman possesses the chastity which cannot be broken.[245]

In 1927 when Ilyop wrote this article redefining chastity, she was renouncing her ties to Christianity and its teachings and speaking from her new association with Buddhism and the practice of meditation.

After becoming a Zen Buddhist nun, she retold the story of her early life as a radical feminist who promoted sexual freedom for women in terms of the Buddhist path—a search for spirituality, truth, and liberation. She advised women to develop themselves and realize their true nature by teaching "the importance of self-worth, self-confidence, self-awareness, self-awakening, and self-realization."[246] Her message focused on helping women benefit from a Buddhist perspective, and she took pains not to distance herself from the life of her readers through her status as a nun and Zen master. The Korean clergy wrote in formal Chinese, basing sermons on Buddhist scriptures or Zen teachings. Ilyop wrote about her love affairs in the Korean alphabet, *han'gul*, so that ordinary people had access to her teachings on Buddhism—on a subject of mutual interest, love and relationship. Recall that Keizan, the early Soto founder translated teachings for his female disciples into *hiragana*, the women's script, for the same reason—accessibility for one who did not read the Chinese characters. In the later chapter on Rengetsu, we will see that she also wrote her poems in *hiragana*. Providing accessible teachings to those without education was a recurrent theme for women Zen teachers.

Conventions stated that it was unacceptable for a nun to write about her love affairs, but Ilyop went ahead. She was convinced that women particularly needed to understand how to pursue their freedom their own way, including the women's world of love and relationships. She wrote about her pursuit of love, happiness, and freedom in the secular realm of relationships, in accessible language, but she wrote from the wisdom of her Buddhist perspective.

Kim Ilyop's message illustrated that love and sexuality were not a hindrance to enlightenment and that an understanding of the human heart and its longing for love could actually deepen one's aspiration and enhance a teacher's ability to help others be free of suffering. Her own experience of longing and rebellion were transformed through Buddhist practice to skillful means for helping others find a way to enter Zen practice.

She felt, in particular, that women needed to be able to love freely, to be able to choose their own lovers. Most important, freedom for Ilyop was a primary condition for becoming fully human. Ilyop believed that the essential work of becoming a human being was to find the real "I." Becoming the true "I" meant not being constrained by conventions or hypocrisy. From her secular position, she challenged sexist conventions of her day that required celibacy prior to marriage for women but not for men. She encouraged women to develop their own standards and find their freedom.

> Only when one finds the original spirit of human beings, which is non-existence, and is able to use it at one's disposal, [does] the life of a human being open up. When that happens, one becomes an independent being who is not being swindled by environments, and thus whenever, wherever, and whatever kind of life with whatever shape of a body, one leads one's life, one finds nirvana.[247]

This life of "nonexistence" is described by Ilyop as the "unified I." This unified I manifests only through courageous effort and strong intention and enables us to experience nirvana, freedom from suffering. Ilyop also stated that "the Buddha is another name for this 'I.'" In other words, the unified I is our buddha-nature, it includes our entire personal existence interacting in a harmonious relationship with all that we encounter in our life. Ilyop challenged conventional roles for women, and she encouraged women to find their own moral standards to free themselves from conventional thinking.

Nonexistence, or the unified I, can arise only when we let go of our attachments, recognize our fears and habitual responses, and clarify our life through the buddha-mind. Ilyop cautioned her audience not to be "swindled" by the environment—not to be tricked by ideas, value-laden customs, and circumstances that seem compelling. She encouraged her readers to continue to look deeply at how cultural conventions can distract one from encountering reality and finding true purpose.

Ilyop struggled to free herself even from Buddhist conventions after finding her place as a nun. After ordination, Ilyop could not keep her promise to her teacher Man'gong to discontinue her writing (and publishing).[248] It is customary for newly ordained priests or nuns to free themselves of their previous worldly identity, to let go of individual preferences—in short to enter the realm of nonexistence. Man'gong requested that his newly ordained writer–celebrity nun give up writing and thereby give up clinging to this self defined by her identity as a writer. Ilyop promised her teacher that she would give up her writing; she promised to enter the Zen Buddhist world wholeheartedly. Even though she had agreed to follow her teacher's instructions, in the end she could not keep her promise to live her life according to his instructions. In Zen, the student needs to "surpass" her teacher. This means that the student needs to take the teacher's practice instruction and make it her own. Clearly, Kim Ilyop followed her teacher and used her own life as the raw material for her Dharma offering for the benefit of others. Both Kim Ilyop's controversial subject matter and work as a writer in the world, done while remaining a nun, offer some inspiration on how we must stay true to our own experience in order to follow our highest ideals. Ilyop's candor and compassion, her unconventional teaching voice on love and intimacy, teach us that there is always a way to bring forth a unique integration of our practice and our life as our dharma offering.

Yoshihime:
Revisiting the Mountain Gate in Kamakura Japan

Miaozong's koan moved geographically to Japan, and was studied four hundred years later in the imperial convent of Tokeiji. The Tokeiji nun Yoshihime,[249] called Devil-girl, enacted Miaozong's koan with the gatekeeper of the nearby Engakuji monastery. Yoshihime had crossed the road from Tokeiji temple to the nearby Engakuji to attend a Zen lecture.

The gatekeeper at Engakuji required an expression of Zen understanding from prospective attendees as the price of admission to the lecture. Yoshihime's response followed the path of her Dharma mother, Miaozong—direct confrontation.

Yoshihime, said to be ugly and exceptionally strong, was the daughter of a general. She was a student of the seventh Tokeiji abbess, Ninpo (d. ca. 1400). The gatekeeper blocking her entry to the Engakuji lecture shouted: "What is the gate through which all buddhas come into the world?" Yoshihime grabbed the gatekeeper's head and forced it down between her legs: "Look, look," she said, implying that the answer was within her vagina and that words were unnecessary.

The gatekeeper, not to be outdone by her direct response, offered his own Zen words: "In the middle there is a fragrance of wind and dew." The monk's words seemed to say, "Given the two sides of duality, the middle way, the Buddha way, is the sweetest."

Yoshihime did not accept his answer: "This monk! He's not fit to keep the gate. He ought to be looking after the garden." The monk's answer was too flowery, too delicate for Yoshihime. When did the Buddha way ever prefer wind and fragrant dew to storms of lightning and thunder? After all these years of exclusion and condemnation, if we still cannot acknowledge the strength of this place or vindicate the purity of the vagina, let us not instead damn it with faint praise—the delicate fragrance of this place is not its essential nature.

The gatekeeper ran back into the temple to bring out reinforcements to address this thorny problem. Perhaps he wanted to see one of his Dharma buddies receive the same treatment from Yoshihime. The abbot's attendant, a more senior monk, came down to solve the problem at the gate. In the spirit of fair play, he probably had not been told what exactly had transpired. He once again posed the same question to Yoshihime. "What is it, the gate through which the buddhas come into the world?"

One might wonder here if these monks were serious defenders of the Dharma or just young monks looking for cheap thrills—or whether there is really any difference. Yoshihime grabbed the head of the abbot's attendant and held it between her legs, saying: "Look, look!" The attendant commented on his view of this place with more substance. "The buddhas of the three worlds come giving light."

This time, Yoshihime approved the attendant and stated, "This monk is one with the eye; he saw the 84,000 Dharma gates thrown open all together." All the paths to enlightenment shine through each and every form. How could the vagina, this most disputed place, be otherwise? Birth and death, man and woman, sexuality and celibacy, conventional and nonconventional, buddha and beast; all 84,000 Dharma gates are in one place, the gate through which all buddhas enter this world! Yoshihime was admitted to Engakuji for the public lecture.

How wonderful: the teaching of "No Attachment" had traveled four hundred years across the seas to surprise and enlighten Japanese Zen monks. Miaozong and Wanan brought the Sung dynasty monastic setting to life; Yoshihime and the gatekeeper portrayed Zen's human face in fifteenth-century Japan. Devil-girl's playfulness and the monk's response tell us that Zen was alive and well, and that monks and nuns were finding ways to enrich and deepen each other's understanding even though they practiced in separate temples.

The Abbess Soshin:
The Buddha in the Harem

The abbess Soshin (1588–1675) turns Buddhism full circle by bringing Zen into the shogun's harem. Buddha Shakyamuni had left the harem to find his spiritual path. The Zen Buddhist nun Soshin entered the shogun's harem to teach the Buddha's way. Soshin's teaching in the women's quarters preceded the great Zen Master Hakuin by one hundred years, but he later (most likely unknowingly) re-enacted her willingness to teach harem women, some of whom were sexual slaves, by teaching the prostitute Ohashi (ca. 1700). Hakuin told Ohashi, who was indentured as a prostitute to support her impoverished family, that she could attain enlightenment under any circumstances. Ohashi proved Hakuin correct, and eventually became an ordained Buddhist nun. Soshin taught women of the harem that being fully aware within their particular circumstances would set them free.

Soshin was born Onaa to a prominent samurai family. Her father, a tea-ceremony student of Sen no Rikyu, died on the way home from a mission in Korea. Onaa was adopted into the Maeda family of Kanazawa and at age fifteen married one of the Maeda sons.

After bearing three sons, she was divorced and sent away from the

Maeda clan. It is not clear why the divorce occurred, although historical conjecture is that Onaa's father had been converted to Christianity, and when Christianity was later banned she became an outcast. After being forced to leave her husband, Onaa took refuge in Saika-in, a sub-temple of Myoshinji. Her birth father had founded and endowed Saika-in, and her uncle was the founding abbot. Onaa studied Zen as a means to survive the devastating loss of her husband and children.

Onaa later remarried, but there were financial difficulties in her husband's clan. Her aunt, Kasuga no Tsubone, sponsored her employment as an advisor to the shogun, Iemitsu Tokugawa. Kasuga no Tsubone had been the shogun's wet nurse and maintained considerable power in his palace as his advisor. Onaa was cultivated by her aunt for that same influential position. Onaa was quieter, less political, and better educated, and she began teaching Zen to the women of the shogun's inner quarters, the *ooku*. Due to the intense political rivalry within the *ooku*, Onaa found herself ejected on charges that she was teaching the forbidden Christianity.

Onaa was allowed to resume teaching within the *ooku* on the condition that she receive formal ordination as a Zen Buddhist nun. Iemitsu had been a harsh persecutor of Christians and did not accept Onaa's previous Zen training as proof that she was a Buddhist. Because of the gossip and suspicion, she returned to her training temple to become formally ordained as the nun Soshin. After her ordination the shogun favored her as a spiritual advisor and had a temple erected for her that included five villages and was spread over eighty-two acres. The temple was called Saishoji. Soshin-ni modestly named her uncle as its founding abbot and took the position of second founder.

Both her Rinzai lineage and a Soto Zen perspective are evident in her writing, *Soshin-ni Hogo* (The Dharma Words of the Nun Soshin). On the Soto side we hear echoes of Dogen's Chinese great-uncle in the Dharma, Hongzhi (1091–1157). Here is a sample of what Soshin wrote:

> As for deluded thoughts, when a single thought arises regarding the unchangeable and unforeseeable, this single thought gives rise to endless or limitless discriminating thoughts. There is no basis for settling on any one of them, because they are all just speculation. As a result natural ease is obscured by gloom.

It is as if the fine, blue sky is completely covered by clouds. Once you make up your mind to turn to the one mind, it's as if the pure wind blows up the clouds and you harmonize with all buddhas and deities as one and your Self.[250]

And here is what Hongzhi had written several hundred years earlier:

Splendid and lustrous like the waters moistening autumn, noble like the moon overwhelming the darkness, from the beginning just beam through all gloom profoundly free from stains. Constantly still and constantly glorious, this stillness is not extinguished by causes.[251]

Adding a little more explanation, Soshin describes Hongzhi's process of "beaming through the gloom" using practice to penetrate the depression caused by getting lost in thoughts and feelings. She describes turning to the one mind, focusing the mind on the awareness itself, and experiencing the buddha-mind as a fine blue sky where clouds have been blown away by a pure wind. We find the same message in Hongzhi's injunction to beam through all gloom: a place profoundly free of all stains, constantly still and constantly glorious.

While Soshin's teachings accord with the Zen tradition, her venue for teaching, the women's quarters, is most unconventional. She taught women who were chosen consorts of the shogun, women who would bear his child, or women who might be traded as a sexual favor to another powerful lord. What is most compelling is that she is a woman teaching other women, some of whom are trapped as sexual slaves, and all of them living in a fiercely political and emotional hotbed of power, intrigue, and seduction. Soshin offered her Zen training to help women calm the suspicions and depressions that arose within this highly charged environment:

If you harbor suspicion for everything, you may feel depressed. Since all the things you guess are just conjecture, how can your suspicion ever be resolved? This is the cause of your discontentment. A person with sincere intention [instead] allows the mind to realize the mistakes of the ego's delusions. This is done through looking into a mirror of unchangeable wisdom. Reflecting the mind in this mirror, you can see your own delusions.[252]

Soshin describes our egotistic, self-centered view and the ensuing emotional projections that distort our ability to discern reality. Her integration of Buddhist practice with an understanding of complex emotional relationships is sophisticated considering that she predates the science of ego psychology by several hundred years. Living in the harem, with its painful and sometimes degrading circumstances, she offers powerful medicine to help women see through their suffering.

From the Buddhist view she teaches that our discontent is not caused by circumstances, even if they are difficult; our unhappiness is caused by our distorted views and expectations of our situation. If we use an accurate mirror to free ourselves of reactivity, the mirror of zazen, we become free of our delusions and may transcend our circumstances. If we rely on our distorted patterns of perceptions as if they were a realistic map for our relationships, we cannot resolve our conflicts or discomforts. These instructions conform to our contemporary understanding of how neurotic patterns lock us in depressed mental states.

She cautioned women of the *ooku* to practice where they lived—right smack in the midst of gossip, intrigue, and the sexuality of the secular world.

But this does not mean that you should devote yourself only to secluded practice, disliking and fearing all the things of the secular world. What I mean is, if you are continuously aware of the constancy of no-thing-ness, that things have no self-function, you will be following the original mind. One moves beyond, one transcends grasping pleasure and averting from suffering to see and follow the original mind. This is finding ease in [the midst of] everyday life; this is true joy.... Therefore, you don't have to go away to the mountain; it is within your own mind.[253]

Regarding the koan practice she had learned in Rinzai Zen, Soshin recommended neither koan study nor monastic training. She suggested that within the *ooku*, studying koans would be less useful than sustaining "the intention to realize the delusions of the ego." What do we make of her practice instructions that recommended training with delusions that arise rather than removing oneself from them—for example, by home leaving?

Leaving the *ooku* was not usually an option for many of the women living there. Soshin stressed the value of practicing right where they were—in the midst of secular (and sexual) activities. Wanting some perfect practice setting was a waste of time and could have become a trap. The opportunity to work with this moment is always at hand. Transforming pleasure, aversion, and anticipation into the constancy of "no-thing-ness" was a perfect practice for the women who had little control over the outer world. Soshin's teaching stressed their ability to practice just as they were, just as they were living in the palace. She was transforming their self-image from that of an object or victim to a practitioner.

These women might have misused koan practice by focusing on a Zen phrase to blot out an unpleasant experience or otherwise find an escape from their life of servitude. This use of koans would not have developed an ability to reconcile the present moment with the original mind. In other words, the koan practice could have been used as a magical mantra to escape or repress unwanted experience.

Soshin's view of palace women, including sexual slaves, as potential buddhas is compassionate and far-reaching. Whereas the Buddha found it necessary to flee his palace and his retinue of women, Soshin had faith that the Buddha's awakened mind could be found even in the midst of the sexual realm. From the time of the Buddha in India, nuns have struggled to make sense of their sexuality in the context of practice. Miaozong tried to help the head monk understand that sexuality was not separate from spiritual practice. Kim Ilyop wanted to reach out to women in the world and show the relevance of Buddhist practice to matters of the heart. Soshin found herself in the shogun's *ooku* teaching women of the shogun's harem. While celibacy was required for monks and nuns, the female teachers believed that sexuality could be included in their teaching and made a point of doing so. This belief reflected women's reality—often they had no choice in whether to be sexual or not—should their circumstances block their buddhahood? Female teachers believed that there is a way to practice and to awaken even in the midst of sexual activity.

Working Nuns   10

The Buddha's Teaching on Work

WHILE THE BUDDHA requested that his renunciant followers beg rather than work for a living, he gave specific instructions to laypeople for earning a living and protecting their wealth. The Buddha recognized that, for his lay followers, protecting material resources and providing for the family were important aspects of adult responsibility. More directly, since the Buddhist sangha completely relied on begging for food, medicine, and other property from lay people, the physical well-being of the monks and nuns was dependent on the wealth of lay people. Monks and nuns were to live day to day, depending entirely on the sincerity of their practice to provide for their needs. They could not work for a living or keep possessions or money. Nuns found it more difficult than monks to support themselves and their convents. Often they earned money by selling crafts or teaching classes rather than relying solely on begging and donations. Because of their financial adversities, nuns functioned in a category that blended monastic practice with lay life; convents too incorporated aspects of lay life for financial support while housing communities of ordained practitioners.

Western Zen Buddhists, particularly those living in monastic institutions, face conditions that make following the Buddha's instructions for ordained monks quite difficult. Most notably, the institutions do not have a broad financial base, and it is difficult for Zen students at monasteries to afford health care while practicing. Often Zen centers cannot provide health insurance. Like contemporary practitioners, historical Zen nuns in particular had difficulty surviving on donations. By reviewing their solutions to financial support, we learn not only about creative and appropriate ways Buddhists have earned money, but also about how they incorporated their spiritual practice into the world of work.

The Buddha instructed his monks to rely on begging as their only means of support and never to handle money. Monks were to beg for daily food, and they were not to accept food in exchange for their teaching. Teaching was to be given freely; there was to be no exchange of teachings for goods of any type.

The begging tradition was alive and well in the time of the Buddha, in part because wealthy lay followers provided the Buddha and his congregation, both monks and nuns, with land and food. Today we see little begging for sustenance among Western Buddhists, including those Theravada monks who still follow the Buddha's original prohibitions on work. Western Zen Buddhists following the later, more adaptive Mahayana schools of Buddhism have never felt constrained by the Buddha's instructions not to work for money and never to handle money.

To develop an authentic and indigenous form of Zen Buddhist practice in the West, it is useful to examine just how the Buddhist path of right livelihood has been adapted in other places and other times. When Buddhism migrated to China and beyond, political circumstances and the Confucian work ethic required Buddhist monks and nuns to find alternatives to begging as a means of support. Chinese Buddhist monks worked the land to sustain themselves through farming and renting their land. While alms-gathering monks still exist in the Southeast Asian tradition, farming and other means of support have spread in the Mahayana tradition. Western Zen practitioners are currently finding alternatives to farming and begging as right livelihood, and they are actively looking for ways to engage their Buddhist practice in activities to help others in need such as hospice projects and teaching children. Today, when Western Zen students (including ordained priests) attempt to follow the Buddha's precept on right livelihood, they apply the standards the Buddha designated for laypeople: support yourself only by legal, nonviolent, and unharmful means.

Zen Convents and Work

Just as Westerners are adapting the meaning of right livelihood to fit our way of life today, many nuns made a similar adaptation historically. Nuns' financial support included work projects that accorded with Buddhist standards for laypeople. Nuns did not limit themselves to the Buddha's rules for monks and nuns or the Mahayana adaptations that included only farming. Nuns worked outside the convent in social assistance projects and other nonfarm activities.

Because the earliest rules for nuns (the Eight Special Rules) barred them from teaching independently, Zen convents have not been funded as well as monasteries. As we've seen, around 1900 the Soto School of Japan gave monks an average stipend of 180,000 yen per year in financial support, while nuns received on average only 600.[254] Additionally, convents were usually smaller than monasteries and therefore lacked sufficient labor force to support themselves. In ancient times, when wandering and begging for alms exposed nuns to the risk of rape and abduction, nuns were less willing than monks to venture out in search of money. More recently, monasteries have received greater financial support than convents through bureaucracies like the Japanese Soto-shu or corporate sponsorship.

Convents survived financially through creative practice-related offerings. Both monasteries and convents, contrary to the Buddha's instructions, have been and are supported by donations for spiritual teaching—lectures, prayer services, funeral and memorial services, and donations from both secular and lineage-based professional organizations[255]—but nuns have traditionally also provided different services that are not specifically spiritual offerings. They have taught classes to maintain cultural arts, they have delivered services for children, and they have provided on-site caregiving for the elderly.

Paula Arai's recent research on the Japanese Soto Zen convent order reveals that nuns are required to learn the traditional arts as part of their training: flower arranging, singing, sewing, Chinese poetry, calligraphy, cooking, and tea ceremony (these arts are not always required for Zen monks' training).[256] This training is expected to help them embody the traditional Japanese womanly virtues through the sensory refinement these arts require. The acquisition of these skills is seen as a way to develop discipline and sensitivity to others, a skill practiced in everyday life activities. Practicing these arts can develop patience and help tame the selfish ego, and teaching them in lay communities has helped the nuns survive economically. For example, in Korea the nuns of the training convent Ummunsa study calligraphy, piano, flower arranging, computers, and the Japanese or English language. This helps them maintain their financial independence and connect with the community.

Teaching classes that preserve traditional culture develops an important bond between laypeople and nuns. People who do not wish to practice Buddhism can find Buddhist values transmitted through nuns' classes on the traditional arts. Families that attend classes develop positive relationships with the nuns and seek their advice during difficult times, deepening their understanding of the Zen Buddhist perspective. Arai's research suggests that nuns are considered more approachable than monks, more able to talk about the family's concerns.

Nuns and Children

In the seventeenth century Ryonen Genso, whom we met earlier, sponsored a school to educate the village children surrounding her temple; probably other convents offered this same service. More recently, the Soto nuns' convent order that followed Ekan Daishi started an orphanage after World War II, taking to heart the male founder Dogen's words on the four virtues of a bodhisattva:

> *Fuse:* giving
>
> *Aigo:* use of loving words
>
> *Rigyo:* completely forgetting oneself in one's effort to help other people
>
> *Doji:* living by helping each other[257]

Dogen's teaching words offer clear-cut methods for bodhisattva training in the midst of everyday life. The Soto Zen nuns took these bodhisattva instructions to be the basis for their spiritual practice and the guide for their service to the world. They used Dogen's specific teaching words to develop work ethics and standards for creating an organization to help orphans. Japanese Zen convent and monastic life describe buddha-nature as revealed through one's everyday behavior. The focus of everyday convent activity is spiritual practices and ceremonies, but here we see another route to buddhahood: perfecting one's character through selfless helping.

In addition to providing orphan care, Soto Zen nuns in Japan today are responsible for giving newborn babies their Buddhist names. The naming ceremony requires creativity and training in calligraphy. The occasion of a baby's naming ceremony provides the nuns with an opportunity to serve families in their neighborhood, to develop the family's relationship to Zen Buddhism, and to open the possibility of the nuns becoming and staying connected to the child's upbringing.

In the eighth-century, Empress Komyo, believing that Buddhism was meant to provide care for the needy, built sanctuaries where impoverished people could receive services. Shelter, care, and medicines were provided for homeless or impoverished people. A devout Buddhist, Empress Komyo sponsored the building of Buddhist monasteries and convents and also a clinic and dispensary (Seyaku-in) and a shelter for the homeless and orphans (Hiden-in). She personally served at these institutions as part of her Buddhist practice. There is a legend that Empress Komyo also built a bathhouse to keep her vow to personally cleanse the bodies of one thousand leprosy sufferers.

In Korea in 1971 the abbess of Pomunsa, Eunyeong, had a house for dispensation of charity constructed just outside the convent's gate. It housed a public bath, a barbershop, a clinic, a dispensary, and a home for elderly women. The nuns of Pomunsa could actively express the Buddhist vow to save all beings by working to care for others through these charitable offerings. They could provide valuable services to the community, continue their development in the bodhisattva tradition (like Japanese Soto nuns), and they could develop their leadership skills within the convent and beyond.

Convents across Asia have a long history of taking in foundlings. At Pomunsa in 1984 there were sixty-two nuns and twenty-seven children living in the community.[258] Most of the children were foundlings, abandoned by their mothers or other family members at the doorsteps of the temple without any identification. Many were likely born from rape or other couplings considered unforgivable in Confucian society. Pomunsa, in the midst of Seoul, surrounded by private homes, provided the children with a chance to be cared for in a loving environment without the shame associated with their personal family histories. The convent only kept the girls, who are harder to place in adoptive families, and encouraged the adoption of the more desirable baby boys. Since many of the nuns themselves came from poor families and were given to convents at early ages, they felt a special rapport with these infants.

Taiwan's Socially Active Nuns

Currently there is a revival of Buddhist practice in Taiwan. In this resurgence, ordained nuns outnumber monks in some orders by as much as six to one and maintain an active social welfare component. The nun Zhengyan (b. 1937), leader of this reinvigorated Buddhism, has created a large network of lay Buddhist institutions. Zhengyan's followers have begun providing health care for those who would otherwise have none. Besides a hospital, Zhengyan has guided her organization to build a Buddhist nursing school and a medical school. A university is also planned.

Zhengyan was ordained by the Chinese master Yinshun (1906–2005). Yinshun's master was Taixu (1890–1947), who had been ordained in the Linji Chan tradition. Both Yinshun and Taixu advocated a Buddhist practice that expressed the values of the Buddha rather than basing practice on esoteric rituals and superstitions, such as funerals performed to appease ghosts and spirits. Both Taixu and Yinshun inspired Zhengyan through their writings, which emphasized Buddhism's need to find expression in everyday life, not in the next life.

Zhengyan's earliest vows included restating Chan master Baizhang Huaihai's dictum "A day without work is a day without food," and her own vow "to extend the spirit of Buddhism to all levels of society."[259] She has kept her vows and lived up to her teacher's values by creating and heading the Buddhist Compassion Relief Tzu Chi Association. The association has more than three million Buddhist followers in Taiwan and internationally. Zhengyan's character, dedication, and clear purpose are the inspiration for her members' conversion to a Buddhism based on keeping the precepts by performing work to help others.

Perhaps the traditional female role as caregiver accounts for the nuns' orientation to hands-on bodhisattva practices. Nuns' caregiving practices highlight important differences between nuns' and monks' activities. Some male Zen masters, most notably Dahui (eleventh-century China), responded to a famine and plague with food and labor. Hakuin Zenji (eighteenth-century Japan) supported and instructed the common folk. Both of these accomplished Zen priests included social action in their teaching. The nuns more frequently fully embodied the practice of hands-on caregiving both inside and outside the convent. Nuns consistently interpreted the bodhisattva's "I vow to save all beings" to mean not just saving beings from their deluded thoughts, but rescuing the hungry and the injured with whatever comforts they could apply. The San Francisco Zen Center's hospice project, and the numerous Zen centers providing dinner for the homeless, grief counseling for survivors, and stress reduction/meditation for inmates, are all examples of how contemporary practitioners provide caregiving to the community.

Zen Nuns and Work in the World Outside the Convent

Not all Zen nuns lived in convents; some were supported by their families or supported themselves by work in the world. Many formally ordained women and others who were self-ordained (who cut their hair, recited vows, and began wearing Buddhist robes without entering a formal relationship with an authorized teacher) lived and worked outside of the convent or monastic setting. Three outstanding nuns were well known for their work: Zhidong (Chih-t'ung, d. 1124), Eunyeong Sunim, and Rengetsu (1791–1875).

Weiju:
Washing Away Ignorance

Weiju was born Zhidong, the daughter of a scholar. She was clever and spiritually inclined, but her family did not allow her ordination. The elder sister-in-law of Miaozong, she was married to the grandson of a prime minister but returned to her family to request ordination. Her family refused, but she practiced her meditation at home for many years. When her parents died she requested that her brother, who according to Confucian custom was to decide her future, allow her to become ordained. Her brother also refused, but she was able to study with various teachers without ordination and was given a Buddhist name as a laywoman (Kongshi). Finally, she was ordained as the nun Weiju at the time of her brother's death.

Even as a laywoman she was recognized and respected by well-known Zen teachers, having attained a deep enlightenment with Linji master Sixin Wuxin (1044–1115). Yuanwu, the compiler of the Blue Cliff Records, and Foyan Qingyuan (1067–1120) were her contemporaries and spoke of her with high regard. Near the end of her life (sometime between 1111 and 1118) Weiju opened a public bathhouse. On the door to the entrance to the bath she wrote her teaching words:

> Nothing exists, so what are you bathing?
> If there is even the slightest bit of dust, where does it
>   come from?
> Say one profound sentence, then you can enter the bath.
> The ancient spirits can only scrub your back;
> How could I, the founder, illuminate your mind?
> If you want to attain the state that is free from dirt,
> You should first let all parts of your body sweat [make
>   effort].
> It is said that the water can wash off the dust,
> Yet how can people understand that the water is also dust?
> Even though you suddenly wipe out [the distinction between]
>   water and dirt,
> You must still wash it off thoroughly when you come here.[260]

Weiju presents the essential Zen dilemma in single sentences—"Nothing exists, so what are you bathing?" or "What is this fleeting life, and how do we live it?"—and connects it to her livelihood of running the bath house. She took her work in the world, the bathhouse, and transformed it into a Zen crucible. Zen teaches that everything changes, that nothing exists in the way that we think it does; why take a bath or why offer a bath? If these impermanent bodies have no inherent self, then what are we doing with them? What is our relationship to our bodies and to our lives? Most of us sleepwalk through this problem—ignoring the deeper question of what this life means.

She commanded her customers to "say one profound sentence and you can enter the bath" in the tradition of the wandering nun Shiji and the tea lady who encountered Deshan. Shiji asked Juzhi (Japanese: Gutei) for "one word of Zen" as the condition for stopping to visit at his monk's hermitage. The tea lady commanded Deshan to answer her question as the condition for receiving his tea cake. Was Weiju familiar with their teaching? She lived about two hundred years later than they did, and could have read about their exploits.

Weiju posed the question to awaken those who entered her bathhouse. Taking a bath with Weiju meant nakedly encountering the question of your life in the deepest sense. The bath transformed into an opportunity for the bather to awaken from delusionary thinking, and it was Weiju's opportunity to realize her function as a Zen teacher in the work world. Weiju instructed her patrons in Zen, and taught Zen practitioners that wherever we work we can help people awaken.

Weiju suggested that ancient spirits, ancient teachers, and unseen beneficial forces can only nudge you in the direction of enlightenment. Even she, a present and willing Zen teacher, cannot help you wake up unless you make great effort. There is a place that is free from "dirt," a way of living that is free from the obscurations and confusions of this worldly life, but you need to make the effort to find this for yourself.

In her last few phrases she worked to move people beyond a superficial understanding of washing away delusions. Using the metaphor of the bath, she referred to the dust of the world that is washed away by the water. She instructed that water can also be dust—we may even become confused and attached to the words and methods of Zen.

Even though you may have a sudden realization of the world of nonduality—free from the distinctions of water and dirt—work to let go of this realization. Awakening to the deepest meaning of life is an ongoing process; she warned her patrons to wash away any traces of their pride or attachment to spiritual understanding.

The last instructions make us wonder if Weiju's bathhouse was positioned near a Zen training monastery. Weiju could have been speaking to those monks who came to bathe covered with an attitude of pride in their practice or enlightenment.[261] Entering the bathhouse, regardless of whether you were a layperson or a monastic, meant encountering Weiju's teaching. From her bathhouse dominion, Weiju commanded one and all to wake up and to clean up their act!

Eunyeong Sunim:
Founder of the First Independent Nun's Order in Korea

Eunyeong Sunim (1910–81) was born to a farming family during the time of the Japanese occupation of Korea (1910–45).[262] Her father, severely beaten by the Japanese police because he resisted Japanese brutality, was disabled and could not work. The family became impoverished. Eunyeong's mother vowed if her husband recovered, one of her children would become ordained to follow the Buddha's way. When Eunyeong's father finally did recover, there was a quiet family conversation regarding the mother's promise. The eight-year-old Eunyeong, overhearing their worry over the fulfillment of her mother's vow, declared that she would be the one to be ordained.

Eunyeong began her training at age eight as the disciple of the nun Kungt'an Sunim of Pomunsa convent. As mentioned earlier, Pomunsa was founded in 1115 by National Teacher Tamjin, expressly for nuns' training. During the Japanese occupation of Korea corruption was rampant, resulting in the theft of monastic properties by Koreans collaborating with the Japanese occupiers. Such was the case with Pomunsa. When Kungt'an heard that the deeds to her temple's fields were stolen, she returned to Pomunsa with her ten-year-old disciple Eunyeong.

Without the farmland that Korean monasteries usually owned for their support, the two nuns went out on begging trips, and through hard work and creative efforts they began to restore the temple. Eunyeong, exhausted by begging trips and missing the temple, found ways besides the traditional begging practice to support the temple financially. She developed a temple restaurant, and repaired and sold discarded objects to benefit the temple. She spent her whole life in fundraising projects to ensure the continuation of the eight-hundred-year-old temple. It was difficult for Eunyeong to find time to study Zen with so much work to do. Her devotion to Pomunsa preserved the convent despite crises and attempts by corrupt officials to steal the land and discredit her.

Pomunsa, like all convents in Korea, was governed by a larger male monastery. Prior to 1945, Korean monasteries were often run by abbots notorious for their collaboration with Japanese authorities. Such was the case of Kang Taeryon, who became the administrative abbot presiding over Pomunsa even after Eunyeong and her teacher had returned to support and maintain the temple. It is alleged that through false promises he swindled the nuns out of their land. When Eunyeong complained to the legal authorities, she was told that she and her teacher were no longer nuns. They were ordered to leave the convent and conduct themselves as laywomen.

They refused to take off their nun's robes and to leave the temple. Repeatedly Eunyeong was told that she could not win this battle. She was verbally abused by legal authorities who called her a crazy woman and a disgrace to the Buddhist community. Eunyeong reportedly stated that she felt like dying from these insults.

After her second meeting with government officials resulted in the same unfairness and verbal abuse, Eunyeong said that she almost fainted from shock; she had to sit down and steady herself. She had no more energy left to endure insult and abuse. She barely made her way onto the street. Dizzy and trembling with shock, she sat down on the street and wept copiously. How could she face the nuns unless she saved their home, Pomunsa? she wondered. She had no place to go and no one to turn to for help. She felt like dying, she said, but she made a vow to fight this injustice to the end. While she felt willing to give up her life for the sake of the Buddhadharma, she was not willing to die on account of unfair treatment. She vowed to herself,

> No matter how weak and frail a woman I am, I cannot allow myself to be trampled down like this. I will show them until I die that there is someone who cares for justice and fairness in the world. Would it make sense to the Buddhist world that the nuns of Pomun-Sa are just thrown out of their nunnery because of the cross temper of some monk?[263]

Through her teaching words we hear the awakened voice of many Zen women who persevered despite discrimination and hardship. Eunyeong continued to plead with authorities on behalf of Pomunsa and filed a suit against Kang Taeryon. She felt troubled by her role, creating legal battles for the Buddhist sangha, but, after prayer and meditation in the Buddha hall, she resolved to go forward. Other nuns were fearful; they felt they should submit to the authorities, no matter how unfair the treatment. Eunyeong realized she had to help the nuns overcome their years of habitual submission and what she perceived to be their misunderstanding of the Zen doctrine of letting go. Letting go of one's self-clinging does not mean we can't take a stand in the face of injustice.

Throughout her legal battles, Eunyeong remained strong for the sake of Pomunsa and the nuns. When her legal complaint resulted in no action, she wanted to change lawyers and appeal her case. When she asked her own lawyer for her file, he refused to give it to her and allegedly throttled her and threw her down, saying, "How dare you take an honorable person to court, you ill-bred woman?" Pursuing her case in the face of corruption, misogyny, and cruelty, Eunyeong vowed to save Pomunsa or to follow the unwritten Asian code and commit suicide because she herself had failed the temple and disgraced her teacher.

Eventually her legal battles prevailed against Kang Taeryon, the temple was returned to the nuns, and Eunyeong and her teacher Kungt'an were reinstated. Even so, Taeryon's influence continued, and he attempted to install a male abbot of Pomunsa to oust Eunyeong and her teacher. The local lay community refused to allow the male abbot entry to Pomunsa. When the Japanese were finally defeated in 1945, Kang Taeryon was punished and expelled by the Koreans for collaborating with the Japanese. After dedicating twenty-five years of her life to the temple, Eunyeong Sunim was elected abbess of Pomunsa when her teacher retired.

As abbess, Eunyeong rebuilt and upgraded Pomunsa, established charitable projects on the temple grounds, and founded the first independent *bhikshuni* order in the world, Pomun-jong (Independent Order of Nuns). From the time of the Buddha, nuns had lived under the guidance of the monks, making Eunyeong Sunim's new independent nuns' order a historical precedent. Her accomplishments as a fundraiser and project manager were enormous. She renovated old buildings and built new ones to provide spaces for the nuns' education and for community cultural activities. She built a clinic and convalescent home for elderly women on the temple grounds. All these projects were carried out during the Korean War (1950–53) and the disruption of postwar Korea.

The Korean Zen teacher Samu Sunim lauded Eunyeong for her charitable work and construction projects during a period of such turmoil. He also asserted that despite the efforts she expended to rebuild Pomunsa, her creation of the Pomun-jong was her foremost accomplishment in a lifetime of struggle. "The founding of the Pomun-jong was a declaration of independence from the monks' control of the sangha by concerned Korean Buddhist nuns under the leadership of Eunyeong Sunim."[264]

Eunyeong established the independent nuns' order to counteract the oppressive behavior of male monastics toward the nuns, behavior that she had personally experienced. She also refocused the nuns' efforts into social engagement and work for the community's benefit.

During the Japanese occupation of Korea, Japanese Zen missionaries had tried to control Korea by reforming Korean Zen into the Japanese model. All Korean monks and nuns were encouraged to marry as the Japanese monks did. Just as the Japanese nuns had refused to marry, so did Korean nuns refuse to give up their celibate status. After the Japanese occupation was defeated, Korean monks who had adopted Japanese Buddhist values were removed from important Korean temples in an effort to reclaim the Korean heritage. The Koreans resumed their style of celibate Zen supported by the work of the nuns who had remained faithful to their Korean vows during the Japanese occupation. But despite the skills and dedication to the Korean celibate order shown by the nuns, none of the twenty-five head monasteries in South Korea were given to nuns. The nuns numbered 5,138 and the monks 7,913, yet the nuns were only given two of the sixty Central Sangha Council positions that were established to govern the Korean monasteries.

Eunyeong Sunim took poison and died in 1981; it was unclear whether she knew the beverage she was offered was poison or not, since she denied having taken poison when her disciples found her ill. She and two disciples drank a beverage that killed two of them. The question of suicide arose because that evening's discussion was with a disciple concerned about the the temple's finances. Was she or the disciple who offered the poisoned beverage depressed because of the temple's level of debt? It was a mysterious and murky ending to a life dedicated to her temple. The Pomun-jong order continued to thrive even after Eunyeong's death. In 1984 the order contained 24 temples, 263 nuns, and more than 110,000 followers. Eunyeong was an amazing force in Korean Buddhism, and we can look forward to learning more about her life and death with a more complete translation of her diary.

Otagaki Rengetsu:
Expressing Zen through Art

3/27/10 tea
Drank out of a Rengetsu
cup. ^ etc

Rengetsu was one of the most famous female artists in history. She is presented in this chapter for her financially successful and critically acclaimed work in the world. Her evocative poetic images and art express Zen teaching in a way that explanatory words can never reach. She created more than fifty thousand pieces of art, which are sought after now as much as they were during her lifetime. Her art, while solidly embedded in Zen Buddhist principles, express the pain and joy of life in the world of family, nature, and work—the world of lay life from the Buddhist point of view. Perhaps the combination of this comprehensible Zen in her poems, and the everyday uses for her pottery (tea, sake, and serving) help to explain the popularity of Rengetsu's work. Her life and work teach us to fully engage just where we are, to express our own life passionately in our work, and to let go of selfishness even as we work to earn our livelihood.

Born Otagaki Nobu, Rengetsu (1791–1875) was orphaned and adopted at a young age. Well educated and twice married, she bore children that did not survive long. Ordained in the Pure Land school of Buddhism, she also studied Zen and expressed her Zen understanding through her poetry. By all accounts, as a young girl she excelled at everything she undertook—martial arts, calligraphy, and all the classical studies. Unfortunately, as we have learned, gifted women were often married into situations that were not always directly conducive to their spiritual or creative development.

Nobu was married at sixteen to a young samurai who may have physically abused her. She had three children who all died at an early age. After her first husband died she remarried, but by the time Nobu was thirty-three her second husband had died as well. She returned to live with her adoptive father, a Pure Land Buddhist priest, on the grounds of Chionji temple with one child, who also died later. There she found a measure of peace, became a Buddhist nun thereafter known as Rengetsu (Lotus Moon), and devoted herself to practice.

Rengetsu's home in the temple was not secure; her dwelling there depended on her adoptive father's position as head priest. She herself was not recognized as a potential leader of the temple. When her adoptive father died eight years later, Rengetsu was forced to leave Chionji and to think about how she could support herself. She considered becoming a tutor of the game of go,[265] but concluded that men would not like to be instructed and surpassed by their female instructor. Instead Rengetsu decided to sell pottery.

Perhaps the pottery and the poetry she inscribed on it were conceived as a moving meditation to resolve the losses she had suffered. She would gather and prepare the clay herself, form the pot by hand (she did not use the potter's wheel), and then on each piece inscribe one of her poems. Even though Rengetsu knew *kanji*, most of her calligraphy was done in the women's script, *hiragana*; the results were simple and stunning in their visual purity and poetic power. Each piece of pottery that Rengetsu created was imbued with her well-developed artistic sensibility, her determination, and her realization, hard won through a life of loss.

Her poetry expressed a tender side of Zen, the *wabi-sabi* aesthetic—the lonely and plain beauty of daily life utterly exposed. Rather than claim, as a Zen master might, that she had severed all attachments through committed Zen practice, she exposed her longing with a Zen voice. From the meditator's cool, quiet, and precise view, she expressed her experience of both suffering and bliss and, in doing so, transcended both.

Rengetsu opens a wide view of human vulnerability and longing, but she does it by stepping out of the evocative picture she creates. We experience her loss not through her emotional response but through its absence. Her poems paint a detailed picture and leave an opening where emotional depth can be fully and personally experienced by the reader. She lets the natural setting and its evocative context speak.

On the subject of her deceased children she chooses the site of a historical battle where father and son said their final goodbye before heading straight into their last battle. In this place, Sakurai Village, the samurai father compared life to the brief but glorious blooming of the cherry blossoms he beheld there. Rengetsu shares her suffering with others but claims nothing special about her loss. How sweet and how heartbreaking this impermanent human condition is for all of us. Consider the following poem, which she introduces with the line "To my beloved children."

My final message:
Flowers blooming

With all their heart
In lovely Sakurai Village.[266]

Rengetsu teaches that no matter how limited a life span, we must blossom
fully to our experience. Each loss we encounter reminds us of the pre-
ciousness of our blooming and our connection, and of the enormous
pleasure we may take in the unfolding of this life. The sadness of her
small children's death, although unmentioned, is keenly felt as part of our
shared experience.

The theme of cherry blossoms also expressed lost love for her husband
in her poem about him. She once again does not hide the human side of
her passion through claiming nonattachment or adopting a Buddhist
view of impermanence. She owns a continuing sadness, even though
years have passed. Consider this poem, "Memories of My Husband."

Together we enjoyed
The cherry blossoms,
And passed long summers
In the mountains:
Standing here such sadness.[267]

Rengetsu did not hide her love for her husband or the effect his absence
had on her heart. The importance of this statement from a Buddhist nun
should not be underestimated. As we in the West learn the meaning of
nonattachment, we sometimes mistake the intended consequences of the
practice and realization of "letting go." Letting go of our attachments
means that we do not look to objects, circumstances, or people as a
means to achieve happiness, but it does not mean we have no feeling.
Through Zen Buddhist meditation practice we realize a deeper and more
stable connection to happiness. Through meditation we can connect with
our "true nature," our ongoing and connected relationship to the entire
universe. The discovery of our true nature sometimes comes with a thrill,
but the experience of knowing our true nature can be counted on in the
most difficult of times to provide stability. Our lack of attachment, our
lack of demand that the universe meet our self-centered needs, enables us
to be more fully present in our relationships.

Rengetsu stands out as an example of poignant realization integrated with tender human feelings. In another poem about her lost husband, "Thirty Years after My Husband's Death," Rengetsu addresses the universality of suffering contained within her bereavement:

> The evanescence of
> This floating world
> I feel over and over:
> It is hardest
> To be the one left behind.[268]

Picturing Rengetsu in Zen samurai culture, with its emphasis on not blinking in the face of death, we more fully appreciate her teaching. While the samurai warrior concentrated on courageous action in the shadow of his own impending death, Rengetsu believed that the widow's or widower's task, living on alone, was far more difficult than that of the samurai's sacrifice. There are many layers of meaning in this message. One meaning is that death and dying are not as difficult as we imagine; cultivating acceptance of our own death is a task to be undertaken, but we will die anyway, whether we accept it or not. Another is that, difficult as it is to carry on, facing our sadness after watching our loved ones die, it is even more difficult to continue to bloom. Rengetsu does not just advise us to do so, she is a living example of what she preaches.

Rengetsu's poem "Heart" offers us a teaching on love and loss. Rather than abstaining from love and family as a way to practice, she finds Buddhist teachings within this world of human relations.

> Coming and going,
> Without beginning or end,
> Like ever changing
> White clouds:
> The heart of things.[269]

In this poem we see Rengetsu's transcendent view of the dualistic concepts of outside/inside and substance/no substance. We are reminded that this work happens within our hearts, through our direct experience and intimate life—not through ideas about practice but through our actual lives. As our own heart transforms, the entire universe reflects what we begin to understand. Our understanding is reflected everywhere we look—in the unending, continually changing flow of phenomena. And, to stretch our view just a little further, she calls this ineffable flow "the heart of things." Usually when we think of the heart or core, we think of something solid. But Rengetsu invokes a view of change itself as both our own center and the core of all existence. If we continue looking without distraction into our own deepest heart, we will only find clouds passing through empty sky.

Rengetsu's poetry and teaching are like these clouds—given away on cups, teapots, and other household objects, they have no solid form. Her message isn't a fixed collection that calls itself a "teaching." It is like the cherry blossoms, the clouds, and the crimson colors of autumn. It is just passing through. It appears without claiming to be anything special. It is up to us to find our heartfelt relationship to her teaching and her inspirational life that has dispersed before our eyes.

In a poem inscribed on a teapot, she describes the waters of Katada Bay on Lake Biwa, a common Japanese metaphor for the travails of a woman, and the peace that meditation may provide:

> Wind blows across
> Katada Bay
> A forsaken boat
> Unmoving on the
> Icy stillness.[270]

In Japan it is said that a woman's life is like being tossed on the waves of Lake Biwa. In this poem Rengetsu conjures up a windy scene, a lonesome boat, and a way to cool the emotions and find a peaceful stillness in the midst of Lake Biwa—perhaps a reference to Buddhist meditation, but certainly an encouragement to find one's own stability in the midst of the waves.

Rengetsu's way—giving away her teaching without collecting and labeling it as Buddhadharma—seems to be the way that Zen women have offered themselves—with little recognition of a collected work. Humility, an admirable quality true to Buddhist practice, should not obscure the

Rengetsu's "Waters of Katada Bay" Teapot

value of teachings freely given. Rengetsu's teachings to both men and women instruct us to realize our unique potential within this life, and to keep on refining this offering until the end.

Clearly, Rengetsu's life of adversity forced her to come to terms with human suffering and the meaning of this life. She never explicitly described her process of awakening—which teacher she studied with and what experiences she had in training. We can only infer the meaning of her experience through knowing her life story and studying the poems she distributed on pottery and calligraphic cards.

There are many stories of Rengetsu's character that describe her humility and simplicity even after she won success as an artist. After her work became popular, she moved her residence often to avoid the crowds. Despite her unsettled life, she was a prolific artist. By the time of her death in 1875 at age eighty-four, Japan had declared her a kind of patron saint of the arts. She was beloved by people from every social class.

She was known to give away money to the poor and to help other artists through collaborating with them so their pieces would also sell.

One story tells us that Rengetsu helped those imitating her work by teaching them how to forge her signature. She had no need for wealth or fame and lived a simple life, which only increased the popularity of her work. There is also a story that when a robber entered her home one night, Rengetsu lit a lamp so he could see better what there was to steal, and then fixed the thief a cup of tea.

Rengetsu taught that in order to live and work authentically, we need to be ourselves. She did not try to imitate what a Buddhist nun was supposed to be; she fully inhabited her own life in manifesting the nun's role. As we find the capacity to accept and transform our suffering, we take our own unique position in the world. Personal gifts and limitations, when recognized with honesty and acceptance, become our unique and authentic offering to this world. We cannot push aside our personal human experience to do something else; all our faults and foibles need to be first known, then transformed through acceptance, and finally incorporated into our lifework as our deepest intention.

Through Rengetsu, and her Buddhist name, Lotus Moon, we are reminded about our function in the world. No matter how corrupt the world is, we can inhabit it with our deepest intention to live a meaningful and beneficial life. The beautiful lotus, the symbol of purity in Buddhism, can bloom only in muddy water. We may express our lives in the world of work in the same way, keeping in mind a phrase in a traditional Zen chant: "May we exist with purity like a lotus in muddy water. Thus we bow to Buddha."

Rengetsu, Eunyeong Sunim, and Zhidong all found ways to pursue their practice and to earn money to support themselves. Their gift was finding a way to pour themselves into their work with creativity and passion. While Buddhism is often practiced through silent meditation in isolated monasteries, we can also see from these examples that sincere and thoroughgoing practice can flower into a life of productive activity.

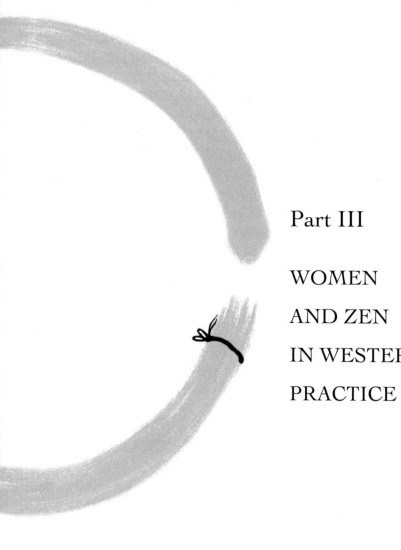

Part III

WOMEN
AND ZEN
IN WESTERN
PRACTICE

Asian Zen for Western Practice   11

THE BASIS for Buddhist practice is dependent not on male or female embodiment, but on seeing the truth of our human existence—the absolute reality of impermanence, the absence of inherent or separate self, the unsatisfactoriness of experience based solely on materialistic goals, and the inherent freedom that is the birthright of all human beings. All schools of Buddhism agree that this basis is irrefutable. It is independent of whether one is male or female, child or elderly, handsome or disfigured, beautiful or plain.

This essential Buddhist understanding, sometimes referred to as "the four marks of existence," acknowledges reality as it is. Visible expressions of formal practice—robes, silence, rituals, bells, incense, altar, Buddha statue—are often mistaken for "holiness" or, worse, absolute reality. In Zen we call this "mistaking the finger pointing at the moon for the moon itself." Dzongar Khyentse Rinpoche,[271] in the Tibetan tradition, likens this tendency to confusing the teacup with the tea it contains.

In Buddhist practice the "tea" is realizing the essential nature of reality. The teacup—skillful means for teaching this essence—is formed by the traditional practices used to experience the tea. The teacup helps to gather and offer the tea so we can taste it for ourselves. The shape of the teacup meets our lips, efficiently or awkwardly, sometimes delivering essence without losing a drop, sometimes deluging us and spilling out practices that we cannot readily take in. The teacup can entice us, challenge us to pay attention and sip mindfully, or turn us away from the tea.

Gathering together fragmented and forgotten stories of Zen's female ancestors creates a Buddhist teacup of a different shape—one created from the women's world of spiritual practice. This particular teacup is suitable for everyday use and is appropriate for informal or formal settings. It can be offered to a variety of people and is imbued with pragmatism, depth, and intimacy. Tasting Buddhist tea from these cups, we imbibe the essence of the Buddha's teaching. This teacup holds Zen's essential teaching, but it is created within a world of family ties—a world strewn with cultural and physical obstacles—and fired in a kiln of faith and effort built to sustain and nurture spiritual development.

This is not a vessel that invokes a world of silent hermit masters, but one that comes instead from a world of determined, presumably defeated, women embedded in family responsibilities, who nonetheless continued their spiritual practice and transformed their lives from the inside out despite cultural and Buddhist prohibitions forbidding them from changing their outer circumstances. This is not a vessel tempered in celibacy and separation from family, work, and love; but one molded by the hands of women who cared for their families, bore children, earned money, and served their communities.

What can we learn from drinking in the Dharma from such a vessel of female Zen ancestors? We specifically learn about Buddhist practice that includes three broad categories: practicing with loved ones, practicing while working in the world, and adapting our training institutions to fit our actual lives. Attending to these three areas of development seems essential for the continuance of Zen in the West.

Zen has benefited its practitioners across time and culture by adapting its teaching methods and venues while maintaining its essential message—that human beings can transform their consciousness and lessen suffering. Zen practice has been portable and able to transform itself as it has traveled from the Buddha's India to our contemporary Western world. As modern Westerners, we cannot expect our world to return to the values of the Buddha's India, Bodhidharma's China, or Dogen's Japan. Rather we need to help transform Zen to come forward and to meet us as we are. Zen Buddhism's long and varied survival under different conditions and cultures tells us that Zen practice truly addresses an essential human need. Language and teaching methods need to continue to deliver the essential message in ways that are culturally appropriate. This is a task at which our female Zen predecessors excelled. Their practice/wisdom teaches us that where there is sincere intention, whatever the circumstances, deep and effective practice will emerge in its own way—appropriate to the moment.

Though there is much good that has come of Zen's encounter with the West, the journey has not been smooth. Several accounts of how a teacher's misbehavior has resulted in harm to students and to their communities have centered on Zen masters engaging in exploitative sexual relationships with their female students. Katy Butler recounts how male Zen teachers, both Western and Japanese, have taken sexual advantage of their female students and also misappropriated other community assets.[272] We need to understand what goes wrong in transferring Asian Zen Buddhism to Western practice and how cultural differences embedded in Zen—its organizational hierarchy and its literature, as opposed to its actual meditative practices—are affecting us in Western Zen centers. For example, while we are taught by our Asian tradition to respect and honor Zen teachers and their position in the lineage, we have no organizational processes through which to address their mistakes, even those that are obviously causing harm. Because we are basing our Western practice on only one half of our tradition's teachers we are missing some essential ingredients.

We need to ask whether the traditional Buddhist view of women practitioners and teachers as inferior to their male counterparts, and our own male-dominated Western culture, not only make women targets for abuse by their teachers, but collude to single out and favor male Western Buddhist teachers. Rita Gross has pointed to a disparity between the equal number of North American female and male Dharma teachers and the disproportionately high number of male teachers who have been pictured in recent publications.[273] One magazine advertised nineteen male teachers and *zero* female teachers. Is Buddhist history repeating itself? Are contemporary women Dharma teachers unsupported, underfunded, undervalued, and becoming less visible? If Western Zen women's presence becomes marginalized as it did in Asia, we will lose Zen's female teaching voice and its more flexible and varied solutions to the problems that Western Zen has been encountering—problems of sexuality, marginalization, and lack of financial support.

We need to find solutions to the problems facing Western Zen. The study of female ancestors and their teachings offers a wider view of how to practice. We encounter the general potential for adaptation and specific adaptations that will support the unfolding of Western Zen. These specific adaptations are: a greater variety of venues and organizational structures; a frank discussion of sexuality and its place in practice; the potential for remunerative work in the world while devoted to Zen practice; a more explicit integration of lay community and practice life; and the inclusion of family in practice life. Both the validity and necessity of adapting practice and the specific adaptations are useful to the development of Buddhism in the West.

When Buddhists have a practice grounded in their actual lives there is not only more opportunity to practice (for example with family and coworkers), but there is less chance that they will simply blindly imitate exotic rituals and thereby mistake the teacup for the tea. Buddhism, like other spiritual traditions that rely on sometimes unquestioned obedience to a religious leader, becomes vulnerable to abuse of practitioners, cult-like isolation, and an overemphasis on status and hierarchy versus the propagation of the Buddha's way.

Zen may be particularly prone to these problems if we add in the factor of allowing the Zen master's "crazy wisdom." Like other religious organizations, Zen Buddhism must open itself to feedback and adaptation from a wide variety of practitioners and interested parties. We have seen evidence that the female ancestors' variety of residential and nonresidential programs, and their strong connection to the community they served, provide contemporary Buddhist institutions with more flexible forms of practice, suitable to a wide audience that offered genuine awakening to the women.

One expects problems to develop in a fledgling institution like Western Buddhist training centers; Asian Buddhist traditions have not just training monasteries and centers, but village temples, training seminaries, universities, and a wide variety of Buddhist-based institutions like hospitals and food banks. How can we address our current institutional problems and adapt to create a more broadly connected and integrated practice in the West? Only with a variety of valid and substantial practice options that are integrated with a larger community can the potential for institutions isolating themselves from honest feedback be lessened and our positive relationship to the community be secured. Besides service to the community we also need committed Zen students, living and supporting themselves outside of Buddhist residential communities. Such practitioners are less dependent financially, socially, and psychologically on these practice institutions. Additionally, monasteries and convents have depended on the community to provide both financial and labor resources to support them. A residential community that explicitly values and supports both its wider community and nonresidential members, whether ordained or lay, who are working in the world, may be more likely to receive much needed support. The importance of monastic practice for training is indisputable; yet, it is not the only way, nor is it a sufficient platform in itself to sustain Buddhism's continuation in the West.

Our female ancestors established the importance of adaptation and provide many examples of the variety of practice, many that resulted in awakening.

The following chapters focus on problems that are arising in Western Buddhist practice centers, and how to remedy these problems with the wisdom gathered by the female tradition and the essential qualities of female spirituality. For Zen Buddhism to survive in the West we need the benefit of both sides of our practice's wisdom—male and female—and we need the ability to adapt practice and institutional life to our actual circumstances.

Women and Sexuality in Western Practice 12

THE FIRST NUNS' pioneering critique of the search for power through beauty and seduction could be immensely useful in articulating the dynamics of sexuality and power from a female perspective and liberating male and female practitioners from the pull of sexual dynamics in Western Zen centers. Sexual attachments all too commonly remain unconscious or are considered off-limits for Buddhist investigation and discussion. The pull of sexuality that arises during monastic or even lay sangha training can result in poor choices and conflict within the sangha. A discussion of the search for power through sexual attraction will help clarify the path for practitioners whether these dynamics arise inside or outside of practice places.[274]

We need more conscious training to understand these dynamics and prevent enactments of sexual relationships between male teachers and female students—affairs that end badly for both teacher and student. While many Zen centers have suffered "scandalous" relationships, these unconsciously driven poor choices are not limited to Zen centers. To repair the damage, often teachers and students have been sent away from their sanghas—a loss to the community. But if we do not really understand what happened and how, we are bound to keep repeating these unfortunate relationships. Studying the early nuns' experiences of their sexual longings and the freedom that resulted from practice may help shine some light on this problem.

Vimala, a nun at the time of the Buddha (see chapter 6 above), disclosed a desire to conquer men and gain power through seduction. Does the complex described by Vimala still entice contemporary women to seek affection or a sexual relationship with their teacher or practice leader? Is this what motivates a woman to draw close to the Western male teacher's power by becoming his "favorite" or even by becoming his sexual partner? A female Zen student may draw on her powers of seduction, wishing to enhance her ego through intimate association with a male she imagines to be spiritually powerful. If she does so, out of habit or cultural conditioning, she misses the chance to transform these unwholesome patterns through Zen training.

Women often have a more difficult time seeing these delusions, especially when a teacher receiving their seductive or ingratiating behavior enjoys the attention. Zen teachers who are flattered by women who flirt with them tend to reward these women. Women need to recognize their tendency to seek power by attracting male attention, and men have to learn to identify this specific personality trait that arises at times with some women. Male teachers need to understand how a woman's seduction may feed into their own hidden needs for affirmation. If they understand this, they might stop taking the woman's attention personally. If they do not, they fail to help the female student see through her favorite ego booster. They also may mistake a neurotic pattern for a genuine affinity and become embroiled in an unwholesome relationship.

The Buddhist nuns' descriptions of internal enslavement to seduction match modern feminists' and psychologists' views on the ways women attract and please to build their ego identity—using beauty and ingratiation in exchange for power. Feminists, writers, and psychologists have explored human craving for power derived from beauty and its ability to seduce those in power. Naomi Wolf, a contemporary scholar and social critic, portrays women as unconsciously playing out their longing for power, recognition, and belonging through their physical attractiveness to gain power.[275] And Polly Young-Eisendrath, a Jungian analyst and Buddhist practitioner, depicts the female expression of desire as a longing to be desired by another, and observes the cultural attribution of "evil" to the power of women's beauty.[276]

Women and men are affected by complex, unconsciously held attitudes regarding women's beauty; the linking of beauty to destructive power occurs in both genders. Timothy Beneke in *Men on Rape* writes of the male sense of being assaulted by the all-powerful forces of women's wiles.[277] Beneke examines how men avoid responsibility for their personal feelings of loneliness and vulnerability and invoke the age-old view of woman's power to conquer through seduction evidenced in colloquial expressions: "she's a knockout," "what a bombshell," "she's strikingly beautiful," "that woman is ravishing," "she's really stunning," "she's a *femme fatale*," "she's dressed to kill."[278] All of these expressions use violent verbalism and convey a coercive power emanating from women's beauty, a power that renders us senseless and helpless.

Vimala, in writing about her transformation through Buddhist practice, exposed her secret thoughts and took responsibility for her lust for power through seduction. Vimala's description of her pattern may help other women and men to see their relationship to the body, desire, and power seeking. As we engage Buddhist practice in a non-celibate practice environment, both men and women need to become aware of unconsciously held attitudes through studying the words of Vimala, and other nuns who described their sexual impulses. Through mutual awareness of unconsciously held longings and their powerful enactment, men and women Buddhist practitioners can become fully liberated together. Women and men, male teachers and female teachers, all need to explore their longings for power and security in the sexual arena if these longings are to cease being reenacted in Zen Buddhist settings.

Male Zen Teachers and Sexuality

Far too often we find that a male Zen master in a training monastery or a lay community has initiated a sexual affair or a pseudo-intimate affair (i.e., a special relationship with a favorite female student or "teacher's pet"). Male Zen teachers not only have had sexual relationships with female students but, less obviously, they have encouraged an unwholesome idealization from their young female assistants. These inappropriate relationships reflect an absence of integration of emotional nourishment—one denies unmet unconscious longings and needs in order to adhere to a strict monastic practice. This process has been referred to as spiritual bypassing, where meditation itself is used to repress rather than to resolve feelings.

These relationships seem to be an inevitable price we will pay in the

West when two genders practice Buddhism together. We need to learn how to pay attention to our own feelings both on and off the cushion and to take responsibility for relationships that arise in the sangha. Although meditation helps us to become more aware of our thoughts and feelings, the process is gradual. Paying attention, educating ourselves, and openly discussing these matters will help reveal hidden tendencies and power plays. Sangha discussions about clandestine relationships may reveal the male and the female sides of male-female power dynamics.

Men's secret longing for contact with their own vulnerability is the shadow side of the public persona of the heroic male Zen master. Described in detail in *Sex in the Forbidden Zone* by Peter Rutter, this craving can be understood as a comfort-seeking impulse or a need to express wholeness as a person. Needing to publicly maintain an idealized position at the top of a power structure, a man loses touch with his own vulnerable feelings. So he seeks to fulfill himself and express his softer side through a relationship with a vulnerable female. To the man in power, his own need for vulnerability appears disguised by a vulnerable female and his unconscious need to accept this side of himself is experienced as attraction to an admiring and dependent female. Since this tendency is often deeply repressed, meditation alone may not readily reveal it. However, if Zen teachers are educated about this hidden impulse they are more likely to suspect this hidden root and recognize it rather than act it out.

Educating the Community

I cannot remember a time when recognizing and working with sexuality was included in a Dharma talk at a Zen community—aside from when I've done it as I have been exploring the topics in this book. Yet the powerful consequences of sexuality in Zen practice places have left little doubt that this is a topic worthy of exploration in the context of Buddhist teaching. Why do teachers avoid it?

Have Zen students become so extremely sensitive through meditation and renunciation that talking about sexuality is like throwing a lighted match into kerosene? Perhaps sexuality is considered too politically difficult and personally revealing to discuss without offending someone or inappropriately exposing oneself. If men spoke, their personal views could be judged; if women spoke, it might be seen as seductive; if heterosexuals spoke, homosexuals might be offended; if homosexuals spoke, they might feel ill at ease; and so on.

In classical Buddhism little is said about integrating sexuality and practice. There are some very general instructions to the Buddha's lay students, but these instructions don't describe how to apply practice awareness with sexual relationships. Many passages refer to women as ensnaring and warn monks to be on guard against them, and other passages, meant to repress sexual feelings, describe the decay of a beautiful and attractive woman's corpse. Including sexuality in Dharma is difficult for these and other reasons, but the fact that female ancestors included this topic in their teachings should encourage us to try.

Using the examples presented in this book, we can start with the female ancestors' teachings on practice and sexual dynamics. We can question whether some of these dynamics are currently being enacted in our own centers. We can observe and comment on the tendency of the Buddhist literature to project sexuality onto women and the female body and make them responsible for men's sexual desires. We can explore the subtle ways that sexual attractions have been played out in our own community of work or sangha. We can seek to learn how such dynamics unfold when we are not in touch with our secret longings. We can talk about sensed flirtations arising between individuals in the community, and the sangha's responsibility to discuss these relationships and set standards for preventing harm. We can discuss the potential damage caused by hidden relationships and hold teachers and senior practitioners accountable, with the aim of rehabilitation and deepening practice rather than expulsion.

Working with Emotions 13

Zen and Human Relationships

WHILE THE BUDDHA required celibacy of his monks and nuns, Western Zen practice does not require this from ordained practitioners; it is possible for Westerners to practice mindfulness in the midst of these relationships. Zen is not a puritanical practice; it is a practice that affirms the whole of human experience and relationships, and thus there is an appropriate place for family and marital relationships. So can we envision a Western monastic training that respects family and marital relationships? Practicing in relationship requires understanding the difference between *detachment* and *nonattachment*. *Detachment* means we cut off our emotional connection to a situation—we turn away or just don't care. *Nonattachment* means that we participate in a situation without a specific demand or expectation for a particular outcome. Detachment may manifest as emotional repression; nonattachment is the fundamental principle of Buddhist practice. We need to make this distinction abundantly clear for Zen practitioners to develop a wholesome practice environment.

A priest's training requires several months, or even years, of monastic seclusion, is this the optimum arrangement for supporting a married priest and his/her family? Is it necessary to create this separation to train priests in the West? How will this requirement limit or support the propagation of Zen in the West? At the moment we are seeing some marriages ended in part because of this requirement. Since the requirement to practice apart from one's marital partner exists, we need to expose, understand, and transform the feelings that arise in separation and in union so that they are used as part of training, and greater awareness of suffering and its transformation arise. Training vows are difficult, but so are marital vows. When I was asked by an American Zen master how I could call myself a priest when I was married, I answered: "I keep all of my vows." He then sheepishly admitted that he had become divorced to explain his own attainment of monk's status. However, I believe that keeping all of our vows—to loved ones and ourselves—as Buddhist practice will help us transplant a rigorous and appropriate training in the West.

As a married trainee at a secluded monastery, I had my own experience of breaking the rules and "going over the wall" to meet my husband. What I experienced in the aftermath of the bliss was the reawakening of craving. The interlude led to heightened clarity about my own intimate process of fantasy and craving. After six weeks of loneliness and separation from my husband, I came face to face with my longing in a fresh light. The sharp pain I experienced helped me more attentively return to the process of letting go all over again. I did so with a clear view of what I had done—how indulging my longing had started the cravings all over again. Attending to the relationship and my longing became useful tools in my practice.

Monastic experience was wonderful training, but I concluded that the lengthy separation, the three-month *ango*, was not good for my marriage. Fortunately, my marriage remained intact; other trainees have not been spared the loss of a relationship because of their training requirements. I subsequently found other ways to train intensively for shorter periods of time that respected the needs of my marriage. Since many Western spiritual leaders are married, wouldn't it be wise for us to find ways to support marriage even during monastic training? Relationships need a wholesome environment to survive and can provide insight into the essential Buddhist cycle of suffering. Long-term relationships provide ongoing training in seeing one's own selfish tendencies, a truly rigorous practice place for married or committed Western Buddhists.

Home Leaving and Home Avoiding

Home leaving has a variety of meanings for Zen Buddhist practitioners: giving up personal comforts in order to devote oneself to community;

maintaining a celibate or unmarried lifestyle; taking vows as the central and guiding principle of one's life; or abandoning one's family responsibilities to pursue the Dharma. All Zen priests affirm home leaving in their ordination ceremony. In the context of priest ordination, home leaving has come to mean freeing oneself of the habitual attachments and tendencies that construct a false self—freeing oneself of the shell of attachment in which we hide to avoid facing each moment with naked awareness.

What is becoming apparent in the larger Western Zen community is that monastic practice (years of "just following the schedule") risks leaving some practitioners clueless when it comes to personal relationships. The personal self remains hidden or repressed, unintegrated with spiritual development. In other words, years of silent monastic training may result in the production of adults unprepared and unable to engage in mature relationships or work in the world. This is an undesirable outcome in that it makes Buddhism look rather unappealing, but it also neglects to make use of the emotions as the source of our transformation. Watching feelings arise and viewing the field in which they are experienced and transformed are essential elements of Buddhist practice.

For monastic practitioners, life structured by rules and schedules provides moment-by-moment opportunities to let go of preferences and manifest no-self, but an over-emphasis on no-self can lead to spiritual bypassing, in which personal feelings and impulses remain repressed and unintegrated. The difficulty arises when the relinquishing of self-clinging thoughts on the meditation cushion, or the abandoning of preferences, is mistakenly translated as *having no feelings* when interacting with other people. Far too often, monastic Zen students may confuse detachment or emotional distancing and repression for noticing with a nonattached mind. As we have seen in the life stories of Zen women, staying connected to loved ones not only did not interfere with their awakening, but it may have provided relationship skills in working with their sanghas.

The Appearance of the Zen Zombie

The home-leaving principle, when combined with the emphasis on no-self, leads some students to erroneously equate the abandonment of feelings with Zen enlightenment. The repression of feeling affords some Zen students a short-term lessening of anxiety, but it is not the path to personal integration of selflessness. Furthermore, using meditation and monastic training to repress feeling is neither an effective tool for developing awareness nor a useful method for resolving interpersonal conflict.

Meditation and monastic life can become a method of repression and a means for hiding from life's work. The malady shows itself when rigid adherence to rules and a disregard for personal engagement passes itself off as Zen training. A simple example of this behavior came to light when a young mother, visiting for the first time a Western Zen residential center, asked several robed practitioners for a refill for a bottle of milk for her baby. After a few encounters in which Zen residents impatiently refused to give her a glass of milk, she turned to me and asked, "Are Zen people this mean to everyone?" Sadly, I had to answer, "Yes, far too often."

Many of us began spiritual practice as a means of resolving trauma. Unfortunately, the image of the unattached, enlightened, fierce Zen master who has transcended self-clinging and happily lives the hermit's life, appealing as it is, may not be so useful to Westerners. We need to integrate meditation's energetic awareness into our personal traumas, our wounds, and our defense mechanisms. Zen practice means finding the mind of meditation in times of fear, anger, and desire, rather than trying to banish fear, anger, and desire from our consciousness. We need to practice what we preach in intimate relationships that affect us on a daily basis. This dimension of practice is not well articulated in the stories that present male ancestors as masters who have completely transcended human needs, but is addressed repeatedly in the lives and teachings of female ancestors.

Buddha Realm
in Everyday Western Life   14

Life's Everyday Teaching

THE WORLD of women's Zen is a world that embraces a variety of awakenings, in which each woman finds her own way in her own circumstances—just as we must learn to do in Western Zen training centers and lay life today. Our study of different women's training experiences and convent styles gives us the examples we need to develop training institutions that appropriately serve Western practitioners male and female, their families, and their communities. We need institutions that offer us realistic training—guidelines that deepen our acceptance of how we actually live right here in this culture rather than encouraging us to look for enlightenment somewhere else. The training we receive should help us bring peace and sustenance to our communities.

We need to train in ways that take Zen out of its Asian institutional containers and pour it into our own teacup: into our own working life which values and is valued by our communities. We need to develop Western Zen institutions that do not imitate ancient Asian monastic images but instead support the integration of practice into our own vernacular.

Zen Training and Worldly Work

In Asia, monasteries have historically enjoyed a broad basis for financial support—temples have been supported by large congregations, governments and corporations. Early Western Zen aimed at building training monasteries, which were supported largely by private donors and the work of their members. Many Zen institutions now find themselves facing financial crisis with inadequate community, institutional, or cultural support for their mission. One reason for this state of crisis is the perception of Zen Buddhists as marginal or insignificant to Western culture—or even worse, as strange or harmful. These perceptions, obviously, do not encourage donations. Western Zen needs to widen its basis for support. It will not survive through just building training monasteries that serve practitioners. Large training monasteries need to redirect more of their efforts to establishing their value to the community in order to transplant Zen to the West.

Some suggestions about how the Buddhist mission might extend to a larger population, and possibly stave off decline, come from Clark Strand writing in the *Wall Street Journal*.[279] Besides including children and families, the Buddhist community might offer useful community services, developed and enhanced by practice. Here again, we may take a page from the female ancestors who found ways to finance their temples through services to their community and beyond.

Female Zen masters developed practices and skills to support themselves financially—in fields like art, writing, and teaching. Currently, Chinese Buddhist monks and nuns are pioneering the integration of worldly work and monastic life by building hospitals and training priests and nuns in the helping professions—as teachers, social workers, doctors, and nurses. Western Buddhists need to honor the early Buddhist injunctions against attachment to wealth and work as a distraction from practice, but at the same time they must face the realities of what is required to develop and support contemporary Buddhism. The practice of female Zen masters offers assurance that we can integrate financial support without sacrificing enlightenment.

The tendency to avoid personal development through seclusion in monastic life can result in the economic dependency of Zen practitioners. The penchant to avoid work in the world, to rely entirely on an institution that is in its infancy, is destructive of institutions and unwholesome for practitioners. If Zen centers unwittingly allow their students to devote their entire adult lives to serving only the monastic community, they will need to be prepared to support these students through their retirement years. And this is beginning to look like an unrealistic if not impossible financial task.

Zen students who do not develop their personal gifts, and who do not thereby mature through work in the world, are also missing an important task of adult development and adjustment. Western psychologists have emphasized the adult task of individuation, becoming more fully oneself, as crucial to finding meaning. Honing one's work abilities and friendships, one continues to develop psychologically and to feel and to be productive in society at large. Monastic seclusion and relationships confined to this specialized setting may not fully facilitate adult development. Avoiding worldly work can be seen as another type of spiritual bypass.

If Zen centers provide long-term residence as compensation they risk encouraging students to become financially dependent, they risk staffing their residential centers with people who are there for some of the wrong reasons—people who stay at the centers because they have lost their ability to support themselves financially in the world. Global financial uncertainty and technological change may make it even more difficult for long-term Zen students to reenter the marketplace. They may become dependent and resentful of the very institution within which they feel trapped.

As the female Zen masters demonstrate, exchanging the fruits of practice for financial support with the community offers a way to engage with the world outside and to remain financially solvent. Zen centers that offer services will draw a greater number of people to our practice. When a monastic schedule makes it difficult to work in the world, a more appropriate schedule might be devised that would still accommodate group practice. Female ancestors formed smaller group homes—a more economically sustainable model that could offer a schedule appropriate for work in the world. This should be encouraged today.

By developing personal gifts and bringing these gifts to the community, individual practitioners can practice nonattachment in their own lives. Work in the world presents occasions for the arising of competitiveness, pride, envy, and resentment. Learning to apply buddha-mind in the midst of worldly turmoil is a wonderful teaching that awaits explicit development for Western practitioners.[280] The understanding of how our female ancestors commonly fused work with Zen helps us value this aspect of our tradition and validate our efforts to integrate Zen training and work in the world.

The Graying of the Zen Center

Some Western Zen centers, having made use of their practitioners' labor over the course of many years, are finding themselves in a bind as these practitioners age and reach retirement. This bind has two key dimensions: declining financial opportunities and declining health. Asian Zen counterparts have had centuries to develop financial support; Western Zen centers do not currently have the means to offer retirement funds, medical coverage, and housing to the large numbers of Zen students who populate their residential centers and are reaching retirement age.

Many students who have faithfully faced the rigors of little sleep, a low-protein community diet, and an absence of rigorous daily exercise find themselves physically and emotionally depleted and sometimes with chronic degenerative diseases related to their Zen lifestyles. Zen centers that have benefited from the long-term commitment of residential students may now find themselves unable to sustain their centers while supporting and housing large numbers of aging students. Some older residents are being asked to leave; those that need medical attention may find their needs unmet.

If Western Zen students examine current Asian models, they will see that monastic training requiring little sleep, early morning arising, and long periods of seated meditation is usually sustained only for a few years. In Japan monastic training is for the young monk only; it is not practiced into old age. Zen monks train for a few years in a strict monastic environment, and then return home to live in a city or village temple with a family-serving community. Western Zen centers encourage practitioners to simply follow monastic training guidelines even as one ages—a practice that may create health problems and shorten the life span. Just as we should not idealize Zen masters, we should not idealize monastic training as a perfect lifestyle for all ages. Medical research suggests that getting enough sleep and a diet appropriate to one's personal needs is important for sustaining health. We should not cultivate attachment to health and fitness, nor should we waste this body that is itself a precious Dharma resource.

Looking to the female ancestors, we find a more sustainable and wholesome model. We find ordained nuns living at home and also in convents where space was created for the elderly as part of their community.

Sustaining health and correcting excesses with healing have often been the domain of female ancestors and female spirituality. To help their students practice appropriately as they age, residential Zen centers in the West may encourage the formation of small group homes for the elderly. Such homes may also enhance a Zen center's economic viability.

Female Spirituality 15

When God Was a Woman

PRACTICE STYLES developed by Zen's female ancestors can be examined within the larger context of female spirituality. In the past, God, often defined today only in masculine terms, has been worshipped as female. For example, consider this from Thebes, Egypt, in the fourteen century B.C.E.:

> In the beginning there was Isis: Oldest of the Old, She was the Goddess from whom all Becoming Arose. She was the Great Lady, Mistress of the two Lands of Egypt, Mistress of Shelter, Mistress of Heaven, Mistress of the House of Life, and Mistress of the word of God. She was the Unique.[281]

And in ancient Sumer the goddess was Inanna; multifaceted, she represented fecundity and the feminine. Beyond the maternal principle, she was heaven and earth, matter and spirit, and energies that cannot be made certain and secure. In one song she is said "to pour forth grains and legumes from her womb."[282] Goddess-worshipping cultures were destroyed by the command of Yahweh and early Jewish ancestors—the pagans that were "smote" by the Israelites.[283] The female God was responsible for bringing forth life on earth, for transforming matter, and for holding that which cannot be named. She represented cosmic pregnancy from which life emerged out of the invisible realm. She offered birth and sustenance, and through her provision is connected to all living things.

And the Great Mother's appearance is not limited to the ancient Middle East; she appeared in the Hindu tradition as Kali Ma, and then later, from a different perspective, in Taoism. Because the Zen tradition is traced through the Buddhist encounter with Chinese Taoists, the Great Mother as she appeared in Lao Tsu's *Tao Te Ching* affected Zen's inception. Consider this quotation from Lao Tsu:

> The Tao is called the Great Mother
> Empty yet inexhaustible,
> It gives birth to infinite worlds.
> It is always present within you.
> You can use it anyway you want.[284]

The Great Way (Tao), essential spiritual development, arises from the mysterious female or Great Mother. She has no form, yet continues to offer life endlessly. We are intimately connected to her; in fact, we are made of her, and may use her essence to create our life.

> [T]he origin of the universe comes from
>   the Great Mother:
> There was something formless and perfect
> Before the universe was born.
> It is serene. Empty.
> Solitary. Unchanging.
> Infinite. Eternally present.
> It is the mother of the universe.
> For lack of a better name,
> I call it the Tao.
> It flows through all things,
> inside and outside, and it returns
> to the origin of all things.[285]

The flow of form from emptiness (and back, form to emptiness) is the Great Mother's movement. She is infinitely empty, infinitely creative, giving and receiving; all life emerges and returns to this source. The Taoist description of the empty source, formless, intimate, and infinite, and the description of the Great Mother evolved to give birth to Zen.

The Great Mother in Buddhism: Prajnaparamita

Even in the West, most if not all Zen centers chant a core verse called the Heart Sutra or Prajnaparamita Heart Sutra. This chant contains the heart of Zen's teaching: Form is emptiness and emptiness is form. The sutra from which this chant is extracted is actually translated from the Sanskrit as "The Great Mother Prajnaparamita Sutra."[286] Early Mahayana Buddhists attributed this sutra to the Buddha, and claim that it was lost for several centuries. The Great Mother Prajnaparamita Sutra, according to Buddhist scripture, was rediscovered when the Buddhist teacher Nagarjuna went down to the *nagas* (dragons) under a lake and discovered a vast treasure trove of Mahayana sutras, among them the many versions of the Great Mother Prajnaparamita Sutra. The passage to the underworld is a cross-cultural image used to describe the descent from the outer world to the world of the Great Mother; it is explored in depth by Jungian scholar Sylvia Brenton Perera in her work *Descent to the Goddess.*

Buddhism teaches that the nagas took the Buddha's lectures on the Great Mother under the sea to protect them from decline. When the nagas saw a worthy Dharma vessel, Nagarjuna, they pulled him down to receive the hidden teachings. Nagarjuna's name is a combination of *naga* and *arjuna*, meaning the protector of the nagas. Nagarjuna studied the Great Mother Prajnaparamita Sutra for fifty years and taught it throughout India. The Heart Sutra practiced in almost every Zen center as "The Great Heart Sutra" is actually a verse from the Great Mother Prajnaparamita Sutra. The renowned Buddhist scholar Robert Thurman gives us a concise overview of the importance of this text:

> The original Prajnaparamita is the text called the *Great Mother: the Prajnaparamita of 100,000 Lines.* It purports to record the full audience given by Shakyamuni Buddha on Vulture Peak with the greatest explicitness and completeness.... Over the centuries various abridged versions have emerged, including the very short *One Letter Sutra* (the letter *A*), the short *Heart Sutra*, the concise *Diamond-cutting Sutra*, the *8,000 Line*, the *18,000* or

20,000 Line, and the *25,000 Line Sutras*, from a total of eighteen Sutras. These are all considered the same Sutra, differing only in length and detail, never in basic import....

These perfect wisdom texts served as the foundation for a systematic curriculum developed over many centuries in the Mahayana Buddhist monastic universities, among the earliest universities on this planet.... This ancient curriculum opened the minds of millions of practitioners for a thousand years in India. In East Asia, it seems clear that Prajnaparamita served as the basis of the Ch'an and Zen traditions.... The famous Sixth Patriarch of Ch'an in China, Hui Neng, recalled his own perfect wisdom upon a single hearing of the *Diamond-cutting* version of the *Prajnaparamita*.[287]

The Prajnaparamita sutra is the essence of perfect wisdom for Buddhists. And the goddess Prajnaparamita, the archetypal embodiment of perfect wisdom and the source of highest enlightenment for all the Buddhas, is represented in female form. Her teaching is form and emptiness inseparable, or the transformation and manifestation of life essence. From her being, our life emerges; to her we return at death for transformation. The Great Mother, as manifested in the Prajnaparamita sutras, permeates and transcends space, time, and all physical dimensions. Her process is synonymous with the Big Bang out of which all physical reality emerged. Both the Zen and the Tibetan traditions are based on the teachings of Prajnaparamita; both traditions claim Nagarjuna, who based his teachings on the Great Mother Sutras, as a founding ancestor.

The Great Mother Prajnaparamita Sutra instructs followers of her teaching about the Mahayana bodhisattva practitioner in decidedly female nurturing terms:

The bodhisattva will always maintain a motherly mind, consecrated to the constant protection, education and maturing of conscious beings, inviting and guiding them along the path of all-embracing love. This Mahayana mind never succumbs to fear, anxiety or depression and is never overwhelmed by the strange adventures of awareness in the three realms of relativity—mundane form, sublime form and formlessness.[288]

Buddhist practitioners are encouraged to strive to become the embodiment of intimacy and nurturing in order to help others and to fulfill their practice. Guided by these principles of devotion to helping others, the bodhisattva follows a steady path in the ordinary, extraordinary, or mysterious emanations that she or he encounters in this life. These Great Mother teachings were lost under the sea once long ago, and now once more need to be rescued from the depths where they are again hidden.

Shunryu Suzuki Describes the Return to Mother

The Great Mother principle surfaces in Zen founder Shunryu Suzuki Roshi's teachings. He described meditation as entering emptiness, as experiencing the *shunyata* of Prajnaparamita, as contact with the Mother. In his lecture "Calmness of Mind," he speaks of returning to our mother's bosom as letting go and letting the Buddha care for us.

> Because we have lost our mother's bosom, we do not feel like her child anymore. Yet fading away into emptiness can feel like being at our mother's bosom, and we will feel as though she will take care of us. Moment after moment, do not lose this practice of *shikantaza* [just sitting, completely present].[289]

Suzuki Roshi described Zen meditation as a return to mother. He explained that striving to accomplish something has created a feeling that we have lost our mother—we have forgotten our basic connection to the matrix of existence. Zen meditation helps us to transform this mental tendency. When within our meditation we let go of mental constructions, relaxing our striving to create a supposedly separate self, we address this suffering. When we are truly engaged in meditation, we experience a "fading away" or dissolving back to our essential intimate connection to our actual existence, our relationship to the Great Mother.

Suzuki expressed Zen meditation as realizing our actual connection to the source of life. This experience of intimate "withness" can best be described in the boundaryless, tactile, and fluid relationship of a mother suckling her child. This essential intimacy underlying our consciousness has become lost through habitual cravings. We have covered our earliest and most vivid sense of connection to mother with a concept of separation and independence.

Suzuki describes the embodied experience of the Great Mother as a return to our mother's bosom, suckling her milk—an intimate, relational, and personified experience of sustenance and contact. His teaching is a far cry from the harshness usually associated with samurai Zen—shouts, blows, and unfeeling silent submission to rules. It is a far cry from the goal of achieving the strict, idealized, unfeeling persona of a great macho Zen hero. His description of practice validates and reinserts the Great Mother principle into Zen and validates the female ancestors' warm and related ways of practice. He positions returning to mother as integral to the Zen tradition.

Indeed, the Zen tradition, based as we have seen on the Great Mother Prajnaparamita Sutra, is fully expressed through the intimacy and relatedness of Zen's female ancestors, a good model for Buddhist practice evolving in the West. We find the depth of practice we seek from zazen within our family and loving relationships, our work in the world, and our hands-on caregiving for the benefit of others. Our embodied fading away into emptiness allows us the back-and-forth movement of form pouring into emptiness, and emptiness becoming form, that has guided our tradition from its inception. This is not a model that we are borrowing or imposing but one that is embodied by the Great Mother, her Prajnaparamita Sutra instructions for bodhisattva training, and Zen's female lineage.

As Buddhism grows up in America, we too are growing up. We realize we can no longer imitate the practice of young Asian monks. Zen is not an Asian practice; it expresses a universal human need. Most of all we need to bring the practice into our very own Western lives, and having begun Buddhist practice later in life, we need to pace ourselves. We need to continue practicing into old age in order to develop. Returning to the Great Mother's bosom, we accept her wisdom to take care of our health, to express ourselves without imitating others, and to constantly let go of our ideas about reality in exchange for the real thing—reality itself. Including female teachings in our developing Western Buddhism nurtures our continuous and deepening practice with loved ones and our communities.

May it be so.

Appendix 1

Index of Women Mentioned

Nuns of India

DATE (approx)	NAME	PAGE
500 B.C.E.	Mahapajapati Gotami	44–51
	Vimala	96–98
	Nanduttara	93–94
	Ambapali	94–96
	Yashodhara	46
300 C.E.	Prasannasila	167

Chinese Nuns

DATE (approx)	NAME	PAGE
292–361	Jingjian	51–53
300–370	Zhixian	53–54
ca. 320	Huizhan	54
ca. 400	Jingchen	100–101
470	Zongji	17–18
625–705	Empress Wu	59–60
808	Lingzhao	168–70

Korean Women

Japanese Nuns

Appendix 2

A Women Ancestors' Lineage Document

Myochi-ni
Yodo-ni
Kakuzan Shido
Mugai Nyodai
Miaohsin
Miaozong
Dianxin Pozi
Shiji
Liu Tiemo
Moshan
Teishin
Lingzhao
Zongji
Jingjian
Uppalavana
Patacara
Sundari-Nanda
Khema
Dhammadina
Mahapajapati

Ekyu-ni
Eshun-ni
Zhiyuan Xinggang
Soshin-ni
Ryonen Genso
Yoshihime
Tachibana no Someko
Otagaki Rengetsu
Nagasawa Sozen
Nogami Senryo
Joshin Kasai
Kojima Kendo
Sumiko Kudo
Ruth Fuller Sasaki
Jiyu Kennett
Jean Ross
Maurine Stuart
Maylie Scott
Kushin Myoan

Appendix 3

A Women's Lineage Paper
Created by Salt Spring Zen Circle

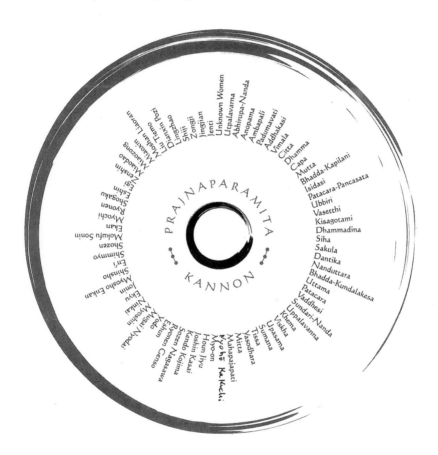

Credit: Norman Fischer, Peter Levitt, and Barbara Cooper

Notes

1 "The Sandokai of Sekito Kisen Daiosho," in Berkeley Zen Center Daily Chant Book.
2 "Patriarchs' Zen" is a term used to describe the history of the transmission of Zen from India to China and Japan. It consists of the teachings of only male Zen masters, and has historically been the accepted basis of Zen Buddhist practice. In this context, by definition, there are no female Zen masters. This version of history was brought from Asia to the West by male Zen founders. A chant of the historical Buddhas and patriarchs is part of the liturgy of most Zen temples in the West.
3 Levering, "Miao-tao and her Teacher Dahui," in Gregory and Getz, Buddhism in the Sung, 188.
4 Mahapajapati is the Pali for her name and will be used throughout. In Sanskrit her name is Mahaprajapati.
5 Murcott, First Buddhist Women, 197.
6 Sponberg, "Attitudes toward Women."
7 Anguttara Nikaya 3.66; Thanissaro, Handful of Leaves, vol. 3, 32.
8 Levering, "Lin-Chi Ch'an and Gender," in Cabezon Buddhism, Sexuality, and Gender, 144.
9 Ferguson, Zen's Chinese Heritage.
10 Ibid., 178.
11 According to Kazuo Osumi ("Historical Notes on Women," xxvii), women's inherent impurity and sinfulness prevented them from attaining enlightenment. The Nirvana Sutra "claims that the sinful obstacles of one woman equal the sum of harmful attachments of all men in the world."
12 Kanter, Men and Women of the Corporation.
13 Cleary, Book of Serenity, 253.
14 Ferguson, Zen's Chinese Heritage, 176.
15 Cleary and Cleary, Blue Cliff Record, 159.
16 Nishijima and Cross, Master Dogen's Shobogenzo, bk. 1, 69.
17 At the time "Raihaitokuzui" was written, women were forbidden to enter Koyasan, Todaiji, and Hieizan, the three main Buddhist headquarters for Shingon, Pure Land, and Tendai Buddhism in Japan.
18 Levering, "Lineage or Family Tree," 160.
19 Yokoi, Japanese English Zen Buddhist Dictionary, 506.
20 Unpublished research emanating from Shasta Abbey suggests that Bodhidharma's own teacher in India, Prajnatara, was a woman. Perhaps Bodhidharma's experience of a woman teacher opened the way early on in China for Zen's women.
21 Tanahashi, Moon in a Dewdrop, 168–74.

22 Levering, "Dogen's Raihaitokuzui."

23 Leighton, *Dogen's Extensive Record*, 110.

24 Gregory and Getz, *Buddhism in the Sung*, 246.

25 Nishiyama, *Shobogenzo*, "Raihaitokuzui," 216–17.

26 Ibid., 218. See Paul, *Women in Buddhism*, 188–89.

27 Cleary, *Blue Cliff Record*, 110.

28 Ibid., 30.

29 The Mumonkan, or Gateless Gate, consists of one hundred teaching stories or koans. It is part of Zen's classic literature.

30 Shibayama, *Gateless Barrier*, 247–48.

31 Stevens, *Lust for Enlightenment*, 125.

32 Seo, *Art of Twentieth-Century Zen*, 60.

33 Green, *Recorded Sayings of Zen Master Joshu*, xi.

34 Ibid., 31.

35 Ibid., 104.

36 Buddhi is the feminine-inflected form the Sanskrit word for "Awakened One," used for the first female teacher and founder of the order of bhikshunis, Mahapajapati.

37 These are the "five obstacles" (*gosho*), an early Buddhist belief that a woman cannot reincarnate as Brahma, Indra, Mara, a world-ruling king, or a buddha. See Ruch, *Engendering Faith*, 74.

38 Ibid., 134.

39 Ibid., 166.

40 Stevens, *Lust for Enlightenment*, 104.

41 Instead of meditative work toward enlightenment, Pure Land Buddhism teaches that through devotion to Amitabha (an important Mahayana buddha, ruler of the western paradise of Sukhavati), one will be reborn in the Pure Land (strictly speaking, not a location, but a state of consciousness) in which enlightenment is guaranteed. Pure Land Buddhism was (and is) popular because it provides a straightforward way of expressing faith. It was popular among those on the outskirts of society, who may have been denied spiritual services but could still find personal solace through devotion.

42 Stevens, *Three Zen Masters*, 84.

43 See note 20 above on the possibility that Bodhidharma, the first Zen patriarch in China, received his authorization to teach from Prajnatara, a woman.

44 McRae, *Seeing through Zen*.

45 Falk and Gross, *Unspoken Worlds*.

46 For example, historians have uncovered examples of female Zen masters in particularly lively Zen eras (e.g., Sung dynasty China) who show up as Dharma heirs in one century, but who disappear from the records one hundred years later. See Levering, "Miao-tao and her Teacher Ta-hui," and also Hsieh, "Buddhist Nuns in Sung China."

47 Murcott, *First Buddhist Women*. There were various ceremonies that nuns were not allowed to perform as a result of the Eight Special Rules.

48 Osumi, "Historical Notes on Women," in *Engendering Faith*, xxx.

49 Murcott, *First Buddhist Women*.

50 Zelliot, "Buddhist Women," 104.

51 Here again each of us must decide for ourselves whether to accept the accounts offered in the Buddhist scriptures that paint the Buddha as limited by his human frailty and perception or to view the Buddha as a perfectly and fully enlightened being whose historical account has been altered by later Buddhists leaders.

52 It is not clear from the historical accounts whether the Buddha initially had refused any ordination for Mahapajapati or had allowed Mahapajapati a limited ordination to follow the path, but resisted allowing her home leaving. The usual version of the story suggests that she had no ordination until after she insisted and tried to join the male order at Vesali after walking 150 miles. Current studies suggest that she had a limited ordination, that did not allow for home leaving, and that the historic walk with her followers resulted in a more complete ordination.

53 Chatsumarn, in ebook *Women in Buddhism*, 30.n.

54 Murcott, *First Buddhist Women*.

55 Walters, "Gotami's Story," in Lopez, *Buddhism in Practice*, 137.

56 Murcott, *First Buddhist Women*, 18–19.

57 Jingjian may have actually been preceded by the nun Ahpan, about whom we have little information. Ahpan may have been ordained under the emperor Ming (r. 58–75). We start with Jingjian because this is where detailed records begin.

58 "Bhikshuni" is the original term used for Buddha's female renunciants and implies that the practitioner is following all of the rules designated for that level of ordination.

59 From the time of the Buddha, ordination rules for monks and nuns differed in number and content. Nuns had to abide by the Eight Special Rules that monks did not have to observe. Overall, nuns had 311 rules to follow; monks had 227. Among the rules that only nuns had to follow were admonitions regarding the subservience of nuns to monks, regardless of their relative experience or spiritual maturity.

60 Tsai, *Lives of the Nuns*, 19.

61 Ibid., 22.

62 Ibid., 27.

63 Osumi, "Historical Notes on Women," in *Engendering Faith*, 30.

64 Ilyon, *Samguk Yusa*, 182. "Ado" may be used for a person whose name is not known.

65 Bays, "Zenshin's Example," in *Buddhadharma*, 5.

66 Nuns were required to stay two years in a convent before ordaining in order to prove they were not pregnant. Apparently, miraculously long gestation periods were feared among the nuns.

67 Mikoshiba, "Empress Komyo's Buddhist Faith," in *Engendering Faith*, 26.

68 Paul, "Empress Wu and the Historians," in Falk and Gross, *Unspoken Worlds*, 152.

69 Confucian values originating in China were adopted in Korea and in Japan.

70 Kim, *Women of Korea*, 42.

71 Arai, *Women Living Zen*, 35.

72 Ruch, *Engendering Faith*, 194.

73 Samu Sunim, "Eunyeong Sunim," 133.

74 Master Yuanwu practiced in the tradition of Linji, whose teaching was characterized by abrupt, harsh encounters with students, aiming to bring about enlightenment. His methods included shouting and striking, most often using the fly-whisk, a symbol of a Zen master's authority. The severity of this practice puts perspective on Xinggang's courage in pursuing spiritual practice.

75 A koan (Chinese: kung-an) is a story, dialog, question, or statement containing aspects that are inaccessible to rational understanding, requiring a direct response from the student as a means of obtaining awakening. For example, "What is the sound of one hand clapping?"

76 Thirteenth Daughter Zheng is described as a young woman (twelve years old) "with a tongue like a sharp sword whose words flow like torrents of water." She was able

to confront a seasoned Chan master "with complete fearlessness and confidence." Her dharma presentation is rejected three times by her teacher, yet her aspiration to practice remains undiminished. (Grant, "Female Holder of the Lineage," 56–57.)

77 Ibid., 58.

78 Ibid., 59.

79 Grant, *Daughters of Emptiness*, 77.

80 Ibid., 60.

81 Ibid., 63.

82 Ibid.

83 Ibid., 69.

84 Ibid., 71.

85 Ibid., 74.

86 "Great Seon Masters of Korean History," Chogye Order website, koreanbuddhism.net.

87 Ruch, *Engendering Faith*, xlvi.

88 Engakuji was a temple in the Rinzai sect. Monastics there relied on and venerated the teaching of its founder, Linji (Japanese: Rinzai).

89 *Days of Discipline and Grace.*

90 Ibid., li.

91 Nishiyama, *Shobogenzo*, "Raihaitokuzui."

92 Sallie King, "Awakening Stories of Zen Buddhist Women," 513.

93 Bodiford, *Soto Zen in Medieval Japan*, 90.

94 Ibid., 96.

95 Ibid., 90.

96 Great Tree Zen Center, established by Teijo Munnich, is the first women's retreat center in the Western Zen tradition.

97 *Nushu* is a secret written and oral language for women only used in China. See note 168.

98 Stevens, *Lust for Enlightenment*, 6.

99 Murcott, *First Buddhist Women*, 48.

100 In this meditation on the body you focus on the physical parts of the body that are identified in the early scriptures: hairs of the head, hairs of the body, nails, teeth, skin, flesh, sinews, bones, marrow, kidneys, heart, liver, diaphragm, spleen, lungs, stomach, bowels, mesentery, and excrement.

101 Murcott, *First Buddhist Women*, 131–34.

102 Ibid., 126–27.

103 Grant, "Through the Empty Gate." Patricia Ebrey has detailed the traditional lives of Sung dynasty Chinese women and their subservient roles within the patrilineal Chinese system in her book *Inner Quarters.*

104 Hsieh, "Buddhist Nuns in Sung China," 78.

105 Tsai, *Lives of the Nuns*, 56.

106 Skillful means (Sanskrit *upaya*) is a practice of adapting wisdom in the moment to support Buddhist teaching.

107 Grant, *Daughters of Emptiness*, 53.

108 Ibid., 121.

109 In 2004 there were about three hundred nuns training at this historic temple, which was established around 557. Nuns began reestablishing and rebuilding this temple in 1958.

110 See chapter 7 below for Manseong Sunim and Man'gong Sunim.

111 Batchelor and Son'gyong Sunim, *Women in Korean Zen*, 112.

112 Mikoshiba, "Empress Komyo's Buddhist Faith," in Ruch, *Engendering Faith*, 21–40.

113 For the four virtues see chapter 10 below.

114 Arai, *Women Living Zen*, 60.

115 Mantokuji is discussed by Diana Wright, "Mantokuji: More than a Divorce Temple," in Ruch, *Engendering Faith*, 247–78.

116 While we may use the contemporary term "women's rights," there was no such concept until the twentieth century.

117 Ruch, *Engendering Faith*, 218.

118 The Tokugawa era or Edo period extended from 1603 to 1867.

119 Morrell and Morrell, *Zen Sanctuary*, 52.

120 Ibid.

121 Ibid., 53.

122 Huineng read a poem by a monk aspiring to lead the community: "The body is the Bodhi tree / The mind is like a mirror bright / Take heed to keep it always clean / And let dust not collect upon it." Huineng responded with "There is no Bodhi-tree / Nor stand of mirror bright / From the first not a thing is / So where can dust alight?"

123 Morrell and Morrell, *Zen Sanctuary*, 53.

124 Ibid., 117.

125 Ibid., 55.

126 Ibid., 53.

127 Women of these warrior families were often married to men from enemy groups as a way of cementing the peace or serving as hostages. Thus Senhime and Tenshu were part of both the Tokugawa clan and the Hideyoshi clan.

128 Hsieh, "Buddhist Nuns in Sung China," 81.

129 Grant, "Lineage and Loyalty."

130 Levering, "Miao-tao and Her Teacher Ta-hui."

131 Ibid., 191.

132 Ibid., 190.

133 Ibid.

134 Other records are *Chiadai* (*Universal Record of the Flame*), *Chienchung Chingkuo* (*Supplementary Record of the Flame*), and *Chingde* (*Record of the Transmission of the Flame*). In all of these records, a flame (or lamplight) is a symbol of awakened mind.

135 In brief, the gradual school suggests that through slow and steady letting go of delusion, the character is polished and awakening appears. The sudden school emphasizes supreme, Herculean effort to suddenly break through delusion, and puts great stock in the sudden enlightenment experience that results.

136 Levering, "Miao-tao and Her Teacher Ta-hui," in Gregory and Getz, *Buddhism and the Sung*, 196.

137 Dahui emphasized sudden awakening through koan practice. Hongzhi (a teacher of Miaodao's original teacher, and also Dogen's teacher) taught realization of nondual awareness through silent meditation. These approaches have been characterized as contrasting (fast versus slow), but Leighton (*Cultivating the Empty Field*) argues that Hongzhi and Dahui were colleagues and friends, that their contrasting styles and practices may be seen as complementary, and that these are living questions for practitioners of today.

138 Levering, "Miao-tao and Her Teacher Ta-hui," in Gregory and Getz, *Buddhism and the Sung*, 196.

139 Ibid., 201.

140 Ibid., 204.

141 Ibid., 207.

142 Ibid., 208.

143 Kodera, *Dogen's Formative Years*, 77.

144 Young Mi Kim, "Chingak's Theory of Women's Enlightenment," 49.

145 King Kangjong was a strong supporter and student of Hyesim.

146 "Zhaozhou's Mu" originated with the Zen master Zhaozhou, and is usually the first koan assigned to a koan student. The question is posed, "Does a dog have buddha-nature or not?" "Mu" was Zhaozhou's answer, meaning "no thing."

147 Samu Sunim, "Manseong Sunim," 190.

148 "Zazen sickness" has been described by various teachers as a kind of energetic imbalance created by excessive effort. (*Sanggi* is not to be confused with the "Zen sickness" described, for instance, by Yunmen in koans.)

149 Samu Sunim, "Manseong Sunim," 192.

150 Ibid., 193.

151 Ibid.

152 Stephen Addiss, "The Zen Nun Ryonen Genso," *Spring Wind* (1986): 180–87.

153 Barbara Ruch, "Burning Iron Against the Cheek," in *Engendering Faith*, lxvii. Gomizuno'o was a close disciple of Isshi Bunchu of the Daitokuji and Myoshinji lineage (see Stephen Addiss, *The Art of Zen*, 36). He also studied with and became a Dharma heir of Ryokei Shosen, a Myoshinji priest who converted to Obaku Zen. According to Dumoulin (*Zen Buddhism: A History—Japan*), Gomizuno'o also supported the Rinzai Zen Master Takuan Soho and the Obaku patriarch Ingen (Chinese: Yinyuan).

154 This 1629 "Purple Robe Incident," a recorded historical event, occurred because of a power struggle between the imperial and shogunal governments over the emperor's right to recognize National Zen Masters and bestow the purple robe. When the shogun overturned this long-standing imperial privilege through a technicality, the emperor left the throne. Dumoulin (in *Zen Buddhism: A History—Japan*) reports that the shogunal government's prerequisite for Purple Robe status was thirty years' experience as a Zen master and the completion of seventeen hundred koans.

155 Fister, *Art by Buddhist Nuns*, 17.

156 Fister, *Japanese Women Artists*, 28.

157 Addiss, *Art of Zen*, 95.

158 Ruch, *Engendering Faith*, lxxv.

159 Barbara Ruch makes the connection between Ryonen Genso studying at an imperial convent and the legend reported at the imperial convent founded by Mugai Nyodai. Mugai Nyodai allegedly had burned her face to enter Tofukuji several centuries earlier. Ruch, while making the connection, notes the earlier alleged burning (of Mugai Nyodai's face) and Ryonen Genso's knowledge of this event lack documentation.

160 According to Dumoulin, the Obaku Zen school developed from the 1620 emigration of Chinese Linji monks to Japan. Obaku Zen was different than the Linji (Japanese: Rinzai) sect that was established after Japanese Zen masters had trained in China in the thirteenth century. It is considered to be somewhere "in between" Soto and Rinzai training.

161 Addiss, *Art of Zen*, 95.

162 Hisamatsu, *Formless Self Society*, 649–65.

163 Cleary, *Immortal Sisters*, 3; Wong, *Seven Taoist Masters*, 57.

164 Bodiford, *Soto Zen in Medieval Japan*, 205.

165 Addiss, *Art of Zen*, 95.

166 Ibid.

167 Ibid., 99.

168 Women were generally not trained in the Chinese characters (*kanji*), but they learned the phonetic *hiragana* instead. Ryonen knew the *kanji*, but she chose to use the more modest *hiragana*, known as "women's script."

169 Addiss, *Art of Zen*, 98.

170 Ibid.

171 Ibid.

172 Ibid.

173 Selkirk, *Buddha's Robe Is Sewn*, 2.

174 Hashimoto Eko Roshi (1890–1965) ordained Yoshida Eshun Roshi, taught Katagiri Roshi, and was considered a leading Zen master along with Sawaki Kodo Roshi.

175 The *nyohoe* style of sewing now used in Soto Zen is traced through the Shingon school. See Figure 1 tracing the lineage of *nyohoe*-style sewing to the Soto Zen teachers from Joshin-san and Yoshida Roshi through Hashimoto Eko Roshi and Sawaki Kodo Roshi.

176 Sano, "Story of Joshin-san."

177 Paying visits to geishas, described here as a dissipating habit, involved drinking in the company of professional female escorts, but not necessarily prostitution.

178 Harada Sogaku Roshi (1871–1961) was abbot of Hosshinji temple, where many Westerners have practiced in Japan. He was the teacher of Yasutani Roshi, a pioneering Zen founder in the West who taught Philip Kapleau Roshi and Maurine Stuart Roshi in America.

179 A *zazenkai* is a group that usually meets weekly and offers Zen meditation instruction to laypeople.

180 Zazen (Zen meditation), *okesa* sewing (hand-sewing of formal Buddhist robes), and *takuhatsu* (formal Buddhist begging practice) are all training activities at formal Japanese Zen practice centers.

181 Kaizenji was the temple of Abbess Yoshida Eshun Roshi, who was also a disciple of Hashimoto Eko Roshi.

182 Ryokan-san (1758–1831) refers to a well-known poet monk who practiced in the same Soto Zen tradition as Joshin-san. He was celebrated for his free and creative spirit, but he never consented to take responsibility for a specific temple. He is also referred to in this book as the teacher of the nun Teishin.

183 Sometimes Japanese individuals will legally adopt an adult in order to provide for them materially in a culturally acceptable way or to continue a family business.

184 Japanese Zen nuns and monks keep their heads shaved as part of their commitment to the Buddha's instructions. Some Soto Zen temples include a ceremony where the priests shave each other's heads. This is a lesson in trust and intimacy. Rev. Sano Kenko shaved her head before her funeral—a formal practice and an intimate goodbye.

185 Braverman, *Living and Dying in Zazen*, 118.

186 Ñanamoli and Bodhi, *Middle Length Discourses*, 179, Sutta 27 verse 12, 272.

187 Diana Paul cites this passage in *Women in Buddhism*, 52, note 14: Anguttara Nikaya, vi 5, III, 56.

188 Walshe, *Long Discourses of the Buddha*, 264.

189 Grant, *Daughters of Emptiness*, 73.

190 Maezawa Catalogue, Kyoto, Mampukuji Scroll; translation by Patricia Fister.

191 Unpublished translation by Miriam Levering, with permission.

192 Addiss, *Art of Zen*, 98.

193 Sasaki et al, *A Man of Zen*, 43.

194 Cook, *Record of Transmitting the Light*, 175.

195 Dan Martin, "The Woman Illusion?" in Gyatso and Havnevik, *Women in Tibet*, 72.

196 Vasubandhu and Asanga are considered important ancestors in the Tibetan and Zen traditions.

197 Kodaiji is now considered a subtemple of the Rinzai-shu Kenninji temple of Kyoto.

198 Fister, *Art by Buddhist Nuns*, 17.

199 Sasaki et al, *A Man of Zen*, 74.

200 Ibid., 75.

201 Ibid., 75.

202 Grant, *Daughters of Emptiness*, 63.

203 Ibid., 53.

204 King and Sueki, *Wastepaper Record*.

205 Bassui Tokusho (1327–87) worked to revive Zen from the two extremes of the faults he perceived: excessive dogma or ceremony, and excessively lax discipline. He was particularly devoted to meditation practice and eschewed formal symbols of rank and status, even refusing to wear a monk's robes after his ordination. A truly inspirational teacher, he gathered many followers toward the end of his life.

206 King and Sueki, *Wastepaper Record*, 56.

207 Sekida, *Two Zen Classics*.

208 King and Sueki, *Wastepaper Record*, 68.

209 Ibid., 82.

210 Merit is the mysterious and ineffable positive energy that results from sincere Buddhist practice. It is customary to give this merit away to others, to dedicate any merit that accrues from practice activity to the well-being of others.

211 Hakuin Ekaku is considered one of the greatest Zen masters in Japanese history. He is recognized for his profound teachings and written discourses, his original art, and his compassionate relationship to the commoners of his village. He is credited with the revival of the Japanese Rinzai school in the eighteenth century, and all current Rinzai temples trace their lineage to Hakuin.

212 Stevens, *Three Zen Masters*, 80.

213 Ibid., 81.

214 Ibid.

215 Ibid.

216 Kodama and Yanagishima, *Zen Fool Ryokan*, 104.

217 Ibid., 105.

218 Ibid., 108.

219 Ibid., 109.

220 Ibid.

221 Ibid., 110.

222 Stevens, *Three Zen Masters*, 158.

223 Ñanamoli and Bodhi, *Middle Length Discourses*, 273.

224 Wilson, *Charming Cadavers*, 23. From the Vinaya Pitaka, 3:20

225 Ñanamoli and Bodhi, *Middle Length Discourses*, 596–97.

226 Hsieh, "Buddhist Nuns in Sung China," in Gregory and Getz, *Buddhism in the Sung*, 157.

227 Thomas Cleary, in *Kahawai Koans*, a publication of the Diamond Sangha, Hawaii.

228 Cleary, *Classics of Buddhism and Zen*, "Transmission of the Light," 141.

229 Cleary, in *Kahawai Koans*.

230 Kodera, *Dogen's Formative Years*.

231 In today's Zen center training, Wanan would be called the *shuso*.

232 This is according to Stevens, *Lust for Enlightenment*; and Covell and Yamada, *Unraveling Zen's Red Thread*.

233 Covell and Yamada, *Unraveling Zen's Red Thread*, 218.

234 Stevens, *Lust for Enlightenment*, 90.

235 Levering, "Stories of Enlightened Women in Ch'an," in King, *Women and Goddess Traditions*, 152.

236 "The Jewel Mirror Samadhi," Berkeley Zen Center Chant Book.

237 Green, *Recorded Sayings of Zen Master Joshu*.

238 Grant, "Lineage and Loyalty," unpublished paper.

239 Dumoulin, *Zen Buddhism*, 224.

240 Park, "Kim Iryop and Korean Buddhism's Encounter," 181.

241 Ibid., 185.

242 "Entering the mountain" is the Korean term for becoming a Buddhist priest or nun.

243 Oh, "Kim Ilyop's Conflicting Worlds," 178.

244 Ibid., 183.

245 Park, "Kim Iryop and Korean Buddhism's Encounter," 185.

246 Ibid., 187.

247 Ibid., 189.

248 Oh, "Kim Ilyop's Conflicting Worlds," 182.

249 Leggett, *Warrior Koans*, 52.

250 Levering, "Zen for the Women's Quarters," 3.

251 Leighton and Wu, *Cultivating the Empty Field*, 41.

252 Levering, "Zen for the Women's Quarters," 4.

253 Ibid.

254 Sallie King, "Awakening Stories of Zen Buddhist Women," in Lopez, *Buddhism in Practice*, 513.

255 The Soto, Rinzai, and Obaku sects in Japan, as well as the Chogye order in Korea, are examples of organizations that administer and may assist individual temples. Currently there is also government support in China for maintaining monasteries, and there is also corporate sponsorship of treasured old convents and monasteries.

256 Arai, *Women Living Zen*. Monks may sometimes learn singing as part of their offering to the congregation on certain occasions and may learn to sew their own *okesa* (priest's robes), but they generally are not expected to master these subjects in order to teach them to their congregations.

257 Arai, *Women Living Zen*, 65.

258 Samu Sunim, "Eunyeong Sunim," 156.

259 Jones, *Buddhism in Taiwan*, 200.

260 Hsieh, "Images of Women," 163.

261 We assume there was no convent nearby or she might have lived there. She located her bathhouse near her teacher's monastery so she could continue to study.

262 Samu Sunim, "Eunyeong Sunim," 129–162.

263 Ibid., 147.
264 Ibid., 156.
265 Go is an incredibly complex game of strategy. Go is to chess as chess is to checkers.
266 Stevens, *Lotus Moon*, 90.
267 Ibid., 126.
268 Ibid., 90.
269 Ibid., 97.
270 Teapot from an anonymous collection; translation by Michiyo Katsura, Meher Macdonald, and Grace Schireson.
271 Khyentse, "Tea and the Teacup," *Buddhadharma*, (Winter 2006): 13.
272 Butler, "Encountering the Shadow in Buddhist America," *Common Boundary*, (May–June 1990): 14–22.
273 Rita Gross, "Are We Equal Yet?" *Buddhadharma*, (Winter 2007): 33.
274 See Peter Rutter, *Sex in the Forbidden Zone*, for a discussion of one view of how this dynamic is enacted in other situations of unequal power such as with doctor, lawyer, or professor.
275 Wolf, *Beauty Myth*, 1991.
276 Young-Eisendrath, *Gender and Desire*.
277 Beneke, *Men on Rape*.
278 Ibid., 21.
279 Strand, "Buddhist Boomers," *Wall Street Journal*.
280 See the Zen priest Lewis Richmond's book, *Work as a Spiritual Practice*.
281 Stone, *When God Was a Woman*, x.
282 Perera, *Descent to the Goddess*, 16.
283 Stone, *When God Was a Woman*, xvii.
284 Mitchell, *Tao Te Ching*, verse 6.
285 Ibid., verse 25.
286 Robert Thurman, foreword to Hixon, *Mother of the Buddhas*, xi.
287 Ibid., xii–xv.
288 Hixon, *Mother of the Buddhas*, 4.
289 Suzuki, *Not Always So*, 7.

Bibliography

Abe, Masao. *A Study of Dogen: His Philosophy and Religion*. Albany: State University of New York Press, 1992.

Addiss, Stephen. *The Art of Zen: Paintings and Calligraphy by Japanese Monks 1600–1925*. New York: Harry N. Abrams, 1998.

———. "The Zen Nun Ryonen Genso," *Spring Wind* (1986): 180–87.

Angier, Natalie. *Woman: An Intimate Geography*. Boston: Houghton Mifflin, 1999.

Arai, Paula Kane Robinson. *Women Living Zen: Japanese Soto Buddhist Nuns*. New York: Oxford University Press, 1999.

Arnold, Sir Edward. *The Light of Asia, or The Great Renunciation (Mahabhinishkramana): Being the Life and Teaching of Gautama, Prince of India and Founder of Buddhism*. Adyar, Chennai, India: Vasanta Press, The Theosophical Society, 1997.

Batchelor, Martine, and Son'gyong Sunim. *Women in Korean Zen: Lives and Practices*. New York: Syracuse University Press, 2006.

———. *Women on the Buddhist Path*. Great Britain: HarperCollins, 1996.

Bays, Jan Chozen. "Zenshin's Example," *Buddhadharma* (Winter 2007).

Beneke, Timothy. *Men on Rape: What They Have to Say about Sexual Violence*. New York: St. Martin's, 1982.

Bennage, Patricia Daien, trans. *Zen Seeds: Reflections of a Female Priest (Aoyama Shundo)*. Tokyo: Kosei, 1990. Fourth printing, 1996.

Berkeley Zen Center Daily Chant Book, an unpublished manual.

Besserman, Perle, and Manfred Steger. *Crazy Clouds: Zen Radicals, Rebels & Reformers*. Boston: Shambhala, 1991.

Blackstone, Kathryn R. *Women in the Footsteps of the Buddha: Struggle for Liberation in the Therigatha*. Richmond, Surrey: Curzon, 1998.

Bodiford, William M. *Soto Zen in Medieval Japan*. Honolulu: Kuroda Institute, University of Hawaii Press, 1993.

Braverman, Arthur. *Living and Dying in Zazen: Five Zen Masters of Modern Japan*. New York: Weatherhill, 2003.

Brizendine, Louann. *The Female Brain*. New York: Morgan Road Books, 2006.

Butler, Katy. "Encountering the Shadow in Buddhist America," *Common Boundary* (May–June 1990): 14–22.

Cabezon, Jose Ignacio. *Buddhism, Sexuality, and Gender.* Albany: State University of New York Press, 1992.

Chadwick, David. *Crooked Cucumber: The Life and Zen Teaching of Shunryu Suzuki.* New York: Broadway Books, 1999.

————, ed. *To Shine One Corner of the World: Moments with Shunryu Suzuki: Stories of a Zen Teacher Told by His Students.* New York: Broadway Books, 2001.

Chang, Chung-Yuan, trans. *Original Teachings of Ch'an Buddhism.* New York: Pantheon Books, 1969.

Chatsumarn Kabilsingh. *Women in Buddhism.* BuddhaNet, 1978.

————. "Voramai Kabilsingh," in *Spring Wind* (1986): 202–9.

Chodorow, Nancy J. *The Reproduction of Mothering.* Berkeley: University of California Press, 1999.

Cleary, J. C., and Thomas Cleary, trans. *The Blue Cliff Record.* Boston: Shambhala, 1992.

————. *Zen Letters: Teachings of Yuanwu.* Boston: Shambhala, 1994.

Cleary, Thomas, ed. *Classics of Buddhism and Zen.* 4 vols. Boston: Shambhala, 2001.

————. *Teachings of Zen.* Boston: Shambhala, 1998.

————, ed. and trans. *Immortal Sisters: Secret Teachings of Taoist Women.* Berkeley, CA: North Atlantic Books, 1996.

————. *The Original Face: An Anthology of Rinzai Zen.* New York: Grove, 1978.

————. *Rational Zen: The Mind of Dogen Zenji.* Boston: Shambhala, 1993.

————. *A Tune beyond the Clouds: Zen Teachings from Old China.* Berkeley, CA: Asian Humanities, 1990.

————, trans. *The Blue Cliff Record.* Berkeley, CA: The Numata Center for Buddhist Translation and Research, 1998.

————. *Book of Serenity: One Hundred Zen Dialogues.* Hudson, NY: Lindisfarne, 1990.

————. *Minding Mind: A Course in Basic Meditation.* Boston: Shambhala, 1995.

————. *Sayings and Doings of Pai-Chang, Ch'an Master of Great Wisdom.* Los Angeles: Center, 1978.

————. *Shobogenzo: Zen Essays by Dogen.* Honolulu: University of Hawaii Press, 1986.

————. *Stopping and Seeing: A Comprehensive Course in Buddhist Meditation by Chih-i.* Boston: Shambhala, 1997.

————. *The Sutra of Hui-Neng, Grand Master of Zen, with Hui-Neng's Commentary on the Diamond Sutra.* Boston: Shambhala, 1998.

————. *Transmission of Light: Zen in the Art of Enlightenment by Zen Master Keizan.* San Francisco: North Point, 1990.

————. *Zen Dawn: Early Zen Texts from Tun Huang.* Boston: Shambhala, 1986.

Cook, Francis Dojun. *How to Raise an Ox: Zen Practice as Taught in Zen Master Dogen's Shobogenzo.* Los Angeles: Center, 1993.

Cook, Francis H., trans. *The Record of Transmitting the Light: Zen Master Keizan's Denkoroku.* Los Angeles: Center, 1991.

————. *Sounds of Valley Streams: Enlightenment in Dogen's Zen.* Albany: State University of New York Press, 1989.

Covell, Jon Carter, and Sobin Yamada. *Unraveling Zen's Red Thread: Ikkyu's Controversial Way.* Elizabeth, NJ: Hollym International, 1980.

Days of Discipline and Grace: Treasures from the Imperial Buddhist Convents of Kyoto. New York: Institute for Medieval Japanese Studies, 1998.

Dinnerstein, Dorothy, *The Mermaid and the Minotaur: Sexual Arrangements and Human Malaise.* New York: Harper and Row. 1976.

Donegan, Patricia, and Yoshie Ishibashi. *Chiyo-Ni: Woman Haiku Master.* Tokyo: Tuttle, 1998.

Dresser, Marianne, ed. *Buddhist Women on the Edge: Contemporary Perspectives from the Western Frontier.* Berkeley, CA: North Atlantic Books, 1996.

Dumoulin, Heinrich. *Zen Buddhism: A History.* Vol. 2, *Japan.* Trans. James by W. Heisig and Paul Knitter. New York: Macmillan, 1990.

Ebrey, Patricia Buckley. *The Inner Quarters: Marriage and the Lives of Chinese Women in the Sung Period.* Berkeley: University of California Press, 1993.

Falk, Nancy Auer, and Rita Gross. *Unspoken Worlds: Women's Religious Lives.* 2nd ed. Belmont: Wadsworth, 2000.

Ferguson, Andrew. *Zen's Chinese Heritage: The Masters and Their Teachings.* Boston: Wisdom, 2000.

Findley, Ellison Banks, ed. *Women's Buddhism, Buddhism's Women: Tradition, Revision, Renewal.* Boston: Wisdom, 2000.

Fister, Patricia. *Art by Buddhist Nuns: Treasures from the Imperial Convents of Japan.* New York: Institute for Medieval Japanese Studies, 1988.

————. *Japanese Women Artists 1600–1900.* New York: Harper and Row, 1988.

Fleur, William R., ed. *Dogen Studies.* Honolulu: Kuroda Institute, University of Hawaii Press, 1985.

Flinders, Carol. *Enduring Grace: Living Portraits of Seven Female Mystics.* New York: HarperOne, 1993.

Foster, Nelson, and Jack Shoemaker. *The Roaring Stream: A New Zen Reader.* Hopewell, NJ: Ecco, 1996.

Friedman, Lenore, and Susan Moon, eds. *Being Bodies: Buddhist Women on the Paradox of Embodiment.* Boston: Shambhala, 1997.

Fronsdal, Gil. *The Issue at Hand: Essays on Buddhist Mindfulness Practice.* 3rd ed. Redwood City, CA: Insight Meditation Center, 2005.

————, ed. *Remembering the Dragon: Recollections of Suzuki Roshi by His Students*. San Francisco: San Francisco Zen Center, 2004.

Grant, Beata. *Daughters of Emptiness: Poems of Chinese Buddhist Nuns*. Boston: Wisdom, 2003.

————. "Female Holder of the Lineage: Linji Chan Master Zhiyuan Xinggang (1597–1654)." *Late Imperial China* 17, no. 2 (December 1996): 51–76.

————. "Lineage and Loyalty." Paper presented to the Association of Asian Studies conference, March 2001, Chicago.

————. "Through the Empty Gate: The Poetry of Buddhist Nuns in Late Imperial China." In *Cultural Intersections in Later Chinese Buddhism*, ed. by Marsha Weidner, 87–113. Honolulu: University of Hawaii Press, 2001.

"Great Seon Masters of Korean History." Official Chogye Order website, http://www.koreanbuddhism.net.

Green, James. *The Recorded Sayings of Zen Master Joshu*. Boston: Shambhala, 1998.

Gregory, Peter N., and Daniel A. Getz, Jr., eds. *Buddhism in the Sung*. Honolulu: Kuroda Institute, University of Hawaii Press, 1999.

Gross, Rita. *Soaring and Settling: Buddhist Perspectives on Contemporary Social and Religious Issues*. New York: Continuum International, 1998.

————. "Are We Equal Yet?" *Buddhadharma* (Winter 2006): 32–36.

Gyatso, Janet, and Hanna Havnevik, eds. *Women in Tibet: Past and Present*. New York: Columbia University Press, 2005.

Hare, E. M., trans. *The Book of the Gradual Sayings (Anguttara-Nikaya)*. Vol. 3, *Book of the Fives and Sixes*. Lancaster: Pali Text Society, 1932.

Harragan, Betty Lehan. *Games Mother Never Taught You*. New York: Warner Books, 1978.

Haskel, Peter. *Letting Go: The Story of Zen Master Tosui*. Honolulu: University of Hawaii Press, 2001.

Heine, Steven. *Dogen and the Koan Tradition: A Tale of Two Shobogenzo Texts*. Albany: State University of New York Press, 1994.

————. *The Zen Poetry of Dogen: Verses from the Mountain of Eternal Peace*. Boston: Tuttle, 1997.

Hisamatsu, Shin'ichi. *Formless Self Society*. Vol. 3. Trans. by Jeff Shore et al. (Japanese text *FAS* #57, May 1965) Tokyo: Rososha, 1971; rev. ed., Kyoto: Hozokan, 1994.

Hixon, Les. *Mother of the Buddhas: Meditation on the Prajnaparamita Sutra*. Wheaton, IL: Quest Books, 1993.

Hsieh, Ding-hwa. "Buddhist Nuns in Sung China (960–1279)." *Journal of Sung-Yuan Studies*, no. 30 (2000): 63–97.

————. "Images of Women in Ch'an Buddhist Literature of the Sung Period."

In *Buddhism in the Sung*, ed. by Peter N. Gregory and Daniel A. Getz, Jr., 148–87. Honolulu: Kuroda Institute, University of Hawaii Press, 1999.

Hyon Gak Sunim. *The Compass of Zen: Zen Master Seung Sahn*. Boston: Shambhala, 1997.

Ilyon. *Samguk Yusa: Legends and History of the Three Kingdoms of Ancient Korea*. Trans. by Ha Tae-Hung and Grafton K. Mintz. Seoul: Yonsei University Press, 2004.

Jones, Charles Brewer. *Buddhism in Taiwan: Religion and the State, 1660–1990*. Honolulu: University of Hawaii Press, 1999.

Kanter, Rosabeth Moss. *Men and Women of the Corporation*. New York: Basic Books, 1977.

Katsuura, Noriko, "Tonsure Forms for Nuns: Classification of Nuns according to Hairstyle." Trans. by Virginia Skord Waters. In *Engendering Faith: Women and Buddhism in Premodern Japan*, ed. by Barbara Ruch, 109–29. Ann Arbor: Center for Japanese Studies, University of Michigan, 2002.

Khyentse, Dzongar. "The Tea and the Teacup." *Buddhadharma* (Winter 2006).

Kim, Young Mi. "National Preceptor Chingak's Theory of Women's Enlightenment and the Life of Buddhist Nuns in the Koryeo Period." Korean Nuns within the Context of East Asian Buddhist Traditions. 2004 International Conference. Seoul: Hanmaum Seoun, 2004.

Kim, Yung-Chung. *Women of Korea*. Seoul: Enwah University Women's Press, 1976.

Kim-Renaud, Young-Key. *Creative Women of Korea: The Fifteenth through the Twentieth Centuries*. Armonk, NY: M. E. Sharpe, 2003.

King, Karen L., ed. *Women and Goddess Traditions: In Antiquity and Today*. Minneapolis: Fortress, 1997.

King, Sallie. "Awakening Stories of Zen Buddhist Women." In *Buddhism in Practice*, ed. Donald S. Lopez. Princeton, NJ: Princeton University Press, 1995.

King, Sallie B., and Sueki Fumihiko, trans. *Tachibana no Someko: Wastepaper Record*. Tokyo: Ko-onji, 2001.

Kodama, Misao, and Hikosaku Yanagishima. *The Zen Fool Ryokan*. Rutland, VT: Charles E. Tuttle, 1999.

Kodera, Takashi James. *Dogen's Formative Years in China: An Historical Study and Annotated Translation of the Hokyo-ki*. Boulder, CO: Prajna, 1980.

Kokushi, Muso. *Dream Conversations: On Buddhism and Zen*. Trans. by Thomas Cleary. Boston: Shambhala, 1996.

Korean Nuns within the Context of East Asian Buddhist Traditions. 2004 International Conference, May 20–24, 2004. Seoul: Hanmaum Seoun, 2004.

Leggett, Trevor. *The Warrior Koans: Early Zen in Japan*. London: Arkana; Routledge & Kegan Paul, 1986.

————. *Zen and the Ways*. Rutland, VT: Charles E. Tuttle, 1987. First published in 1987 by Routledge and Kegan Paul.

Leighton, Taigen Dan, ed. *Dogen's Extensive Record: A Translation of the Eihei Koroku*. Trans. by Taigen Dan Leighton and Shohaku Okumura. Boston: Wisdom, 2004.

————. *Dogen's Pure Standards for the Zen Community: A Translation of Eihei Shingi*. Trans. by Taigen Daniel Leighton and Shohaku Okumura. Albany: State University of New York, 1996.

Leighton, Taigen Daniel, and Yi Wu, trans. *Cultivating the Empty Field: The Silent Illumination of Zen Master Hongzhi*. San Francisco: North Point, 1991.

Levering, Miriam. "Dogen's Raihaitokuzui and Women Teaching in Sung Ch'an." *Journal of the International Association of Buddhist Studies* 21, no. 1 (1998): 77–110.

————. "Lin-Chi (Rinzai) Ch'an and Gender: The Rhetoric of Equality and the Rhetoric of Heroism." In *Buddhism, Sexuality, and Gender*, ed. by Jose Ignacio Cabezon. Albany: State University of New York Press, 1992.

————. "Lineage or Family Tree: The Implications for Gender." In *Innovative Buddhist Women Swimming against the Stream*, ed. by Karma Lekshe Tsomo. Richmond, Surrey, England: Curzon, 2000.

————. "Miao-tao and Her Teacher Ta-hui." In *Buddhism in the Sung*, ed. Peter Gregory and Daniel Getz, Jr., 188–219. Honolulu: Kuroda Institute, University of Hawaii Press, 1999.

————. "Stories of Enlightened Women in Ch'an and the Chinese Buddhist Female Bodhisattva / Goddess Tradition." In *Women and Goddess Traditions: In Antiquity and Today*, ed. by Karen King, 137–76. Minneapolis: Fortress, 1997.

————. "Zen for the Women's Quarters: The Teachings of Soshin-ni." Paper presented to the American Academy of Religion Conference, November 21–23, 2004, San Antonio.

Lopez, Donald S., ed. *Buddhism in Practice*. Princeton, NJ: Princeton University Press, 1995.

Masunaga, Reiho, trans. *A Primer of Soto Zen: A Translation of Dogen's Shobogenzo Zuimonki*. Honolulu: University of Hawaii Press, 1990.

McRae, John R. *Seeing through Zen: Encounter, Transformation, and Genealogy in Chinese Chan Buddhism*. Berkeley: University of California Press, 2003.

Mikoshiba, Daisuke, "Empress Komyo's Buddhist Faith." In Barbara Ruch, ed., *Engendering Faith: Women and Buddhism in Premodern Japan*, 26. Ann Arbor: Center for Japanese Studies, University of Michigan, 2002.

Mitchell, Stephen, trans. *Tao Te Ching*. New York, HarperCollins, 1992.

Morrell, Sachiko Kaneko, and Robert E. Morrell. *Zen Sanctuary of the Purple Robes: Japan's Tokeiji Convent since 1285*. Albany: State University of New York Press, 2006.

Murcott, Susan. *The First Buddhist Women: Translations and Commentary on the Therigatha*. Berkeley, CA: Parallax, 1991.

Murcott, Susan, and Deborah Hopkinson, eds. *Kahawai Journal of Women and Zen* 3, no. 3 (1981) (Newsletter of Diamond Sangha).

Ñanamoli Bhikkhu and Bhikkhu Bodhi, trans. *The Middle Length Discourses of the Buddha: A New Translation of the Majjhima Nikaya*. Boston: Wisdom, 1995.

Nishijima, Gudo, and Chodo Cross, trans. *Master Dogen's Shobogenzo*. Books 1–4. London: Windbell, 1994–99.

Nishiyama, Kosen, trans. *Shobogenzo: The Eye and Treasury of the True Law*. Japan: Sasaki, 1988.

"Nuns of Hokkeji." *Institute for Medieval Japanese Studies (IMJS) Reports*. New York: April 2005.

Ogata, Sohaku, trans. *The Transmission of the Lamp: Early Masters*. Durango, CO: Longwood Academic, 1991. First published in 1986 by Hummingbird Press.

Oh, Bonnie. "Kim Ilyop's Conflicting Worlds." In *Creative Women of Korea: The Fifteenth through the Twentieth Centuries*, ed. by Young-Key Kim-Renaud. Armonk, NY: M. E. Sharpe, 2003.

O'Halloran, Maura. *Pure Heart, Enlightened Mind: The Life and Letters of an Irish Zen Saint*. Boston: Wisdom, 2007. First published in 1994 by Charles E. Tuttle.

Okumura, Shohaku, trans. *Dogen Zen*. Kyoto: Kyoto Soto Zen Center, 1988.

————. *Shobogenzo-zuimonki: Sayings of Eihei Dogen Zenji Recorded by Koun Ejo*. Tokyo: Sotosho Shumucho, 2004.

Okumura, Shohaku, and Taigen Dan Leighton, trans. *Bendowa: Talk on Whole-hearted Practice of the Way*, by Eihei Dogen Zenji. Kyoto: Kyoto Soto Zen Center, 1992.

————. *The Wholehearted Way: A Translation of Eihei Dogen's Bendowa*. Boston: Tuttle, 1997.

Osumi, Kazuo, "Historical Notes on Women and Japanization of Buddhism." In Barbara Ruch, ed., *Engendering Faith: Women and Buddhism in Premodern Japan*, xxvii-xlii. Ann Arbor: Center for Japanese Studies, University of Michigan, 2002.

Park, Jin Y. "Kim Iryop and Korean Buddhism's Encounter with Modernity." Paper presented at the 2004 International Conference "Korean Nuns within the Context of East Asian Buddhist Traditions," Seoul, Korea.

Paul, Diana Y. *Women in Buddhism: Images of the Feminine in the Mahayana Tradition*. Berkeley: University of California Press, 1985. First published in 1979 by Asian Humanities Press.

Pekarik, Andrew J., trans. *The Thirty-six Immortal Women Poets: A Poetry Album with Illustrations by Chobunsai Eishi*. New York: George Braziller, 1991.

Perera, Sylvia Brinton. *Descent to the Goddess*. Toronto: Inner City Books, 1981.

Porter, Bill. *Road to Heaven: Encounters with Chinese Hermits*. San Francisco: Mercury House, 1993.

Powell, William F., trans. *The Record of Tung-shan*. Kuroda Institute, University of Hawaii Press, 1986.

"Program Commemorating the 35th Anniversary of the Institute for Medieval Japanese Studies." New York: Columbia University, October 2003.

Reps, Paul. *Zen Flesh, Zen Bones: A Collection of Zen and Pre-Zen Writings*. Boston: Tuttle, 1999.

Rhys Davids, C. A. F., and K. R. Norman. *Poems of Early Buddhist Nuns (Therigatha)*. Oxford: Pali Text Society, 1997.

Richmond, Lewis. *Work as a Spiritual Practice*. New York: Broadway Books, 1999.

Ruch, Barbara, ed. *Engendering Faith: Women and Buddhism in Premodern Japan*. Ann Arbor: Center for Japanese Studies, University of Michigan, 2002.

————. "Burning Iron Against the Cheek." In *Engendering Faith: Women and Buddhism in Premodern Japan*, lxv-lxxviii. Ann Arbor: Center for Japanese Studies, University of Michigan, 2002.

————. "Obstructions and Obligations." In *Engendering Faith: Women and Buddhism in Premodern Japan*, xliii-lxiii. Ann Arbor: Center for Japanese Studies, University of Michigan, 2002.

Rutter, Peter. *Sex in the Forbidden Zone: When Men in Power—Therapists, Doctors, Teachers, Clergy and Others—Betray Women's Trust*. Los Angeles: Jeremy P. Tarcher, 1989.

Samu Sunim. "Eunyeong Sunim and the Founding of Pomun-Jong," in *Spring Wind* (1986): 129–62.

————. "Manseong Sunim, a Woman Zen Master of Modern Korea," *Spring Wind* (1986): 188–93.

Sano, Kenko. "The Story of Joshin-san." Trans. Yuko Okumura. In *Totakuji Temple Newsletter*, Kiryu-shi, Japan, January 2007.

Sasaki, Ruth Fuller, Yoshitaka Iriya, and Dana R. Fraser, trans. *A Man of Zen: The Recorded Sayings of Layman P'ang*. New York: Weatherhill, 1971.

Schmidt, Amy. *Knee Deep in Grace: The Extraordinary Life and Teaching of Dipa Ma*. Lake Junaluska, NC: Present Perfect Books, 2002.

Sekida, Katsuki, trans. *Two Zen Classics: Momunkan and Hekiganroku*. New York: Weatherhill, 1996.

_____. *Zen Training: Methods and Philosophy.* Ed. by A. V. Grimstone. New York: Weatherhill, 1981.

Selkirk, Jean. *Buddha's Robe Is Sewn*, Berkeley, CA: Mountain Moon, 2005.

Senzaki, Nyogen. *Like a Dream, Like a Fantasy: The Zen Writings and Translations of Nyogen Senzaki.* Boston: Wisdom, 2005.

Seo, Audrey Yoshiko. *The Art of Twentieth-Century Zen: Paintings and Calligraphy by Japanese Masters.* Boston: Shambhala, 1998.

Shibayama, Zenkei. *A Flower Does Not Talk: Zen Essays.* Trans. by Sumiko Komo. Rutland, VT: Charles E. Tuttle, 1980.

_____. *Gateless Barrier: Zen Comments on the Mumonkan.* Boston: Shambhala, 2000.

_____. *Zen Comments on the Mumonkan.* Translated by Sumiko Kudo. New York: Harper and Row, 1974.

Sidor, Ellen S., ed. *A Gathering of Spirit: Women Teaching in American Buddhism.* Cumberland, RI: Primary Point, 1987.

Simmer-Brown, Judith. *Dakini's Warm Breath: The Feminine Principle in Tibetan Buddhism.* Boston: Shambhala, 2001.

Sponberg, Alan. "Attitudes toward Women and the Feminine in Early Buddhism." In *Buddhism, Sexuality, and Gender*, ed. Jose Ignacio Cabezon, 3–36. Albany: State University of New York Press, 1992.

Stevens, John. *Lust for Enlightenment: Buddhism and Sex.* Boston: Shambhala, 1990.

_____. *Three Zen Masters: Ikkyu, Hakuin, Ryokan.* Tokyo: Kodansha International, 1993.

_____, trans. *Lotus Moon: The Poetry of Rengetsu.* Buffalo: White Pine Press, 2005.

_____. *One Robe, One Bowl: The Zen Poetry of Ryokan.* New York: Weatherhill, 1988.

_____. *Wild Ways: Zen Poems of Ikkyu.* Boston: Shambhala, 1995.

Stone, Merlin. *When God Was a Woman*, New York: Harcourt, 1976.

Strand, Clark. "Buddhist Boomers: A Meditation on How to Stave off Decline." *Wall Street Journal*, November 9, 2007.

Suzuki, Shunryu. *Not Always So: Practicing the True Spirit of Zen.* Ed. by Edward Espe Brown. New York: HarperCollins, 2002.

Tanahashi, Kazuaki. *Enlightenment Unfolds: The Essential Teachings of Zen Master Dogen.* Boston: Shambhala, 1999.

_____, ed. *Moon in a Dewdrop: The Writings of Zen Master Dogen.* San Francisco: North Point, 1985.

Thanissaro Bhikkhu (Geoffrey DeGraff). *Handful of Leaves.* 4 vols. Redwood City, CA: The Sati Center for Buddhist Studies and Metta Forest Monastery,

2002–3. (Selections from the Digha and Majjhima Nikayas, Samyutta Nikaya, Anguttara Nikaya, and Khuddaka Nikaya.)

———. *Meditations 2: Dhamma Talks.* Redwood City, CA: The Sati Center for Buddhist Studies, 2006.

Tisdale, Sallie. *Women of the Way: Discovering 2,500 Years of Buddhist Wisdom.* New York: HarperSanFrancisco, 2005.

Tsai, Kathryn Ann, trans. *Lives of the Nuns: Biographies of Chinese Buddhist Nuns from the Fourth to Sixth Centuries.* Honolulu: University of Hawaii Press, 1994.

Tsomo, Karma Lekshe, ed. *Buddhism through American Women's Eyes.* Ithaca, NY: Snow Lion, 1995.

———. *Innovative Buddhist Women Swimming against the Stream.* Richmond, Surrey: Curzon, 2000.

———. *Sakyadhita: Daughters of the Buddha.* Ithaca, NY: Snow Lion, 1988.

Uchiyama, Kosho. *Opening the Hand of Thought: Foundations of Zen Buddhist Practice.* Ed. and trans. by Tom Wright, Jisho Warner, and Shohaku Okumura. Boston: Wisdom, 2004.

Uchiyama, Kosho, and Eihei Dogen Zenji. *From the Zen Kitchen to Enlightenment: Refining Your Life.* Trans. by Thomas Wright. New York: Weatherhill, 1983.

Waddell, Norman, trans. *The Essential Teachings of Zen Master Hakuin.* Boston: Shambhala, 1994.

———. *Wild Ivy: The Spiritual Autobiography of Zen Master Hakuin.* Boston: Shambhala, 1999.

Waddell, Norman, and Masao Abe, trans. *The Heart of Dogen's Shobogenzo.* Albany: State University of New York Press, 2002.

Walshe, Maurice, trans. *The Long Discourses of the Buddha: A Translation of the Digha Nikaya.* Boston: Wisdom, 1995.

Walters, Jonathan. "A Voice from the Silence: The Buddha's Mother's Story." *History of Religions* 33, no. 4 (May 1994): 358–79.

Watson, Burton, trans. *The Zen Teachings of Master Lin-Chi.* Boston: Shambhala, 1993.

Weidner, Marsha, ed. *Cultural Intersections in Later Chinese Buddhism.* Honolulu: University of Hawai'i Press, 2001.

Welch, Holmes. *The Practice of Chinese Buddhism.* Cambridge, MA: Harvard University Press, 1961.

Wilson, Liz. *Charming Cadavers: Horrific Figurations of the Feminine in Indian Buddhist Hagiographic Literature.* Chicago: University of Chicago Press, 1996.

Wolf, Naomi. *The Beauty Myth: How Images of Beauty Are Used against Women.* New York: William Morrow, 1991.

"Women and Buddhism." *Spring Wind–Buddhist Cultural Forum* 6, no. 3 (1986): 1–3.

Wong, Eva. *Seven Taoist Masters: A Folk Novel of China*. Boston: Shambhala, 1990.

Wright, Diana. "Mantokuji: More than a Divorce Temple." In *Engendering Faith: Women and Buddhism in Premodern Japan*, 247–78. Ann Arbor: Center for Japanese Studies, University of Michigan, 2002.

Wu, John C. H. *The Golden Age of Zen: The Classic Work on the Foundation of Zen Philosophy*. New York: Image Books, Doubleday, 1996.

Yamada, Koun, trans. *Gateless Gate*. Tucson, AZ: University of Arizona Press, 1990.

Yampolsky, Philip B., trans. *The Platform Sutra of the Sixth Patriarch: The Text of the Tun-Huang Manuscript*. New York: Columbia University Press, 1967.

———. *The Zen Master Hakuin: Selected Writings*. New York: Columbia University Press, 1971.

Yokoi, Yuho. *The First Step to Dogen's Zen: Shobogenzo-zuimonki*. Tokyo: Sankibo Busshorin, 1988.

———. *The Japanese English Zen Buddhist Dictionary*. Tokyo: Sankibo Busshorin, 1991.

Young-Eisendrath, Polly. *Gender and Desire: Uncursing Pandora*. College Station: Texas A&M University Press, 1997.

Zelliot, Eleanor. "Buddhist Women of the Baharashtrian Conversion Movement." In *Buddhism, Sexuality, and Gender*, ed. by Jose Cabezon. Albany: State University of New York Press, 1992.

Index

misspelled

About the Author

GRACE SCHIRESON is a Dharma teacher in the Suzuki Roshi lineage empowered by Sojun Mel Weitsman Roshi, abbot of Berkeley Zen Center. She has also been empowered to teach koans by Keido Fukushima Roshi, chief abbot of Tofukuji Monastery in Kyoto, Japan. Grace is the head teacher of the Central Valley Zen Foundation and has founded and leads three Zen groups and a Zen retreat center in California. Grace is a clinical psychologist who has specialized in women and families. She has been married for forty-one years and has two grown sons and three grandchildren.

About Wisdom

WISDOM PUBLICATIONS is dedicated to making available authentic Buddhist works for the benefit of all. We publish translations of the sutras and tantras, commentaries and teachings of past and contemporary Buddhist masters, and original works by the world's leading Buddhist scholars. We publish our titles with the appreciation of Buddhism as a living philosophy and with the special commitment to preserve and transmit important works from all the major Buddhist traditions.

Wisdom Publications
199 Elm Street
Somerville, Massachusetts 02144 USA
Telephone: 617-776-7416
Fax: 617-776-7841
Email: info@wisdompubs.org
www.wisdompubs.org

The Wisdom Trust

As a nonprofit publisher, Wisdom is dedicated to the publication of Dharma books for the benefit of all sentient beings and dependent upon the kindness and generosity of sponsors in order to do so. If you would like to make a donation to Wisdom, you may do so through our website or our Somerville office. If you would like to help sponsor the publication of a book, please write or email us at the address above.

Thank you.

Wisdom is a nonprofit, charitable 501(c)(3) organization affiliated with the Foundation for the Preservation of the Mahayana Tradition (FPMT)